AUSTRALIAN FEDERALISM

AUSTRALIAN FEDERALISM

Edited by Brian Galligan

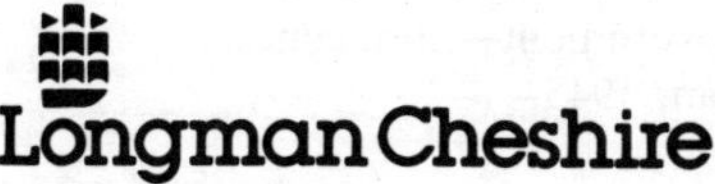

Longman Cheshire Pty Limited
Longman House
Kings Gardens
95 Coventry Street
Melbourne 3205 Australia

Offices in Sydney, Brisbane, Adelaide
and Perth. Associated companies, branches,
and representatives throughout the world.

First published 1989

Designed by Paul Carland
Set in 9/11 Times Roman (Linotron 202)
Printed in Malaysia
by Sun U Book Co. Sdn. Bhd., Petaling Jaya,
Selangor Darul Ehsan.

National Library of Australia
Cataloguing-in-Publication data
Australian federalism.

ISBN 0 582 71188 6.

1. Federal government—Australia. 2. Australia
—Politics and government—20th century.
I. Galligan, Brian, 1945–

320.494

For Geoffrey Sawer, Rae Else-Mitchell,
Robert Parker and Russell Mathews,
eminent scholars of federalism and
veterans of earlier reviews.

CONTENTS

PREFACE

The Bicentenary has been a time not only for celebration of nationhood but also for critical reflection and national stocktaking. Major research and writing projects, including the monumental ten-volume history of *Australians* and several studies of the national parliament, have been published. The Constitutional Commission, which has been reviewing the Constitution, is soon to report to the government and select amendment proposals will likely be put to referendum before the end of the year. Hence the Bicentenary seemed an appropriate occasion for those who have a special interest in our federal constitutional system to review the way it has developed in recent decades, to examine how well it has coped in response to political, social and economic changes, and to assess its suitability for the perceived needs of the future. It was envisaged that such a review would provide a suitable occasion for critically examining how leading practitioners and commentators have viewed federalism during the post-war period and how their ideas may have influenced practice.

A special seminar on Australian federalism was organised at the Australian National University on 2 and 3 July 1987 to undertake a major review of our federal system comparable to those undertaken in 1949 and 1951. The 1949 review was by Geoffrey Sawer, Gordon Greenwood, Robert Parker et al., for the summer school of the Australian Institute of Political Science and published as *Federalism in Australia* (Melbourne: F.W. Cheshire, 1949). That review occurred during post-war reconstruction following the Second World War, and updated an earlier review undertaken in 1933 when Australia was emerging from the Great Depression. While the events immediately preceding this review are less traumatic, changes over the last few decades have been substantial. The occasion of the 1951 review was the Jubilee of the Australian Commonwealth. Two seminars were organised by the recently established Australian National University. The collection included papers by eminent overseas and local scholars, including K.C. Wheare, P.H.

Partridge, Colin Clark and Douglas Copland, and was edited by Geoffrey Sawer as *Federalism: An Australian Jubilee Study* (Melbourne: F.W. Cheshire, 1952). As well Rae Else-Mitchell edited a special collection of essays on constitutional law for the 1951 Jubilee, *Essays on the Australian Constitution* (Sydney: Law Book Company, 1952).

The 1987 seminar was jointly sponsored by the Faculty of Law, the Centre for Research on Federal Financial Relations and the Department of Political Science in the Research School of Social Sciences at the Australian National University. In planning the seminar Les Zines, Geoffrey Brennan and I decided it should serve two purposes: one, provide the forum for a wide-ranging review of Australian federalism and two, stimulate interdisciplinary discussion. The contributing papers were drawn from the disciplines of political science, constitutional law and economics, while the topics were chosen to ensure that the perspectives of the various disciplines were brought to bear on common themes and issues. The papers were circulated in advance to participants and stimulated a good deal of comment and lively discussion across disciplines. Unfortunately it has not been possible to include the commentaries in this volume so I should like to thank all the commentators for their written and verbal presentations at the seminar. Their commentaries made that a notable occasion and helped authors in revising their papers for publication.

The participation of four of the 'veterans' from the mid-century reviews, Geoffrey Sawer, Rae Else-Mitchell, Robert Parker and Russell Mathews, added a venerable quality to the meeting, while Geoff Sawer's after-dinner address was for many the highlight of the proceedings.

Special thanks to Linda Gosnell for helping organise the seminar, Stephanie Hancock for typing many of the final papers and Gillian O'Loghlin for proof-reading. Thanks also to Neil Ryan and Ron Harper from Longman Cheshire, who were enthusiastic in supporting the project, and Moira Anderson for her editorial work.

Brian Galligan
Canberra, April 1988.

FOREWORD

First, I would like to thank those responsible for giving me the opportunity to open this seminar. Retired appellate judges do not necessarily pine for a return to the law, for a return to seemingly endless lawyers' arguments, to the literally ceaseless writing of judgments or, for that matter, to what proved to be the almost invariable epilogue to my judgments at all events—merciless exposure by unkind academics of my errors of logic and mistakes of principle. But there remains, nevertheless, a lingering, bitter-sweet nostalgia for matters even vaguely constitutional. That nostalgia is for me assuaged today by seeing some of those same unkind academics around me and knowing that this time it is each other they will be bent on demolishing.

An opening ceremony should, however, begin not with maudlin introspection but with a welcome and I do warmly welcome all to this seminar, this Bicentenary review of Australian federalism. My welcome is the warmer for the reckless valour you have all displayed in venturing, on a mid-winter morning, to attack the intractable, and at the same time amorphous, topic of Australian federalism and in being prepared to do so, moreover, in what might be thought to be hostile territory, here in Canberra, surely the citadel of centralism, even if it has for the moment been deserted and left quite undefended by its politicians, who are for the moment intent on other battlefields.

It is the occasion of their desertion which prompts me to an initial observation. Is there not something a little eerie about our gathering here together to discuss federalism, the foundation upon which rests our whole Australian polity, our system of government, while at this very moment all around the nation, at meetings and through the media, those who aspire to govern us are ceaselessly exhorting those who are to be governed, yet are doing so with, as I read and hear them, not a single mention of our federalism, of whether it be in good shape or in bad, in need of reform or beyond reproach?

There are, of course, cynical explanations for this phenomenon; cynics have ready, if not always constructive, answers to all such questions. But another kind of answer may, I suppose, be that federalism—by which I mean the overall system, I don't suggest for a moment that there is no room for amendments to our Constitution—that federalism as it now operates in Australia, however grotesquely different its present day operation is from the model which we may deduce that its architects of the 1890s had in mind, still operates relatively well. So well, as world standards of these things go, that it provokes no keen debate at all, let alone any manifestation of what has become the common currency of mass dissatisfaction, whether expressed in peaceful demonstrations, violent riots in clouds of tear gas or urban guerilla warfare. If we were to test present day Australian federalism by public reaction to it or, rather, by the lack of *any* reaction to it, perhaps we should conclude that it is generally regarded as an acceptable enough structure of government, not profitable matter for election-time debate simply because it does not present any major problem for any concerned sector of society.

Another possible explanation, which also, I think, rises above the level of the merely cynical, is that the state of Australian federalism is not really seen as existing as any distinct topic capable of being grappled with by the citizen. Instead, if it is mentioned at all, it is usually only as the arena within which one's particular hobby horses may appropriately be exercised. Those hobby horses range from Canberra's remote and over-mighty bureaucracy, through our unnecessary second tier of parish pump state governments or, per contra, the threatened misuse of treaties to subvert the true sovereignty of those same, but now admirable, state governments, all the way to the now familiar picture of our creaking horse and buggy Constitution, their only proper destinations the knacker's yard and the scrap-heap respectively.

There is, surely, some justification for what seems to be this reluctance on the part of even the politically aware citizen to treat the institution of federalism itself as a suitable subject of discussion, capable of being wrestled with as a distinct concept with an identifiable content and a life force of its own. No more than a nodding acquaintance with some of federalism's innumerable variants in countries around the globe may suggest that the often-attempted task of even defining federalism resolves itself into the unprofitable exercise of searching for some meagre lowest common denominator, defining for definition's sake. Federalism sometimes seems no more than an imprecise label, to be applied indifferently to any one in a great range of instances of power-sharing within the polity of an internationally recognised nation-state. And what the ordinary citizen, being no federal theorist, is interested in is, perhaps, not the label but the substance: he is interested in how close to or distant from those who govern him a particular system puts him.

Perhaps the exception of Switzerland, an exception explicable on historical grounds, does prove a rule: that to the citizens of a nation small both in size and population, federalism may have neither appeal nor utility, having little to offer to, for example, countries such as present day Austria or Denmark or New Zealand. Whereas to the far-flung populations of the great land masses of the USA or of Australia it has obvious attractions, if only as combining the attainment of a nationhood significant in world terms with the virtue of regional governments which remain within reach of and in touch with the governed.

There seems, too, to be a relationship between federalism and that modern phenomenon: the co-existence of centripetal and centrifugal forces in the western world. McWhinney has written of decentralisation as the key word in the existing western style nation-state, with its emphasis on devolution of decision-making on a regional basis; yet this is accompanied by the growth of supra-national institutions which are given wide powers to establish common fiscal and economic policies and to set standards in fields as varied as human rights and trade practices. Of course, mere decentralisation without guaranteed autonomy of the regional organs is not federalism within Geoffrey Sawer's widely accepted description of it; nor does the supra-national institution replicate the classic federalised nation-state; but one wonders whether those same forces which led to classic federalism are now at work on a wide scale and in a rather different international context.

Federalism certainly, of itself, provides no perfect solution to the problem of groupings of distinct and perhaps mutually hostile communities which yet seek the advantages on the world stage of one shared and potent nationhood: several federal nations to the present day show that to be so. Yet something akin to classic federalism, conferring a single and significant nationhood plus the relative accessibility and the decentralisation of power which regional governments offer, may, if suitably modified, meet the needs not only of homogeneous communities like Australia. It may, with modifications, also accommodate the quite different demands which stridently ethnic regionalism makes upon a nation and the stresses which it imposes upon national unity. This seems to me to be suggested by the movements towards devolution of power to regions that we see emerging in a number of nations possessing diverse ethnic regions.

In sum, then, I suggest that federalism in its widest sense is no mere outmoded legacy of the last century. It can provide, in suitable circumstances, a sound model for the democratic governance of very differently situated communities. More than that, its concepts may also be contributing something to the shape of the supra-national entities which we see emerging.

All this may seem a far cry from the subject of this seminar, Australian federalism and its state of health as we teeter on the brink of the Bicentennial year, but the very mention of brink suggests that what I have said is perhaps as close to the subject of this seminar as a

Governor-General should venture in the midst of an election campaign. I am delighted to declare open this seminar and look forward to reading its printed product.

Sir Ninian Stephen
Governor-General of Australia.

CONTRIBUTORS

His Excellency Sir Ninian Stephen	Governor-General of Australia.
Henry Burmester	Attorney-General's Department, Canberra.
Hugh Collins	Professor, School of Social Sciences, Murdoch University.
Brian Galligan	Deputy Director, Centre for Research on Federal Financial Relations, Australian National University.
Bhajan Grewal	Director, Intergovernmental Economic and Trade Relations, Department of Management and Budget, Government of Victoria.
Brian Head	Associate Professor, School of Humanities, Griffith University.
Geoffrey Lindell	Reader, Faculty of Law, Australian National University.
Joan Rydon	Professor, Department of Politics, La Trobe University.
Peter Self	Emeritus Professor, London School of Economics and Political Science and Visiting Fellow, Australian National University.
Campbell Sharman	Senior Lecturer, Department of Politics, University of Western Australia.
Cliff Walsh	Director, Centre for Research on Federal Financial Relations, Australian National University.
Leslie Zines	Professor, Faculty of Law, Australian National University.

INTRODUCTION

1

AUSTRALIAN FEDERALISM: PERCEPTIONS AND ISSUES

Brian Galligan

There can be little doubt that Australia's federal Constitution is so deeply embodied in the political culture and habits of the country and its people that it is largely taken for granted. As Sir Ninian Stephen points out in the foreword to this book, federalism is 'the foundation upon which rests our whole Australian polity, our system of government'. Despite its significance, however, there is little popular enthusiasm for federalism as such nor much interest on the part of politicians to introduce federal issues into the hurly-burly of electoral politics. This suggests, as Sir Ninian comments, that federalism is operating 'relatively well', that 'it is generally regarded as an acceptable enough structure of government' and 'does not present any major problem for any concerned sector of society'. But, as well, Australian political and constitutional history shows that federal issues, when raised, arouse strong and emotive conservative reactions so are probably best left undisturbed.

Federalism pervades Australian life to an extent that many Australians do not appreciate, as David Butler emphasised to this seminar:

> I don't think most of you realise how deeply federal you are; how much you assimilated a federal system with your mothers' milk. You all have dual loyalties to Victoria or West Australia or, heaven help you, to Queensland and to Australia, while I grew up just as an Englishman.

And yet among the select group of élites who have a professional interest in the subject and for serious students of Australian politics federalism is an important and lively topic. Federalism is important because it is the main structuring feature of Australian politics. It remains topical because it is a dynamic rather than a static structure that is itself changed, even if usually in incremental ways, in the ongoing interactive process of shaping Australian politics. As well political institutions once put in place in a congenial host polity tend to have an institutional life of their own, increasing or declining in relative strength and influence or perhaps even changing direction, depending on the energy and ideas of those who work them and the opportunities and constraints that they face. Even if basic structures remain intact and relatively stable, as has Australia's federal system of government for more than three-quarters of a century, significant changes may occur in particular institutions or in directional trends that need to be articulated and critically assessed. For example, the High Court's controversial interpretation of the external affairs power in the 1983 Tasmanian *Dams* case was a landmark constitutional decision that greatly expanded formal Commonwealth power, but whose overall political significance is more difficult to assess.

Federalism remains a controversial topic for a number of reasons, not least among which is the fact that it produces a highly complex system of government that is often the subject of varying and conflicting interpretations. Moreover, federalism, like any system of government, embodies basic normative values over which participants in federal politics and interested observers of the system often differ. Some favour stronger national government but others are avid states' righters; some are happy with the *status quo* while others prefer either more or less centralisation or decentralisation of powers; and some are opportunistic in seeking to exploit the opportunities of multiple political centres that federalism offers in pursuit of particular policy goals and preferences.

In addition there are considerable conceptual and methodological problems in coming to grips with such a large and messy subject as federalism. It is difficult to define the topic in any exclusive way that limits it from other broad aspects of politics, political history and political culture. Most would agree that the essence of federalism is the division of political power and government institutions between two levels of government, both of which are sovereign in limited fields and neither of which is subject to the other in certain core areas. But there is little agreement on precisely where the division ought to be made and what constitutes the basic core of sovereignty that is required for each level of government.

Confronted with all these difficulties some dismiss the whole enterprise of studying federalism as a waste of time and advocate taking up other more manageable topics (for example, Riker, 1970). But federalism is so pervasive in the politics of a federal country like Australia that opting out is hardly feasible. Australia's political and constitutional systems, its public finance and political economy, and its political history and culture are all so thoroughly federalised that it would be a superficial approach indeed that did not have a major focus and emphasis on federalism.

The more normal course, that is typical of the social sciences generally, is to render the topic manageable through disciplinary fragmentation. Each interested discipline considers only those aspects of federalism that come within its accepted field of study and are of professional concern: constitutional lawyers take up federal issues that are the subject of judicial review; fiscal economists focus on federal financial arrangements; and political scientists study select governmental institutions and processes. Since the earlier reviews of federalism around 1950 (Sawer et al., 1949; Sawer, 1952) the disciplines that have a major interest in federalism have become more sophisticated and specialised, but also more select and narrow in their views. As Geoff Sawer pointed out at this seminar, despite enhanced specialised knowledge of the interested disciplines it can no longer be taken for granted that everyone has read the *Engineers'* decision.

The unfortunate consequence, given the tendency of any discipline towards a holistic view, is that each discipline tends to generalise its findings about select aspects of federalism to the whole topic. The result is a number of discrete but inconsistent overviews of federalism which, when popularised, are usually misleading. As well, particular disciplines have been working with partial and cramped concepts of federalism. Until the recent resurgence in the study of Australian federalism among political scientists, the field was dominated by fiscal economists and constitutional lawyers whose leading theme was the ever-increasing centralisation of power in the Commonwealth. This finding was based on the trends in formal constitutional interpretation and fiscal finance but took little account of actual legislative and executive power exercised by the states nor of policy processes and intergovernmental relations.

For example, it is by no means clear that 'tied' or 'specific purpose' grants, made under section 96 of the Constitution which has been broadly interpreted by the High Court to allow the Commonwealth to enter policy areas of the states by specifying terms and conditions attaching to financial grants, can be simply equated with central control. States may initiate requests for such grants as a strategy for boosting their funds (although this is largely undercut by the Grants Commission's equalisation procedures); such grants may free up state funds for alternative purposes (there is evidence for this in areas such as housing policy); and in any case there is little follow-up by the Commonwealth to ensure state compliance. In short one cannot generalise from dominance in fiscal federalism to dominance of the federal system overall. Nor can one generalise about real power relations from formal constitutional trends. The Court may open up potential areas for expansion of Commonwealth power, but countervailing political pressures that keep the Commonwealth largely in check will likely be activated. We cannot tell without supplementing our knowledge of more formal constitutional structures and fiscal arrangements with close study of the politics and policy processes of federalism.

Thus because of the complexity of the subject, its dynamic character, and also because of the different disciplinary frameworks, interpretative views and value preferences of those who study it, Australian federalism remains a difficult and controversial topic that warrants periodic attention in interdisciplinary forums such as the one that formed the basis for this collection. In the various chapters of the book broad aspects of federalism are canvassed in some depth by scholars from the disciplines of law, politics and economics. In the concluding chapter Joan Rydon draws together some of the main themes and points that were raised and puts these into historical perspective. My purpose in this introductory chapter is to highlight certain key issues that were addressed and to suggest something of the range of views that were put. The discussion necessarily reflects my own view on what the key issues were and on the state of opinion among those who participated in the 1987 Federalism Review Seminar (including those whose commentaries are not published in this book).

Federal theory and Australian federalism

There is a venerable tradition in Australian scholarship and commentary that emphasises pragmatism in public affairs and understates the role of theory. It is pointed out that Australians are predominantly utilitarians who pioneered state socialism without doctrine in order to alleviate the harsh conditions of a sparsely populated and unfriendly country and to help cushion the impact of volatile international markets. In due course the separate colonies federated for practical reasons of commerce, convenience and defence, using a hybrid combination of existing English and American models of government.

The pragmatism of the Australian story is usually mirrored by that of the Australian storytellers, with the chapter on federalism being no exception. Douglas Copland was not atypical of Australian social scientists when he rejected outright Kenneth Wheare's modestly theoretical attempt at drawing out the preconditions of 'When Federal Government is Justifiable' at the 1951 Jubilee seminar. Copland (1952: 124) insisted:

> It is not much use exploring the more remote realms of the theory of federalism in relation to effectiveness of administration or of comparing the details of federation, as we know it in this country, with the details of federation in other countries. We must always bear in mind that forms of government are almost invariably the products of the history and geography of a particular area.

Joan Rydon quotes Copland approvingly and also insists that 'the particular nature of Australian federalism has been determined by local conditions'. She lists the four most important local determinants as the pre-existing constitutions of the states, the small and fixed number of states, the dominance of state capitals and relative sparseness of border hinterlands, and the centralised nature of government services. Such local conditions are major determinants of the *particular* nature of Australian federalism, but hardly a complete or adequate account of our *federal* structure.

For that it is necessary, in my view as explained in Chapter 3, to go back to the constitutional theory of the American federalists that is structurally embodied in the federal system of government that the Australian founders copied. Federalism within a liberal democratic polity does enhance democratic participation because it sets up, in addition to national government, subnational governments which deal with the bulk of local issues and are closer to the people. But in addition federalism embodies liberal constitutional values of fragmenting, checking and thereby restraining government power by setting up multiple levels and branches of government. Such characteristics of a federal system are plainly manifest in Australian political and constitutional history and have been as potent in shaping Australian politics as the particular determinants listed by Rydon. The enduring stability of Australian federalism is due in large part to the enhanced democratic participation it allows, particularly at the subnational or state level. The strong anti-federal tradition in Australian politics, manifest until recently in the Labor Party's formal commitment to the abolition of federalism, has been the reaction of populist majoritarianism against liberal constitutionalism.

The Australian Constitution at both the theoretical and constitutional levels is an uneasy combination of two traditions: the British Westminster system of parliamentary responsible government and the American federal system of constitutional divisions of powers. As Leslie Zines explains in Chapter 2, the Australian High Court has adopted an interpretative method drawn from the British system to interpret the American system. In the leading *Engineers'* case (1920) that still encapsulates the Court's interpretative orthodoxy and leads it to sanction Commonwealth incursions deep into the jurisdictional heartland of the states, '"federal" notions [were] ousted as aids to interpretation' in favour of full and plenary interpretation of Commonwealth powers regardless of the impact on federalism and the states (short of discriminating against or destroying them). As Zines puts it:

> [J]ust as a unitary colonial legislature was left free by the courts to pursue its own policies (subject to impartial laws and interests) and to enact its own laws to operate within the limits of its territory, no matter how damaging, so the federal parliament could do so within the limits of the subjects of power granted to it. The British legal notion of the supremacy of parliament with its concomitant consequence of political rather than legal checks on power is the clear philosophy of the *Engineers'* case.

There is something incongruous about a court using an interpretative method that is derived from a politico–legal model alien to federalism to interpret a federal system. Whereas in the Australian Constitution the Commonwealth's powers are spelt out and the residue reserved for the states, the *Engineers'* method produces an inexorable expansion of overall federal power and a corresponding reduction of residual state power. Judges and lawyers admit this consequence but claim there is no satisfactory alternative. Geoff Lindell documents how the so-called 'literal' method of the court has produced a 'dramatic expansion of national legislative power' over the last couple of decades. Despite a certain unease with this outcome, Lindell stands firm on the orthodox line taken by Australian lawyers that 'federalism, at least as hitherto analysed, fails to yield a workable judicial standard or test for limiting the scope of Commonwealth powers'.

There is surely a challenge for lawyers and judges, particularly the dissenting ones in major constitutional cases like the *Dams* case, as well as for political scientists to come up with a method of interpretation that is more suitable for a federal Constitution. It is hardly satisfactory for judges to stick with an anti-federal method because it fits their other doctrinal presuppositions and is easy to apply. Nor is it sufficient, in my view, to sanction the formal centralisation of federal powers that results inevitably from the application of an anti-federal method on the grounds that the political process might redress the Commonwealth's increased constitutional powers and maintain the federal system.

It is ironic that lawyers persist in eschewing federal theory when political scientists and economists are rediscovering it. Committed federalists generally and rational choice economists in particular distrust democratic political processes that are unrestrained by limiting constitutional rules. In Cliff Walsh's restatement of classic federalist theory:

> [O]ne of the most important features of federal constitutions is their role in constraining the ability of governments to use in an exploitative way the coercive powers that are necessarily given to them . . . On this view, the coercive powers of central governments are, and are intended to be, constrained both by the constitutionally defined limits on their roles and functions and by the fact that they are in effect put into competition with subnational governments that are given essentially equal rights in their own domains and given concurrent access to major revenue sources. The coercive powers of subnational governments are further constrained by their being put into political competition with one another, voters (and businesses) having the power to vote with their feet as well as through the ballot box.

Clearly the constitutional constraint on central government in Australia has been severely undermined by the High Court and sanctioned by lawyers. They have adopted an anti-constitutional method of expansive literal interpretation that, given the written form of the Constitution in spelling out Commonwealth and not state powers, favours the Commonwealth, as both Lindell and Zines document in their chapters. That puts considerably greater weight on the processes of political federalism to sustain the system.

Fiscal imbalance and federal balance

A leading theme in commentaries on Australian federalism, that has been developed in detail by Russell Mathews and others associated with the Centre for Research on Federal Financial Relations, is the financial dominance of the Commonwealth. Since the sanctioning of the Commonwealth's monopoly over income tax in the *Uniform Tax* case (1942), Australian fiscal federalism has been characterised by a high level of vertical fiscal imbalance. The ratio of taxation to expenditure is higher for national government and lower for subnational governments in Australia than for other western federal democracies. Walsh and Grewal are both highly critical of this state of affairs in their respective chapters.

According to Grewal the Commonwealth's fiscal dominance is 'an unnecessary, avoidable and harmful feature of the Australian federation that has adversely affected the roles of major intergovernmental fiscal institutions'. The major intergovernmental forums of Premiers' Conference and Loan Council are dominated by the Commonwealth and narrowly concerned with fiscal matters rather than intergovernmental co-ordination. Fiscal imbalance undermines responsibility and accountability on the part of the states because such a high proportion of their expenditure is funded by Commonwealth grants. It also leaves the states vulnerable to excessive restraint imposed by the Commonwealth: for example, for the decade ending 1986–87 the Commonwealth's own purpose outlays increased at 13.6 per cent annually while grants to the states were kept to 9.4 per cent annually. In a decade of fiscal constraint, the Commonwealth has been squeezing the states more than itself.

Walsh too is strongly critical of the Commonwealth's fiscal dominance and the states' corresponding lack of responsibility. He argues that the present system of fiscal dependence encourages grant seeking rather than efficient policy formation and delivery. It produces a 'fiscal club' or 'taxation revenue cartel' characterised more by cosy arrangements among participating élites than by competition that federalism is supposed to promote, and political accountability in fiscal matters that is the hallmark of sound government.

Undoubtedly the least satisfactory part of fiscal federalism as it has developed in recent decades is the high proportion of special purpose, or section 96, grants. An inordinate amount of Commonwealth ministerial and bureaucratic energy goes into this dubious practice of designing and funding specific policy programmes and projects that fall within the ordinary jurisdictional domain and competence of the states. Here, *par excellence*, is the domain of special pleading, pork-barrelling, unnecessary Commonwealth government interference and duplication of functions. The states have obvious incentive to accept such grants; indeed, as Norman Fisher pointed out and illustrated to the seminar, the states, or special interests from the states, often instigate such grants. Except for expanding the Commonwealth's policy domain at the expense of the states and serving the special interests of granting ministers and officials and recipient groups—all of which are detrimental to sound government—special purpose grants serve little purpose. As Grewal points out, they occur in an 'institutional vacuum' without proper co-ordination or review. The amounts that states receive in earmarked funds are offset by national decreases in general purpose funds, and in any case the Grants Commission includes the bulk of such special grants in its equalisation formula that adjusts the amount of general purpose funds to be received. While more systematic research needs to be done on the rationale and processes of special purpose grants, it is likely that that would only strengthen the case for their abolition.

There can be no doubt that the Commonwealth's dominance in fiscal and formal constitutional powers has been expanded and consolidated in the post-war period. That is extensively documented in the chapters by Grewal and Walsh on fiscal federalism and by Zines and Lindell on constitutional federalism. But does that mean that the real power and position of the states has declined proportionately? It has been commonly assumed by those who do not study federalism or the states carefully that that has been the case. But such a superficial conclusion presupposes two dubious steps: one, that formal power can be equated with real power; and two, that the Commonwealth and states are linked in a see-saw balance or zero-sum game in which the increase in one implies a corresponding decrease in the other. Both of these fallacies are strongly rejected by the contributors to this book.

As already pointed out, the constitutional lawyers document the inexorable centralisation of constitutional power that flows from application of the *Engineers'* interpretative method, but emphasise that the political process is available to counterbalance and redress such formal tendencies towards greater power in Canberra. Henry Burmester concludes his analysis of the area of external affairs, where the Commonwealth's powers have undergone probably the most spectacular increase, with the proviso that:

> At the same time, the Australian federal system at the political level has been strong enough to ensure that in many instances the Commonwealth does not assert its undoubted power, but relies on state co-operation to enact legislation, or voluntarily to restrict their trade and investment policies or take other particular action. If, however, national interest is considered to require it, the Commonwealth has shown its willingness to intervene. The use of the World Heritage Convention both to stop the building of a dam in Tasmania and, most recently, to establish an inquiry into certain forestry issues in Tasmania indicates the extent to which a determined federal government can go in reliance on its external affairs power. These are, however, isolated examples. One can point to many more examples where the federal government has deferred to state concerns or sensitivities and only acted with the concurrence or agreement of the states.

The second point that federalism does not work as a see-saw balance or zero-sum game is strongly emphasised by political science contributors. Campbell Sharman rejects the notion of federal balance on a number of grounds: it presupposes a mechanistic view of political relations; it assumes that clear boundaries can be drawn between functions of government and precise weights assigned to components on each side; and it usually assumes the desirability of some equilibrium point in the relationship between governments. But the Australian federal system is much more complex and contentious with both levels of government growing considerably in the post-war decades. Both Brian Head and Joan Rydon reiterate the point that federalism is better approached as a complex web of interactions than a relationship of balance or of dominance and subservience. As Joan Rydon concludes:

> National and state activities and interests become increasingly interconnected. The result is neither the domination of national bodies nor the destruction of the states. Instead there is an increasing variety of organisations combining state and national interests. Within each there may be conflict, competition and co-operation, shifts in the balance of power or of bargaining strengths.

Such a view implies the continuing health and resilience of the states and places considerable weight on intergovernmental relations for the functioning of federalism. These two areas which receive extensive consideration in this collection are considered in the next section.

The states and intergovernmental relations

Despite the formal increase in Commonwealth powers, the states retain an impressive array of powers and functions. Zines points out that despite the large increase in federal power as a result of judicial review, the states have not been reduced to insignificance:

> If the widest scope currently conceivable were given to federal powers, the Commonwealth would be unable comprehensively to legislate for codes on most of the basic subjects of law taught at Australian law schools, such as contracts, torts, criminal law, land law, personal property law, trusts, equity, state administrative law, the law of evidence and so on. This is also true of a number of specialised subjects such as those that relate to the police, local government, town planning, landlord and tenant, etc.

Sharman reiterates a theme that he has developed elsewhere (Sharman, 1988), that the states are not only not subservient to the Commonwealth but are politically dominant. The Whitlam government's challenge to the states failed politically and also enhanced the states' financial budgets and the growth of their administrative expertise. He argues that such political, financial and administrative gains by the states have more than offset the Commonwealth's increase in formal constitutional powers.

Rydon draws a somewhat similar political lesson from the Whitlam experience: 'that the states could be neither side-stepped nor coerced'. Rather through specific grants and their participation in joint programmes the states have been strengthened in their finances, bureaucracies and bargaining powers. Rydon emphasises the importance of electoral politics for federalism, explaining how state elections in Western Australia and South Australia forced modification to key policies of the Hawke federal government on Aboriginal land rights and restrictions on further uranium mining.

In the area of economic management, where the Commonwealth's role has expanded considerably in the post-war period, Brian Head shows that the states 'remain very important regulators and promoters of economic activity in their respective regions'. The states exercise considerable power over an array of important policy areas and in industry policy and resource development are key players. In economic as well as other policy areas, there is no obvious line of demarcation between state and federal powers or roles but rather overlapping and intermeshing that promotes and allows competition and rivalry but, according to Head's argument, also requires co-operation and co-ordination.

The continued vitality of the states and the growth in size and complexity of both levels of government has produced a corresponding increase in intergovernmental relations. In fact intergovernmental relations are probably the most significant but least studied area of contemporary Australian politics. The various contributors to this volume tackle aspects of this large and complex topic, emphasising its significance, illustrating with examples some of the salient issues, and highlighting the problems. As with federalism itself there is no consensus among the various authors about how well intergovernmental relations are working nor how they ought to function.

Sharman describes the explosion in intergovernmental relations as a 'luxuriant flowering' which demonstrates the ability of the federal system to respond to new problems. Grewal is dissatisfied with the way fiscal matters dominate the peak intergovernmental forums and proposes an alternative model that would emphasise policy co-ordination. Walsh, however, suggests an alternative model of more competition between governments whose fiscal powers ought to match their policy responsibilities. Opposed to Walsh, Head and Self make strong cases for a major continuing role for the Commonwealth in ensuring national equity and productivity goals. The inherent tensions and competition that federalism ensures and promotes need to be offset, Head argues, by more intricate processes of co-ordination and consultation. The issue between greater competition or more co-ordination is a fundamental one that involves a potent mix of personal preference and diagnosis on each side and is likely to be a central issue in future debate over Australian federalism.

Nor is co-operative federalism absent from the area of constitutional law, which is arguably the most co-ordinate part of Australian federalism for the reasons Zines explains. Both Lindell and Burmester give examples of co-operative arrangements that modify federal dominance. The pressure of states has recently led to agreement for cross-vesting of jurisdiction that will enable state supreme courts to recover some of the ground occupied by the Federal Court and help resolve undesirable jurisdictional wrangles that have marred the dual system of state and federal courts for a decade. Even in matters of external affairs where the Commonwealth's superiority has been repeatedly sanctioned by the courts, the states are often included in a variety of ways. As Hugh Collins indicates, the states have persisted in minor international roles themselves, and as Burmester makes clear they have not been excluded entirely by the Commonwealth, even at times participating in the process of legislative enactment of treaty obligations.

If the proliferation of intergovernmental relations reflects the adaptability of our federal system in handling big and complex government, it also exacerbates the problems of responsibility and accountability in goverment. Most specialised intergovernmental forums are closed to public scrutiny and once-removed from parliament. Walsh is sceptical about cosy relations within the fiscal finance 'club' despite the rhetorical antagonism that surrounds Premiers' and Loan Council meetings. Rydon is disturbed about the weakening of parliamentary and electoral accountability that intergovernmental arrangements entail. It seems that intergovernmental relations within a federal system do constitute a shadowy 'fourth branch' of government that requires more intensive monitoring and critical scrutiny.

Australian federalism: settled but still controversial

There have been two important changes in the political attitudes of Australians over the last decade or so: one is the 'normalisation' of Labor as a party of routine government; the other is a general acceptance of federalism. The two are related in a number of ways. Besides finally abandoning in the 1970s a hollow formal commitment to abolish federalism, Labor has governed in four of the six states and nationally since 1982–83 (in New South Wales from 1975 to 1988). Not only have there not been significant challenges to federalism during that period, but state Labor governments and leaders like Premier John Cain from Victoria have been in the forefront in overhauling and upgrading state administrations and in advocating reforms for Australian federalism (Cain, 1987). If 'Labor versus the federal Constitution' aptly summed up earlier periods of turbulent Labor politics (see Whitlam, 1957), 'Labor working the federal Constitution' is now the unexceptional state of affairs.

The attitudes of academic commentators have also changed as was clear at the federalism review seminar. There is now fairly general acceptance of, and in some instances enthusiasm for, Australia's federal system. Geoff Sawer said there had been a revolution in attitudes towards federalism, while Robert Parker contrasted the large pro-federal contingent, probably a majority, at this seminar with the predominantly anti-federal majorities at the 1950s seminars. Much energy has been wasted in the past debating whether Australia should have a federal system or not, and in wishful speculation about alternative types of government. There is now a more realistic acceptance of the existing system, and a concern with its actual functioning and improvement.

Arguments against federalism in the past, particularly in the post-war period when most progressives favoured national concentration of powers for economic management and welfare purposes, were based mainly on macro-economic reasons. In his contribution to this collection Peter Self gives a sophisticated critique of Australian federalism that draws on public choice economic theory as well as the more traditional macro-economic considerations. Self's use of public choice theory for this purpose warrants attention because it is rather novel and his conclusions are at odds with those of other contributors.

The functional decentralisation that federalism provides is preferred by public choice economists on micro-economic grounds of improving the capacity of the political system to register preferences for public goods. The test for the vitality and worthwhileness of federalism that Self draws from this is actual diversity of public choices by the various states. Australian federalism fails this test, he argues, because the states all have relatively similar policy outcomes. Self acknowledges that there are a number of powerful factors such as the lack of state fiscal autonomy and the equalisation procedures of the Commonwealth Grants Commission that tend to produce uniformity. Nevertheless, Australian federalism fails the diversity test because state outcomes are so much alike.

Others place more store on the extent and significance of policy differences among the various states (see numerous contributors to Galligan, 1988). But leaving that whole matter aside, the point at issue is whether diversity of outcomes is a valid test of a federal system. In my view and that of other contributors like Walsh, it is not. The justification for liberal democracy generally or a federal constitutional system in particular does not depend on outcomes but process. Federalism is to be preferred not because it produces different outcomes but because it enhances democratic participation and choice. It does not count against a federal system that state majorities all make the same choice; the advantage is that they choose. Whether such public choice is vitiated in practice by the sheer complications, overlapping and duplication of government responsibilities and functions that modern federalism entails or is overridden by intergovernmental arrangements that are removed from public accountability are separate questions, at least in principle.

Australian federalism remains a rich topic for continuing research and political argument. I hope that this collection of essays indicates the significance and diversity of the subject, provides a representative slice of current thinking and debate, and stimulates others to take up the issues raised here that are of abiding national importance.

References

Cain, J. (1987), 'Towards a Federal Reformation: the Renaissance of the Australian States', in M. Birrell (ed.), *The Australian States: Towards a Renaissance*, Longman Cheshire, Melbourne: 1–17.

Copland, D. (1952), Discussion in G. Sawer (ed.), *Federalism: An Australian Jubilee Study*, F.W. Cheshire, Melbourne: 123–24.

Galligan, B. (ed.) (1988), *Comparative State Policies*, Longman Cheshire, Melbourne.

Riker, W.H. (1970), 'The Triviality of Federalism', *Politics* 5: 239–41.

Sawer, G. et al. (1949), *Federalism in Australia*, F.W. Cheshire, Melbourne.

—— (ed.) (1952), *Federalism: An Australian Jubilee Study*, F.W. Cheshire, Melbourne.

Sharman, C. (1988), 'The Study of the States', in Galligan (ed.): 2–17.

Whitlam, E.G. (1957), 'The Constitution versus Labor', in E.G. Whitlam, *On Australia's Constitution*, Widescope, Camberwell, Vic.: 15–46.

FEDERAL THEORY AND AUSTRALIAN FEDERALISM

2

A LEGAL PERSPECTIVE

Leslie Zines

Those who framed the Australian Constitution were not given to over much theorising about the nature of federalism. They were all colonial politicians; many were lawyers; a large number believed in the excellence of British governmental institutions and, in particular, the concept of responsible parliamentary government, which had fairly recently received its classic description in Dicey's *The Law and the Constitution*.

In determining the terms of union, one might have expected them, therefore, to have turned to the only British federation then in existence, namely Canada. Indeed, in inviting the other governments to send representatives to a conference to discuss a federal union, Sir Henry Parkes said that he assumed that it 'would necessarily follow close upon the type of the Dominion Government of Canada' (La Nauze, 1974: 14). In a very short time, however, the Canadian model was rejected. It seemed to the delegates that Canada represented a more centralised system than they were prepared to accept. Two aspects of the British North America Act were disparaged. The first was a group of provisions that gave the federal government control over provincial affairs. Vice-regal representatives of the provinces were appointed by the Governor-General in Council and that body had power to disallow provincial legislation and require the Lieutenant-Governor to 'reserve' bills for assent and, therefore, for consideration in effect by the federal government. The Australians would have none of this. Secondly, the powers granted to the provinces seemed, by and large, to be of a minor nature compared with those expressly conferred on the central legislature. In this respect the framers did not pay sufficient regard to the provincial power over 'property and civil rights' and the state of judicial interpretation by the Privy Council at the time (*Citizens Insurance Co.* v *Parsons* 1881).

The Australian delegates quickly found the United States Constitution more to their liking, less centralised and more 'federal'. The principle followed at both the 1891 and 1897–98 conventions was that the powers and the territories of the existing colonies should remain intact 'except in respect of such surrenders as may be agreed upon to secure uniformity of law and administration in matters of common concern' (Aust. Fed. Conv. Deb., 1897: 17). The Canadian Constitution, however, proved useful in relation to marrying a federal system with parliamentary government, monarchical institutions and the imperial connection. For the rest, it was the United States Constitution that provided the powerful beacon light. Years later, Sir Owen Dixon was to declare that the framers of the Australian Constitution 'found the American instrument of government an incomparable model. They could not escape from its fascination. Its contemplation damped the smouldering fires of their originality' (quoted in Cowen and Zines, 1978: v).

Australia thus chose the form which has often been described as 'classic' federalism. Professor Wheare, for example, has said: 'the federal principle has come to mean what it does because the United States came to be what it is' (Wheare, 1946: 12). At any rate, that was the view of Lord Haldane in his judgment in *Attorney-General (Cth) v Colonial Sugar Refining Co. Ltd* (1914: 252–4). He referred to the Constitutions of the USA and Australia as 'federal in the strict sense' and of Canada as federal 'in a loose sense'. That was because 'the natural and literal interpretation of the word confines its application to cases in which these states, while agreeing on a measure of delegation, yet in the main continue to preserve their original constitutions'. In this respect, Canada 'departs widely from the true federal model'. (The difference, however, does not seem of any great importance in examining the meaning and operation of federal systems.)

The preamble to the Australian Constitution recites that the people of the various colonies have agreed to unite in a 'Federal Commonwealth'. Section 3 of the Constitution Act gives power to the Queen in Council to proclaim that the people in those colonies 'shall be united in a Federal Commonwealth'. No explanation of the term is given. This has led to two divergent views. One is that in construing the Constitution, it is necessary to have regard to its federal nature—which in turn requires an examination of what the federal principle means. The other approach is to say that the framers regarded their handiwork as creating a federal Commonwealth. In order to discover what they meant by that, one should simply examine the Constitution, without regard to any preconceived notions of what is essential to federalism. If the result is a society that does not conform to a theory of federalism, then, so much the worse for the theory.

Despite the rubbishing that it has received in recent decades (for example, Riker, 1964: 36, n.10) as an inclusive and exclusive description of the federal principle, no one would deny that a community that conformed to Wheare's formulation of the federal principle was likely to be a federal state. He said: 'By the federal principle I mean the method of dividing powers so that the general and regional government are each, within a sphere, co-ordinate and independent' (Wheare,

1946: 11). This assumes separate organisations or institutions of government; a relationship between them that is not purely hierarchical, but to a degree co-ordinate, and a 'sphere' of power and responsibility in each level of government that is not revocable at the will of the other. What Wheare's definition does not say much about is the size of each 'sphere', the extent of power pertaining to the governments concerned. (He said 'there must be some matter, even if only one matter' which comes within the exclusive control of the central or regional governments. 'If there is not, that would be the end of federalism': Wheare, 1946: 79.) Some, perhaps, would only admit to the ranks of federal states those which ensured a degree of exclusive power to each level of government that was 'substantial', 'not insubstantial' or 'significant'. All these issues have been the subject of legal, or more particularly judicial, argument and debate in Australia. They occupied much of the energy of the High Court in the first two decades of the Commonwealth, and in recent years, as constitutional issues, they have been shown to be still alive and well, even if weaker in strength.

The provisions of the Constitution that point to its federal nature are, of course, the restriction of the power of federal parliament and government to the matters specified (for example, sections 51, 52, 122), the continuation of state constitutions and legislative powers, subject to the provisions of the Commonwealth Constitution (sections 106 and 107), and the guarantee of the limits of territory of the states (section 123). Other provisions, while not ingredients of a federal state, reflect its nature, such as provisions preventing in certain cases the Commonwealth discriminating against, or granting preferences to, states or parts of states, or requiring uniformity of operation throughout the Commonwealth (for example, sections 51(ii) (iii), 99), and section 117 preventing the states and possibly the Commonwealth from discriminating against subjects of the Queen on the basis of residence in another state.

While it cannot be argued that a Senate with equal membership for all the original states is an essential ingredient of a federal state, it is constantly referred to as a federal feature of the Constitution. It does clearly reflect the fact that the Constitution owed its existence to the agreement of the majority of the people in each of the separately organised colonies. That this was the important point is perhaps indicated by the fact that equal representation in the Senate is not guaranteed to new states. It is left to the will of the federal parliament (section 121).

There are, however, a number of departures from the 'independent and co-ordinate' version of federalism. For the first ten years of the federation the Commonwealth was required to give three-quarters of its collection of customs and excise duties to the states. These were the major sources of revenue and constituted a large proportion of state budgets. The Commonwealth is also empowered to invest federal jurisdiction in state courts (sections 71, 77). The states are required to receive into their prisons persons convicted of federal offences (section

120). The most significant departure of all from the federal model (and it might be added from the concept of responsible government) occurred as a result of the insertion of section 105A of the Constitution in 1929 which gave constitutional force to the financial agreement. The Loans Council set up by that agreement is the only national institution (apart from the monarchy and the High Court) dealing with matters pertaining to both the Commonwealth and states recognised by the Constitution.

The only constitutional provision which specifically prevents a Commonwealth law from affecting the states and vice versa is section 114 which, *inter alia*, prohibits a state, without the consent of federal parliament, from imposing any tax on the property of the Commonwealth and prevents the Commonwealth from imposing any tax on the property of a state. Some provisions seem to assume that Commonwealth powers are binding on state governments unless otherwise indicated. For example, section 51(xiii) and (xiv) provide as follows:

> (xiii) Banking, other than state banking; also state banking extending beyond the limits of the state concerned, the incorporation of banks, and the issue of paper money,
>
> (xiv) Insurance, other than state insurance; also state insurance extending beyond the limits of the state concerned.

On the other hand, other provisions specifically mention the states as being within a federal head of power, leading perhaps to the conclusion that otherwise they would not have bound the states. For example, section 51(xxxi) provides for acquisition on just terms 'from any state or person'. Similarly, section 98 extends the commerce power to 'navigation and shipping, and to the railways the property of any state'.

Throughout our federal judicial history, the concept of federalism has had to vie with the notion of parliamentary supremacy and responsible government. All swings and turns of constitutional doctrines have involved emphasising one at the expense of the other. I do not mean by that that there has ever been any doubt in the minds of the judges that it was for the court to prescribe the limits of governmental power of the Commonwealth and the states. Dr Galligan has shown that the founders certainly intended and expected that the courts would play that role (Galligan, 1987: ch. 2). As Fullagar J. once said, the principle of judicial review of legislation is accepted in Australia as 'axiomatic' (*Australian Communist Party v Commonwealth*, 1951: 262). The question has been rather whether in interpreting the scope of powers (usually those of the Commonwealth) the Court should, to a greater or lesser extent, have regard to the place within the federal system of the other level of government or whether the maintenance of the power and position of those governments should be treated as primarily a political issue to be left to political forces and ultimately the electorate to determine.

The earlier judges clearly saw it as their duty to maintain the Commonwealth and the states as independent and co-ordinate organisations of government. Neither government could use its power to hamper, fetter or control the other government in the exercise of its functions. The states were declared constitutionally unable to tax the income of federal public servants or members of parliament (*Deakin v Webb* 1904; *Commissioners of Taxation (NSW) v Baxter* 1907).

The Commonwealth could not subject industrial disputes involving state governments to the regime of the Court of Conciliation and Arbitration (*Railway Servants*' case, 1906). This 'implied immunities' doctrine was principally aimed at preserving the autonomy of the executive functions of each government from being hampered by the other. The fear was that the federal object of the Constitution would be threatened if each government were permitted to exercise its powers to the full, with the effect or purpose of substantially impairing or even destroying the functions of the other government. Mutual crippling was avoided by keeping the Commonwealth and states clear from each other's reach.

While the doctrine can be said to have been motivated by the federal principle, as Wheare later formulated it, another legal doctrine went beyond it. It was concerned with the area of exclusive legislative power retained by the states, and was known as the 'reserved powers' doctrine. Whereas the immunities principle was conceived as mutual, and could clearly be related to federalism as a dual system, the reserved powers doctrine operated to enhance state power at the expense of that of the Commonwealth. The court inferred from the Constitution that it was intended that the states should, unless otherwise clearly indicated, retain exclusive control of local trade and industry—'the domestic affairs of the states' (*R v Barger*, 1908: 69). The result was that if a subject of Commonwealth power could on one interpretation intrude into that area, and on another would not (or would do so to a lesser degree) the narrower interpretation should be adopted. It was held, therefore, that the Commonwealth could not, under the corporations power (section 51(xx)), control the restrictive practices in domestic trade of corporations (*Huddart Parker & Co. Pty Ltd v Moorehead*, 1908); it could not under the trade marks power (section 51 (xviii)) provide for a mark indicating the workers who produced the goods were members of a trade union which was proprietor of the mark (*Union Label* case, 1908). The taxation power did not support a tax on manufacturers coupled with an exemption for those who gave their employees specified terms and conditions of employment (*Barger* case, 1908).

The early High Court's view of co-ordinate and independent governments not interfering in the slightest degree with each other was, of course, impossible in practice. The formulation of the immunities doctrine provided a let-out. It was subject to any indication to the contrary. Such an indication was seen in the nature of the customs powers. One policy that the founders clearly intended to be left for exclusive determination by the Commonwealth was tariff policy. Free trade or protection—the great debate of the nineteenth century—was to depend on the political judgment of the federal parliament and government. If the states could not be taxed under the Customs Act, any policy would be destroyed by a state's importation of goods, perhaps with the intention of employing them in trade and commerce. The 'necessity' upon which it was said the doctrine of mutual non-interference rested clashed with another necessity, that of upholding federal customs policy (*Steel Rails* case, 1908).

Similar arguments were in fact raised about other powers. Higgins J. complained that the immunities doctrine meant that he, as Arbitration Court judge, could not fulfil the intended function of industrial conciliation and arbitration in relation to private persons and corporations. Because of competing state enterprises, beyond the reach of the Arbitration Court, that court could not lay down, and employers could not agree to, terms and conditions that were otherwise seen as fair and which would settle a dispute (*Engineers*' case, 1920: 163–4).

The decisions of the High Court had a profound political effect in the first decade. The Labor Party was led to support a protectionist tariff on the principle of the 'new protection', i.e. that those receiving the benefit of tariff protection or other assistance such as bounties would be required to share the benefit with the workers. *Barger's* case put an end to that. Labor went its own way. In 1909 the Deakinite Liberals joined forces with the Conservatives (who had seen free trade as a lost cause). A two-party system operated for the first time in the federal sphere.

The *Engineers'* case in 1920 provided a revolution in constitutional interpretation, something akin in result, but not in method, to the 'New Deal' volte face of the United States Supreme Court in 1936. With only one dissent (and that of a Labor appointee, Gavan Duffy J.) the High Court held that the states were subject to the conciliation and arbitration power. The court denounced both of the earlier doctrines. While the main joint judgment seems confused in its detailed reasoning and is badly expressed, its general thrust and direction are clear. It is not the proper business of the courts to create and develop principles and doctrines which are not expressed in the Constitution for the sole purpose of maintaining a federal structure or balance. Full scope must be allowed federal and state powers without regard to possible 'abuse' of such powers or their exercise in an anti-federal way. The political system rather than the judiciary provides the means for checking such actions. In a joint judgment of four judges it was said:

> [T]he extravagant use of the granted powers and the actual working of the Constitution is a matter to be guarded against by the constituencies and not by the courts. When the people of Australia, to use the words of the Constitution itself, 'united in a Federal Commonwealth', they took power to control by ordinary constitutional means any attempt on the part of the national parliament to misuse its powers. If it is conceivable that the representatives of the people of Australia as a whole would ever proceed to use

> their national powers to injure the people of Australia considered sectionally, it is certainly within the power of the people themselves to resent and reverse what may be done. No protection of this court in such a case is necessary or proper (*Engineers'* case, 1920: 151–2).

American notions—upon which the implied doctrines were based—were declared to be alien. British institutions, form of government and constitutional principles provided the appropriate model. The two distinctive features lacking in the American system were responsible government and the one and indivisible crown. While much discussion has occurred about the relevance of these institutions to the issues under discussion in the *Engineers'* case (Zines, 1987: 10–12; Sawer, 1962: 580), they appear to relate to the later emphasis on political action and accountability to the electorate. Dicey had declared the British parliament to be the legal sovereign and the electorate to be the political sovereign. The Privy Council had emphasised that in colonial constitutions, local representative legislatures had been granted all the power that the imperial parliament in the plenitude of its power possessed or could bestow (*Hodge v The Queen*, 1983; *Attorney-General for Canada v. Cain*, 1906). There were no constitutional checks on colonial internal government, only those provided by responsible government and democratic elections.

The Commonwealth parliament was not of course 'sovereign' in the sense that the British parliament was or even in the sense that the New South Wales parliament was before federation. The point was that just as a unitary colonial legislature was left free by the courts to pursue its own policies (subject to imperial laws and interests) and to enact its own laws to operate within the limits of its territory, no matter how damaging, so the federal parliament could do so within the limits of the subjects of power granted to it. The British legal notion of the supremacy of parliament with its concomitant consequence of political rather than legal checks on power is the clear philosophy of the *Engineers'* case.

With 'federal' notions ousted as aids to interpretation, the High Court emphasised the express provisions of the Constitution and a large and liberal construction. This is where, ironically, the rejection of the Canadian system, granting express exclusive powers to the provinces, led to greater central power in Australia rather than the reverse, contrary to what the framers had expected. By concentrating mainly on express provisions (although at one point the judgment referred to what was 'necessarily implied': 151) the job of the Court was simply to determine the width of the federal power. There were no state powers to construe. The states simply retained as exclusive power whatever the Court determined was not within the power of the Commonwealth. It was declared to be 'a fundamental and fatal error' to endeavour to determine, by implication, what exclusive powers were granted to the states and so cut down federal power accordingly (154). (Of course the states retained large concurrent powers, but they were subject to inconsistent federal laws [s. 109].)

But federalism as a legal principle continued to haunt. Significantly, however, the first suggestion that a state might have protection from a law otherwise properly described as being on a subject of Commonwealth power related to the operation of responsible government and the deep-seated British principle that the executive cannot spend funds that parliament has not appropriated for a specific purpose. If a federal award was binding on a state, did that mean that the state was obliged to pay the prescribed wage even though the state parliament refused to appropriate funds for the purpose? The judges reconciled the principle in the *Engineers*' case with a negative answer to this question by declaring that there was a legal obligation to pay the wage, but it was subject to parliamentary appropriation (*Australian Railways Union v Victorian Railways Commissioners*, 1930: 389, 352). In doing so, they purported to rely on the express provision in section 106 which is as follows:

> The Constitution of each state of the Commonwealth shall, subject to this Constitution, continue as at the establishment of the Commonwealth, or as at the admission or establishment of the state, as the case may be, until altered in accordance with the Constitution of the state.

Two years later, the Court in fact did uphold a federal law directly seizing state revenue in satisfaction of the obligations imposed on New South Wales by the financial agreement. However, the Court (Evatt and Gavan Duffy JJ. dissenting) recognised the special nature of that agreement as overriding all other provisions of the Constitution. Section 105A(5) declares that the agreement is binding on the parties 'notwithstanding anything contained in this Constitution or the Constitution of the several states . . .' (*Garnishee* case, 1932).

The revival of federalism as a legal issue, however, was not to be centred on the construction of section 106. Indeed, that provision all but disappeared from judicial discourse. The judges instead relied on the general structure of the Constitution and what was to be inferred from it. Judges such as Dixon and Evatt JJ. expressed irritation at the suggestion that if one followed the *Engineers*' case no implications could be made about the relationship of the two levels of government (for example, *West v Commissioner of Taxation (NSW)*, 1937: 681, 688). Dixon J. seized on certain remarks in the *Engineers*' case which suggested some doubts about the extent to which the Commonwealth could affect a crown prerogative of a state or tax a state. He thought that there was a third 'reservation' from the principle in the *Engineers*' case, namely, an attempt by either government to discriminate against the other. It was on this ground that a law requiring states and local governments to bank with the Commonwealth Bank was held invalid (*State Banking* case 1947). Most of the judges did not deny that the provision was within the scope of the power with respect to banking. The law was bad because, by discriminating, it showed a purpose of controlling the states in the exercise of their functions. This restriction, Dixon declared, was founded on 'the federal system itself'. A federal power could not be used for 'a purpose of restricting or binding the state in the exercise of its executive powers' (80). It was argued that if the Commonwealth had nationalised the banks the states would be in the same position. The reply to this was that:

> at bottom the principle upon which the states become subject to Commonwealth laws is that when a state avails itself of any part of the established organisation of the Australian community it must take it as it finds it . . . If there be a monopoly in banking lawfully established by the Commonwealth the state must put up with it. But it is the contrary of this principle to attempt to isolate the state from the general system . . . (84).

This principle was affirmed in *Queensland Electricity Commission v Commonwealth* (1985), where the Commonwealth attempted to make special provisions regarding the determination of an industrial dispute in the electricity industry in Queensland. The provisions were held invalid (Brennan J. dissenting) on the ground that the only criterion for the special procedures was the possibility of making an award binding on Queensland state electricity authorities.

It has throughout this time been made clear that a law discriminating against one or more states *vis-à-vis* the general community is not the only ground which is based on 'federal implications' that can be used for invalidating federal legislation. All the judges have declared that the Commonwealth cannot use its powers to make a law (even though it is 'general' in character) that would threaten the existence of a state or its capacity to function as a state (*Payroll Tax* case, 1971; *Koowarta v Bjelke-Petersen*, 1982; *Franklin Dam* case, 1983). This ground is certainly at the heart of Wheare's notion of the federal principle and indeed of most theories of federalism. But there is great uncertainty about its scope. No federal law has been held invalid on that basis. The principle has, however, been constantly reiterated in recent times.

It seems then that there has been an attempt to extract from the federal concept an essential element of separate and independent state *organisations* of government, divorced from the powers and functions exercisable by the organs and instrumentalities of those governments. Regard is not had to the *extent* of the legislative, executive or judicial authority of the states. The principle requires the states to remain independent entities with a capacity to exercise whatever powers and functions are committed to them, but it has nothing to say about what, if any, powers and functions they have. What is protected has been expressed in various ways—'capacity to function', 'the structural integrity of the state components of the federal framework, state legislatures and state executives', 'the continued functioning of the state as an essential constituent element in the federal system', 'the processes by which its powers are exercised' (*Koowarta v Bjelke-Petersen*, 1982: 216, 480, 433; *Franklin Dam* case, 1983: 703–4, 767).

The degree to which the concept of federalism has been regarded as having anything to say about the scope of state powers is something I shall refer to later. For present purposes, it is necessary to note that the particular doctrine I am referring to is confined to the independence of state organisations and machinery of government. This conforms to the dichotomy of Dixon J. in the *State Banking* case in the following passage:

> The foundation of the Constitution is the conception of a central government and a number of state governments separately organised. The Constitution predicates their continued existence as independent entities. Among them it distributes powers of governing the country. The framers of the Constitution do not appear to have considered that power itself forms part of the conception of a government. They appear rather to have conceived the states as bodies politic whose existence and nature are independent of the powers allocated to them (82).

The effect of this restriction on federal power has been very limited. It has been held, for example, that in the absence of 'discrimination' it does not prevent the Commonwealth:

1 levying payroll tax on the states as employers (*Payroll Tax* case, 1971);
2 prohibiting all development of state-owned land that is part of the 'natural or cultural heritage' without the consent of the Commonwealth government (*Franklin Dam* case, 1983);
3 laying down the terms of employment of, at any rate, most state officers and employees (*Re Lee; ex parte Minister for Justice (Qld)*, 1986); and
4 requiring the state to abide by rules relating to racial discrimination (*Koowarta v Bjelke-Petersen*, 1982).

In applying this restriction on the power of the Commonwealth, the Court has looked at the practical effect of the law on state independence rather than declaring that certain areas are *per se* beyond federal control. For example, it is clear that certain impositions of taxation on the states could seriously threaten the state's capacity to govern. Yet in the *Payroll Tax* case, the High Court refused to conclude from this that the states were not subject to the taxation power at all. They examined the operation of the particular tax and pointed out that states had continued to function, despite it, for thirty years.

In my book, *The High Court and the Constitution* (Zines, 1987: 295–6), I summed up the sort of areas that would come within the scope of the protection as follows:

> Laws which prohibited the appointment or employment of various persons as ministers, judges, or officers of 'central departments of state' might be seen as *prima facie* within this category. A number of other matters can be considered, generally speaking, as necessary to the operation and processes of an independent state government: advice to ministers by the civil service, the relationship of the Governor to ministers and to parliament, parliamen-

tary debate and the internal procedures of parliament, the operation of 'responsible government', and the freedom of the state judiciary.

Included among the matters referred to by the judges as involving special consideration is the taxation of the 'ordinary revenues of the state' (*Payroll Tax* case, 1971: 385, 393).

It is still orthodox doctrine followed by a majority of the court that federal theory has nothing to contribute to the construction of the powers of the Commonwealth. The principles laid down in the *Engineers*' case have retained their strength in this area. In the *State Banking* case, for example, Dixon J., while affirming the relevance of the federal system to constitutional interpretation, was careful to disavow any notion that the Constitution had by implication reserved any particular legislative power to the states—a view which he said 'lacked a foundation in logic' (83). The result is that federal powers have been judicially expanded by virtue of an interpretation that might be described as 'literal'. The effect of any particular construction on the residue of state powers has traditionally been regarded as irrelevant.

As Mr Lindell's paper shows, the result has been the entry of the Commonwealth into fields that even twenty years ago would have been regarded as surprising. For those who believe that federalism requires a guaranteed area of exclusive power for the states, whether legislative, executive or even administrative, the problem has been to find how this could be achieved judicially in Australia, having regard to the structure of the Constitution. No federal theory of which I am aware can assist. Presumably, one would have to see whether the guaranteed states' sphere was substantial enough to entitle the system to be called federal, or whether it was so insignificant that 'token federalism' might be a better description.

As explained above, the first judges of the High Court deduced that the Constitution had, unless the contrary was shown, left matters of domestic trade and industry to the states. Their task, therefore, might in any particular case be seen to be one of 'federal balance'. You weighed and balanced the powers expressly granted to the Commonwealth against those granted, by implication, to the states. Sometimes (and usually) federal power would have to give way, as in the case of using the tax power, the trade marks or the corporation power as a means of regulating directly domestic trade and industry. On other occasions, national policy required an intrusion into the state sphere as in the case of customs and defence. This method of approach is the one followed in Canada where, for example, the court has to decide whether a law that relates both to, say, trade and commerce (exclusive federal subject) and property and civil rights (exclusive state subject) belongs to one or the other category (this is subject to a rather limited 'double aspect' doctrine).

Since the overthrow of that doctrine, the issue has become more intractable. For the framers of the Australian Constitution it would no doubt have come as a surprise to learn that the limited powers they gave to the Commonwealth parliament could result in the states' exclusive legislative power being reduced to insignificance. In fact, despite the large increase in federal power as a result of judicial interpretation over the past sixty years, it has not happened. It is indeed difficult in the case of nearly all the subjects of Commonwealth power to say that it could happen. (It has, however, been suggested that the external affairs power in section 51 (xxix), as currently interpreted, leads to this result. I shall deal with that particular power later, and for the present leave it aside.) If the widest scope currently conceivable were given to federal powers, the Commonwealth would be unable comprehensively to legislate for codes on most of the basic subjects of law taught at Australian law schools, such as contracts, torts, criminal law, land law, personal property law, trusts, equity, state administrative law, the law of evidence and so on. This is also true of a number of specialised subjects such as those that relate to the police, local government, town planning, landlord and tenant, etc. This is not to suggest that the Commonwealth cannot, or on the hypothesis stated could not, intrude into those areas to a greater or lesser degree. For example, there is a federal criminal law; the *Franklin Dam* case upheld certain controls related to land use; if the corporations power is given its widest construction all the subjects mentioned above would be within the regulatory power of the Commonwealth to the extent that foreign corporations or trading or financial corporations were concerned. But only the states could make a general law relating to many of the subjects mentioned. In quite a number of areas, therefore, the states clearly have the primary and the Commonwealth a secondary role. Many of these matters are of course not such as to excite the imagination of the public, politicians or journalists. But no one could rationally deny their fundamental and long-term importance to social life.

Nevertheless, some judges in recent times have shown concern at applying principles that would require them to construe Commonwealth powers broadly and generously and without regard to what remains for the states. It has been suggested that the concept of federalism may have some part to play in the process, known as 'characterisation' of a law for the purpose of determining whether it is within a power of the Commonwealth. These are at present minority views.

In *Gazzo v Comptroller of Stamps (Vic.)* (1981), the court held invalid, as not being authorised by the marriage power or the matrimonial causes power, a federal law that purported to exempt from state stamp duty a transfer of land executed in accordance with an order of the Family Court (Gibbs CJ., Stephen and Aickin JJ.; Mason and Murphy JJ. dissenting). Gibbs CJ. declared that: 'In considering whether a law is incidental to the subject matter of a Commonwealth power it is not always irrelevant that the effect of the law is to invade state power' (240). He added that, 'That of course would not be relevant if the law were clearly within the substantive power expressly granted'.

His Honour took the matter further in *Actors Equity v Fontana* (1982). He was replying to the argument that the power in section 51 (xx) to make laws with respect to 'foreign corporations and trading and financial corporations formed within the limits of the Commonwealth' authorised the Commonwealth to make laws on any subject directed to such corporations. He denied this, referring to the need 'to achieve a proper reconciliation between the apparent width of section 51(xx) and the maintenance of the federal balance which the Constitution requires' (181–2) (compare Mason J.'s reference to a 'competing hypothesis' that the corporations power 'was intended to confer comprehensive power with respect to the subject matter so as to ensure that all conceivable matters of national concern would be comprehended' [207–8]). The problem is to determine, in relation to the first statement, what is 'state power' and, in relation to the second, what are being weighed to produce the 'federal balance'. Federal theory does not seem to help here. All one can do is to regard the functions in fact exercised by the states at any particular time as one of the weights in the balance. Having regard to the fact that the states have concurrent power in relation to most subjects this places the bias in favour of the current situation. Alternatively, the judge is left to his or her own political views about what matters should desirably be left exclusively to the states, without any guidance from the Constitution (see editorial note, 'The Concept of "Federal Balance"' [1986, 60 ALJ 653]).

In Canada, the concept of 'federal balance' might have a clearer meaning because the Constitution itself gives express and exclusive power to both the federal and provincial legislatures. In dealing with a law licensing a business, for example, the court might be regarded as 'balancing' federal power over 'trade and commerce' with provincial power over 'property and civil rights'.

It is worthwhile inquiring, however, whether the plea that the High Court should interpret the scope of a Commonwealth power 'having regard to the federal system' has some meaning other than one based on an assumption of state implied reserved powers over particular subjects. An argument that it has would assume that a particular broad interpretation of the power is possible, but because of the federal system a narrower one should be adopted. In the absence of a reserved powers doctrine the argument must, I think, relate to functional considerations.

One illustration of this is the reasoning of Higgins J. (a supporter of a literal construction of federal powers and an opponent of the doctrine of reserved powers) in *Huddart Parker & Co. Pty Ltd v Moorehead* (1908). He went along with the majority (who were reserved powers supporters) in holding that the corporations power did not enable the parliament to control the trade, and more particularly the monopolistic practices, of the corporations mentioned in section 51(xx). His reasoning was not however based on the view of the majority that intrastate trade was a matter exclusively for the states. It was, rather, the absurdity, as he saw it, of declaring that the Commonwealth could control all activities in relation to section 51(xx) corporations, leaving the states to control those same activities when conducted by individuals and other sorts of corporations. Thus, he said, if the plaintiff's arguments were correct, the Commonwealth could legislate for defamation by or against a newspaper which was owned by a trading corporation, while the states had exclusive power to do so in relation to newspapers that were controlled by partnerships. Similarly, the Commonwealth could enact licensing laws for hotels owned by corporations and the states for those owned by individuals. Higgins' view was, therefore, that the broader interpretation should be rejected because it led to a crazy distribution of powers. It produced what were, in his opinion, bizarre results. It is not my purpose to discuss the Higgins approach or the present state of the law, but merely the nature of the argument.

I used a similar form of reasoning in relation to another aspect of the corporations power. The earlier judgment in *Huddart Parker* held that the Commonwealth could not create a corporation under that power because it referred to corporations 'formed' within the Commonwealth. They held that this meant that the power assumed the existence of a corporation created under some other (usually state) law. This argument is not conclusive and the matter has not been determined. If, however, the Court so decided, there could still be an argument that while the Commonwealth could not under section 51(xx) create trading and financial corporations, it could control their internal structure and even put an end to them. Such a law could easily be described as on the subject of the corporations concerned.

In *The High Court and the Constitution* (89), I said that, on the assumption made,

> [i]f the interpretation of s.51(xx) results in the state having sole authority to create those trading and financial corporations that cannot be created under another head of Commonwealth power, it is not an unreasonable argument that those matters that are part and parcel of creating a corporation and without which the corporation would be an empty shell, incapable of functioning as a juristic person at all, are similarly outside Commonwealth power. As far as dissolution is concerned, it would seem a startling result from the point of view of the structuring of our governmental system to give the state sole power to create a corporation and the Commonwealth the power to destroy it. One is reminded of Marshal CJ.'s comment (in a completely different context) that the power to create implies the power to preserve: *McCulloch v Maryland* (1819) 4 Wheat 316 at 426. Despite the reasoning given above, therefore, if the court regarded the formation of a corporation to be outside the power, there would be a great deal to be said for it excluding not merely a stark act of creation but also such body of law as can be regarded as concerned with its creation, survival and dissolution.

The point is that arguments of this sort do have regard to the particular sort of constitutional arrangements operating in Australia; but they are not necessarily motivated by, or premised upon, the necessity of having states with particular exclusive powers, nor on any federal theory. It is merely assumed, or it is otherwise clear, that certain matters in fact lie within the states' sphere. It is then reasoned that, as a matter of policy or efficiency, a certain construction of federal power is desirable.

It is, however, possible to take a different view on the policy issue and say that the federal power should be given its broadest construction without regard to the considerations I have mentioned. How the government will use the power is a political issue better left to the political organs. This is in the *Engineers'* case, and it is attacked by Dr Galligan. In his book, *Politics of the High Court* (246), he refers to an argument in the *Franklin Dam* case that the corporations power should be read 'within the context of the federal Constitution'. Galligan describes this as 'a perfectly reasonable request except for the *Engineers'* dogma'. Assuming the argument was otherwise reasonable, it is difficult to see why the argument in *Engineers'* relying on democratic controls was not also reasonable. Why is it necessarily 'dogma'? Both federalism and responsible government are broad and fuzzy political assumptions on which principles of interpretation may be based.

Perhaps a better, though different, example of where the federal system might have been seen as a relevant consideration lies in the field of excise duties (granted exclusively to the Commonwealth under section 90). Gibbs CJ. made a plea (unsuccessfully) for a narrow interpretation of this exclusive Commonwealth power based on the plight of the states as a result of uniform taxation and the views of Mathews and Jay in *Federal Finance*, (1972: 318) that the wide view is 'one of the greatest impediments preventing the achievement of a rational and lasting division of financial powers in the Australian federal system' (*Hematite Petroleum Pty Ltd* v *Victoria*, 1983: 617). This is an area where 'having regard to the federal system' might be clearly seen as involving the balancing of state and federal interests, as indeed Gibbs CJ. did in that case. The issue here is more directly related to state independence. Again, however, it does not logically prevent a judge from concluding that the dominant policy of section 90 is ensuring Commonwealth control of taxation in relation to commodities. The main complaint that can be made is that with the exception of Gibbs CJ. (and unusually for him) there was no discussion and debate about the weighing of the different interests. The mere assertion of the other judges of a particular policy as the correct one might properly be described as 'dogma'.

In recent times, however, external affairs power has seemed to many people a particular threat to the federal system. The majority in the *Franklin Dam* case held that it authorised the Commonwealth parliament to implement legislatively any obligation arising under a treaty. It is clear that it also extends to other matters involving international relations where there is no international agreement. It is the first aspect that has caused the greatest concern.

A number of views have been expressed by judges about the scope of section 51(xxxix) in relation to treaties. Some of them are as follows.

1 It extends only to the implementation of a treaty the provisions of which could be described as a matter of external affairs, apart from the fact that it gives effect to an international obligation or arises out of matters that are of concern to other countries. What is required is that the law should deal with the rights or obligations of residents, nationals, enterprises or governments, etc. of other countries (Gibbs CJ., Aickin and Wilson JJ., dissenting judges in *Koowarta v Bjelke-Petersen*).

2 It encompasses the implementation of treaties on any subject that is of 'international concern' or that comes within 1. In the former case, it is necessary to look at the history of the matter including diplomatic action, resolutions of international bodies, the state of international customary law, etc. (Stephen J. in *Koowarta v Bjelke-Petersen*).

3 It extends to (but is not confined to) the implementation of any obligation under any *bona fide* international agreement (Mason, Murphy, Brennan and Deane JJ. in the *Franklin Dam* case).

The minority judges supported the first construction in *Koowarta* and they reluctantly went along with the second construction in *Franklin Dam* in light of the actual decision in *Koowarta*, upholding the validity of the Racial Discrimination Act. In each case they relied heavily on the danger to the federal system that would occur if the third construction was adopted. In their view, this construction would enable the Commonwealth to pass a law on any subject, dependent only on the decision of the executive to become a party to an agreement. This threat was strengthened by the fact that in modern times any subject might give rise to an international agreement (*Franklin Dam* case, 1983: 668–9 per Gibbs J.; 732–33 per Wilson J.; 484 per Dawson J.). These judges, rightly in my view, denied that their reasoning constituted an application of the doctrine of reserved powers. What was at stake was not an implication that any particular subjects were exclusively within state competence. It was rather that a federal system assumed that *some* subjects must be within that category. They reasoned that the broad construction would in effect give the Commonwealth universal power because the government could decide to enlarge Commonwealth legislative power at will.

I do not know that the majority judges (who relied on the Commonwealth's responsibility for international relations) expressly answered this argument. I think that the most probable conclusion from their judgments is that they considered it to be irrelevant. That is to say, they regarded the extent to which the concept of federalism was relevant to legal principles as confined to ensuring the existence and functioning of the state as an independent organisation of government. This is summed up in a phrase of Mason J. who, after referring to this implied immunity, said (694–95): 'So much and no more can be distilled from the federal nature of the Constitution and the ritual invocations of "the federal balance"'. (Contrast Wilson J. [752] who said 'of what significance is the continued formal existence of the states if a great many of their traditional functions are liable to become the responsibility of the Commonwealth?')

Nevertheless, some remarks of Mason J. do suggest a reply which I think would be along the following lines (*Franklin Dam* case, 1983: 692–3). One cannot argue that because the founders wanted a federal state they could not have intended to give the Commonwealth the power to implement treaties. Because of the comparatively narrow range the treaties covered in 1900, it would not have occurred to anyone at the time that such a federal power had the potential to reduce considerably the scope of state exclusive authority. What has changed has been the factual context. If the result of increased international activity leads to a great reduction of state exclusive power, that is merely an inevitable consequence of the increase in international action. Certainly it appears that it was not until the 1920s that the Canadian power in section 132 to legislate in respect of treaties binding on Canada 'as part of the British Empire' was seen as a threat to the provinces (this power was reduced to an outmoded provision by the decision in *Attorney-General (Canada) v Attorney-General (Ontario)* [1937] that it did not apply to treaties entered into by Canada as a sovereign state).

Of course, the argument suggested above is not conclusive in favour of federal power. A believer in upholding federalism as conceived by the minority judges could perhaps argue that the judicial task of keeping the Constitution incrementally in line with changes in society and of regarding the Constitution as an organic instrument fit for a dynamic community does not work only one way, namely in favour of expanding Commonwealth power.

Another argument that might be used against the minority view is that the present interpretation of the external affairs power does not, strictly speaking, lead to the result stated by them. In order to successfully use the power in respect of treaty implementation:

1 there must be a treaty which deals with the matter in a way that conforms to the policy which the Commonwealth wishes to pursue;
2 the treaty must be *bona fide*; and
3 the law must be a reasonable and appropriate means of giving effect to the treaty.

If these conditions are not satisfied, and the law does not come within any other power of the Commonwealth, it remains within the exclusive power of the states.

I agree with Gibbs CJ. (*Koowarta v Bjelke-Petersen* 1982, 300) that condition 2 is 'a frail shield'. Condition 3 is not, as evidenced by the fact that two of the four majority judges found most of the provisions of the Act, which were based on the external affairs power, invalid on that ground. The ease with which the Commonwealth may find an existing agreement or find a country to enter into an agreement with it in relation to a policy the Commonwealth wishes to pursue is a matter of conjecture. One might argue that, despite the restrictions on the exercise of the power, what remains to the states is too insignificant to satisfy what is required by 'a federal state'. Any discussion in those terms, however, must rely on practical considerations relating to the difficulty or otherwise of the federal government obtaining all or most of what it wants by entering into or acceding to international agreements. I suspect that government by international agreement is not as simple as it sounds. It is important to point out, however, that the majority judges did not advert to such considerations (Mason J. in *Koowarta*, however, indicated some scepticism at 229).

There are, of course, modes of protecting and guaranteeing regional interests in addition to, or other than, demarcating the limits of powers of each and leaving it to the judiciary to adjudicate. Many federations provide institutions for the insertion of state interests into the affairs of the federal legislature. The degree to which this is done might, in some cases, have an effect on one's perception of whether a state is entitled to be described as 'federal', particularly where the scope of exclusive power conferred on the regions seems comparatively small. This is certainly the case with West Germany, which, when regard is had to the vast area of power given to the federal authorities, seems clearly at the unitary end of the federal spectrum. This perception, however, might change when one takes into account the direct representation of the states in the Bundesrat—the upper house of federal parliament. Members of that house are appointed, and can be recalled, by state governments. The Bundesrat does not have a veto over all legislation, but the Constitutional Court has given a wide interpretation to the area over which it has such a veto. It was estimated in 1981 that the power of veto extended to over half of the laws passed since 1948 (Blair, 1981: 93). Each state's votes are cast as a block. The members are mandated delegates of the government of their state (see generally J Alwes in Mathews, 1980: ch. III).

The Senate of the USA was perceived as a states' house. Each state has two senators and, until 1913, they were elected by state legislatures. Since then they have been elected directly by the people. All legislation (as in Australia) requires the consent of the Senate. The United States Supreme Court has relied on the position of the Senate, and indeed of the political processes of both houses of Congress, as a reason for not limiting the legislative powers of Congress by reference to federal principles.

In 1976 the Supreme Court of the USA, for the first time in about forty years, declared a federal law invalid on 'federal grounds' (*League of Cities v Usery*). It was held that wages and overtime provisions in a federal Act could not validly apply to bind the states 'in areas of traditional governmental functions'. In *Garcia v San Antonio Metropolitan Transit Authority* (1985), that case was overruled. The majority were of the view that the position of the states as essential units of the federal system was protected by the nature of the federal legislature and the processes through which it operated. The influence of the states was said to be evidenced by a great deal of social legislation which did not bind the states and further by the specific purpose grants that over the decades had been made to the states. That the latter should be regarded as manifesting the strength of the states in the system sounds strange to Australian ears. Indeed, three of the dissenting judges in that case referred to 'coercive grants programmes' (587). In doubting the capacity of political institutions to preserve state autonomy they made reference to 'the expanded influence of national interest groups' (584).

Whether or not the federal political process provides sufficient support for the position of the states in the American federal system, I am not sufficiently experienced to know. The proposition, in any case, has a degree of ambiguity. By 'states' do we mean state governments, state constitutional powers or state social and economic interests? In *Garcia*, the court seemed to merge all three. It is rather ironical that in the *Engineers*' case one of the main grounds for rejecting American doctrines was the existence of responsible government in Australia and its absence in the USA. As explained above, this seems to refer to the emphasis given in the joint judgment to the democratic control of the political machinery. But the position of the Senate did not rate a mention. It has been argued by an American constitutional lawyer, Professor Barrett (1985), that in fact the federal system is far better protected by the political system in the USA than in Australia because of the existence here of responsible and cabinet government. This has led to more centralised and controlled political parties, the dominance of the executive over the House of Representatives, and the control of the Senate by whatever party or parties predominate in that House. The interests of state groups and state governments cannot therefore be exerted in the same way that they can in the USA where, it is said, the senator's or congressman's continuation in office will depend on the vigour he or she displays in pressing for the interests of his or her state or constituency, respectively (Tribe, 1978: 240–2; Zines, 1987: 384–5).

The predominance of opinion in Australia is that the Senate is not a safeguard for the protection of the states (for example, Wiltshire in Mathews, 1980, 75: 9). Yet the disagreement that occurred in the High Court over the voting rights of territorial senators seemed to revolve around the importance of the Senate to the federal system. In determining the apparent inconsistency between section 7 and section 122 of the Constitution, the dissenting judges gave predominance to section 7 by relying in large part upon the existence of a Senate as the major federal feature of the Constitution. These sections (as far as relevant) are as follows:

s.7 The Senate shall be composed of senators for each state, directly chosen by the people of the state . . .

s.122 The Parliament may make laws for the government of any territory

> . . . and may allow the representation of such territory in either House of the Parliament to the extent and on the terms which it thinks fit.

Barwick CJ. and Gibbs J. considered that an upper house representing the states was 'indispensable' to federalism. To alter the nature of the Senate was to alter 'the essential features of the federation' (*Western Australia v Commonwealth* 1975: 175). To uphold territory senators with full voting rights would 'subvert the Constitution and seriously impair its federal character' (176). The Senate was seen by the framers 'as a means of enabling the states to protect their vital interests and integrity'. The majority, on the other hand, preferred a literal construction of section 122, emphasising the framers' experience of and trust in parliamentary government, and the importance of democratic principles.

Whether the Senate was in any substantial degree a protection for the states was not discussed. All that seemed important to the minority judges was the intention of the founders. Indeed, in interpreting the Constitution, the position and function of the Senate does not seem to have been a factor that has ever been taken into account by the Court in respect of the characterisation of federal laws or intergovernmental relations.

While the existence of political parties has been regarded as a reason why the Senate has failed to fulfil its function as a vehicle of state interests, there may be an argument that the parties have in fact inherited that function. Their membership (like that of many groups in Australia) is highly federalised. State branches are strong and, as a result of the organisation of the federal bodies, presumably have great influence in determining party policy. The provisions for equal representation of the states in the Senate no doubt also gives the smaller states a greater proportion of members in the party rooms of both sides of politics. The extent to which these factors have helped to keep federal tensions alive and fairly well in the Australian system is better answered by political scientists than by me.

Much of the above discussion in relation to attempts by the High Court to preserve the independence of the states may seem unreal in the light of the decisions in the two *Uniform Tax* cases (*First Uniform Tax* case, 1942; *Second Uniform Tax* case, 1957). Certainly those judicially created restrictions on federal power pale into insignificance when put against the undoubted predominance of the Commonwealth in all financial affairs, produced by use of its taxation powers and the power in section 96 of the Constitution to grant financial assistance to any state on such terms as the parliament thinks fit.

The judges who upheld the uniform income tax scheme in 1942 had no doubt of the possible effect of their decision. Latham CJ. pointed out that the Commonwealth could use a similar method to deprive the states, in practical terms, of all their revenue-raising potential, and so convert them into administrative arms of federal policy. The answer given by him was:

> Such a result cannot be prevented by any legal decision. The determination of the propriety of any such policy must rest with the Commonwealth parliament and ultimately the people. The remedy . . . is to be found in the political arena and not in the courts (*First Uniform Tax* case, 1942: 429).

An attack, fifteen years later, on the power of the Commonwealth to attach a condition to a grant that the state should not impose income tax failed. But a provision prohibiting a taxpayer from paying state income tax until he had discharged his liability for federal income tax (upheld in the *First Uniform Tax* case) was declared to be invalid (*Second Uniform Tax* case, 1957).

The main reason given for not applying the principle referred to above, namely that the Commonwealth cannot aim its legislation at the control of the states, was that financial assistance under section 96 did not act as a command to the states. It merely offered them an inducement to give up imposing income tax. 'There is no command that they shall not impose such a tax' (*First Uniform Tax* case, 1942: 419). '[T]emptation is not compulsion' (*First Uniform Tax* case, 1942: 417). '[T]here is nothing which would enable the making of a coercive law' (*Second Uniform Tax* case, 1957: 610).

It is easy to point to the unreality of this dichotomy, as Starke J. did in the *First Uniform Tax* case (443), when he held the condition of the grant obnoxious to the federal policy of the Constitution.

Most of the elements of the uniform tax scheme were upheld on grounds which had nothing to do with the wartime power of the Commonwealth with respect to defence (that power was, however, relied on to uphold an Act providing for the Commonwealth taking over state taxation offices, officers, furniture and files). Some, however, suggest that the Court was heavily influenced by the state of affairs in 1942 and by 'legalism'. Dr Galligan has said (1987: 127):

> The *Uniform Tax* case indicates the extremes to which judges were prepared to go in time of national crisis and demonstrated the absurdities to which a legalistic jurisprudence can lead if it is not tempered with prudence and common sense.

The suggestion is that if the High Court had not been dominated by the spirit of the *Engineers'* case and had had regard to the federal system established by the Constitution, state autonomy in fiscal matters might have been better preserved. (For present purposes, I can ignore the possibility that the entire scheme might have been upheld simply as an exercise of the wartime defence power.)

Assuming that the Court had more regard to the concept of federalism than it did, what might it have done? Would it have been able to prevent a Commonwealth monopoly of income tax or indeed any other tax?

Within the range of legal possibilities, the Court could have held:

1 That the Wartime Arrangements Act providing for the taking over of all state income tax offices and officers was not within the defence

power. (This was so held in dissent by Latham CJ. and Starke J.)

2 That the Grants Act conditioning the grants on a state abstaining from levying income tax was invalid, because it manifested a purpose of controlling the state in the exercise of its functions (as held by Starke J.); and because it threatened the existence of a state or its capacity to function as an independent unit of the federation. (A formula reiterated by many judges in the past fifteen years.)

3 That for the purposes of 2 above, the Income Tax Act and the Grants Act should be read together showing a scheme to bring about the purpose manifested in the Grants Act. Therefore, it could have held that the Income Tax Act was also invalid. (No judge so held.)

4 That the priority provision in the Assessment Act was invalid. (So held in the *Second Uniform Tax* case.)

What might the government have done in the light of such a decision invalidating all elements of the scheme? It might have considered (1) re-enacting the income tax legislation, apart from the priority provision, and (2) legislating to make grants to the states, without imposing any conditions. If this legislation were upheld as valid I think that it is probable that it would have brought about a system of uniform taxation of the sort we have today. Indeed, that is all the present system rests on. The condition attached to the grants—upheld in the *Second Uniform Tax* case—was repealed in 1959. The High Court is certainly in no position to determine that the tax rates are too high. If it was prepared to have regard to the amount of the grants as evidence of the 'unreasonableness' of the rates, it would have to take upon itself the task of determining the reasonableness of the grants. In the face of section 96, it could hardly hold that the Commonwealth could not provide *any* financial assistance to deal with a situation of financial embarrassment to a state caused by competing tax levies of the federal and state governments. In other words, given the Commonwealth power to impose all forms of taxation at any rates it chooses and its power to make grants of financial assistance to the states, whether on conditions or not, I believe it is impossible to rely on the High Court to prevent a federal monopoly of taxation if the Commonwealth government has the will and political circumstances permit. This may be 'legalism' but it is legalism which regards the courts as having to take as given the provisions of the Constitution and accepts that there are limits to the effectiveness of judicial methods in restraining the use of undoubted powers for particular political ends, even where the autonomy of the states is involved.

Theoretically, I think, the same situation pertains in respect to the United States and the Canadian Constitutions where, however, federal power to make grants is inferred from other provisions. Had section 96 not been inserted in the Constitution Bill as a side-wind resulting from the Premiers' Conference of 1899, it is likely that a power to make grants to the states would have been inferred (*Australian Assistance Plan* case, 1975: 395 per Mason J.). The loss of the power by the Commonwealth to impose terms and conditions would at the most, I think, make it more politically difficult for the Commonwealth to make many of the specific grants that it does; but I doubt whether it would render it impossible for the federal government to achieve the effectuation of its policies in many cases.

Given section 96, it might have been possible, however, to have interpreted that provision differently, and in a way which had regard to the distribution of responsibilities between the Commonwealth and the states. Dixon CJ. pointed this out in the *Second Uniform Tax* case. He said that if the interpretation of section 96 had come before the Court for the first time it might have been held that section 96 'did not admit of any attempt to influence the direction of the exercise by the state of its legislative or executive powers' (*Second Uniform Tax* case, 1957: 609). He declared that section 96 was probably conceived by the framers as (1) a transitional provision, (2) confined to supplementing the resources of the treasury of the state by particular subventions when some special or particular need or occasion arose, and (3) imposing terms or conditions relevant to the situation. There would be considerable difficulty in formulating legal principles in accordance with this object, but no doubt an interpretation along these lines might have prevented the legal imposition of many conditions on specific purpose grants. Whether it would have prevented them in any practical sense I do not know. I should have thought, however, that the imposition of high federal tax rates would have created a 'need or occasion' to supplement the resources of state treasuries in the manner in which the uniform tax scheme does, subject to what was meant by 'special or particular' need.

In short, the lack of guaranteed sources of revenue to the states might, I think, fairly be seen as a departure from a federal principle that requires legally independent and co-ordinate regional governments. I have doubts about whether any court could have construed the Constitution so as to ensure this. The legal possibility of achieving what was done in Australia, I think, exists potentially in other federations. It seems that political forces rather than legal power or legal provisions have resulted in different experiences in other countries. (Although it is possible, for example, that some of the states who wanted it might have successfully had their taxing power returned in a practical sense if it had not been felt that this action was impeded by section 51(ii) preventing the imposition of federal tax rates in different states. The Fraser 'new federalism' tax machinery, however, may provide a method for achieving this.)

Recently, however, some suggestions have been made by judges that the Commonwealth might have direct power to regulate (or prevent) state taxation, and not merely by way of 'inducement'. In both the USA and Australia, it has always been assumed that the federal legislative power with respect to taxation refers to taxation levied by the federal legislature for federal purposes. This was so held in the *Second Uniform Tax* case. It formed the basis for holding invalid the provision of the Income Tax Assessment Act that purported to prohibit a person from paying state tax before he paid his federal tax. Dixon CJ. declared.:

> The power to make laws with respect to taxation has never been, and consistently with the federal character of the Constitution could not be, construed as a power over the whole subject of taxation, throughout Australia, whatever parliament or other authority imposed taxation (614).

Murphy J., however, declared that this view was wrong, and that under section 51(ii) the Commonwealth could exclude the states from tax fields (*Hematite Petroleum Pty Ltd v Victoria*, 1983: 637). Gibbs CJ. and Mason J. also made some comments that pointed in the same direction (617, 631). These were, however, incidental remarks and showed no consciousness that the view expressed was contrary to the *Second Uniform Tax* case and the assumptions behind many cases determined since the beginning of federation. I do not believe that these remarks reflected their considered judgment.

Although the principles relating to the implied restrictions on federal power to affect the states do not have regard to the extent of state legislative powers, the legislative power of taxation is different in that it provides the means of exercising all other powers. It relates very much, therefore, to the survival of the states as independent governments. If the view expounded by Murphy J. were correct much of the elaborate structure of the uniform tax scheme, involving four pieces of legislation, would have been unnecessary. While it cannot be said that state independence requires all fields of taxation to be available to it, the difficulty of the court determining the issue in any particular case—or more particularly as a result of a series of federal attempts—would, and should in my view, work in favour of confining the taxation power to federal taxation. (I have elaborated on this question in Zines, 1987:301–8.)

It will be noted that I have concentrated (though not exclusively) on constitutional issues relating to the structure of federal government in Australia. This goes against the tide of most writings by social scientists on federalism, which appears to be a reaction to the long period during which the field was dominated by legal scholars (Livingston, 1967). It was natural and desirable that political scientists, political philosophers and economists should emphasise and illustrate the shortcomings of the legal or judicial approach in understanding how a federal state operates, the forces and interests that sustain it (or impair it), and its virtues and vices. If the outline of Australian federalism I have attempted to convey is too much about 'structure' and not enough about 'processes', too much about legal power and not enough about political forces, and too much a description of the 'layer cake' and not enough of the 'marble cake' (Grodzins, 1964), I must admit it.

My first reason for this emphasis is that others more skilled than I am in politics and economics will no doubt be dealing with the other issues. Secondly, what I have done is probably what is expected of a lawyer and what might be seen as the 'legal perspective' of federalism. But those are not the main reasons. I believe that, at times, many of those who purport to describe federalism as a living, dynamic system or write of its merits and its weaknesses show a tendency to be impatient of constitutional rules and judicial adjudication. Legal and constitutional power is sometimes referred to as 'formal', as if the possession of such power was not a matter of political or social substance, i.e. a factor that is part of the political scene and something to be used in the political battle.

There are times, of course, when 'formal' might be an appropriate term to use in relation to powers of various sorts. In 1943, for example, the legal power of the states to levy income tax might properly be described as formal because of the countervailing forces that prevented any such imposition. The same, however, might be true of economic power, for example, the power of the Commonwealth to starve the states into submission if they do not follow policies demanded by the Commonwealth. The *Franklin Dam* dispute was political, but the legal contest over whether the policies of the Commonwealth or Tasmania would prevail could hardly be described as a dispute over 'formal' powers.

Much of the modern literature emphasises the amount of sharing of tasks and co-operation that goes on among the levels of government in any federation. Indeed in upholding the validity of joint schemes and enterprises, some Australian judges have declared such activity to be inherent in our federal system. '[T]he Constitution . . . necessarily contemplates that there will be joint co-operative action to deal with matters that lie beyond the competence of any single legislature' (*Re Duncan*, 1983: 38 per Mason J.). '[C]o-operation is a positive objective of the Constitution' (Dean J., 59). If one begins, however, with the fact of co-operation, interaction and interdependence of the levels of government, it is too easy to move away from the type of governmental structure we are considering, namely a federal one. If the structure of federalism is ignored or underrated the discussion leads to a topic that extends to governmental processes in western society. I have assumed that not only is our subject more limited, but that it is of some importance that, when 'co-operation' cannot be obtained, the Commonwealth cannot abolish the governmental structure of Tasmania as Britain did with that of Northern Ireland and Greater London.

Concentration on co-operation and interdependence might also lead one to obscure the issue of duress, coercion and accountability. A state with guaranteed autonomy and some area of exclusive power will more often be in a position to 'co-operate' in the sense of deciding whether it is in its best interest to do so, as distinct from having no option. That does not mean, of course, that our states have always been in the former position. The states in 1942 had 'no option' in relation to whether they would impose income tax. Somewhat less extreme, but nevertheless quite heavy, was the pressure on them to enter into the financial agreement. But in that case, having regard to the existence of state governments with powers of borrowing, there were, I imagine, limits on what the federal government would have been able to get them to accept for the sake of the financial benefits involved. I assume that other arrangements have been made as a result of varying degrees of 'pressure', 'inducement' or coercion by the Commonwealth. Some writers have pointed out, and I agree with them, that one can hardly talk in any real sense of 'co-operative federalism' without taking account of one essential feature of the older notion of co-ordinate federalism, namely, some degree of independence and bargaining power. As Professor S.R. Davis has said: 'One can hardly speak of co-operation between master and slave, except in the voice of poetry' (Davis, 1978: 186). Professor Sawer (1976: 102) has put it this way: 'There must be a pretty wide range for over-persuasion or strong pressure exerted by one party in relation to another but there must also be a point of retreat beyond which the weaker party cannot be pushed'. If I remember correctly, Mr Fraser offered Tasmania about $500 million to refrain from building the Franklin Dam. As it happened, the Commonwealth got its way by direct legislation that was held to be within its power, but the example remains illustrative, I think, of the point Sawer was making.

Before I am accused, however, of supporting legalism and formalism at the expense of reality, I wish to state that my purpose is merely to indicate that constitutional considerations are of importance in considering the total picture of federalism. It is not suggested that political and economic factors be downgraded in the pursuit of understanding in this area. In Australia, Dr Galligan, for example, has in his book produced a cogent study of the relationship of constitutional and political issues.

Even purely constitutional issues cannot be appreciated or sometimes resolved without regard being had to how things in fact operate. The recognition by the courts of those political practices and conventions associated with responsible government and intra-imperial relations constitute early examples of this. It is, as I indicated before, difficult to consider whether the exposition of the external affairs power in the *Franklin Dam* case produces the result the minority claims without considering practical and political matters. Similarly, if the political situation in the Australian Senate was similar to that in the USA it might have been used by the Australian judges as an argument, or a further argument, for not reading down federal power, as has happened in the USA. Another example is the United States position that it is for the federal Attorney-General and not a state Attorney-General to act for the protection of the public rights of citizens in resisting federal legislation. This was met with the comment by Gibbs J. that 'I would, in

Australia, think it somewhat visionary to suppose that the citizens of the states could confidently rely on the Commonwealth to protect them against unconstitutional actions for which the Commonwealth itself is responsible' (*Victoria* v *Commonwealth and Hayden*, 1975: 383).

Despite the financial dependence of the states and the growth of federal legal powers at their expense, the states appear to be alive and fairly active. Latham CJ.'s view, expressed forty-five years ago, that uniform taxation could lead to 'the end of the political independence of the states' has not happened. Deakin's prediction, eighty-five years ago, that 'even the greatest and most prosperous [of the states] will, however reluctantly, be brought to heel' (Deakin in La Nauze, 1968: 97) remains to be fulfilled. The states have refused to fold their tents and steal silently away. No doubt this is all the result of political and social forces rather than the somewhat feeble protection afforded by High Court doctrines. But political strength has clustered around and grown out of institutions designed for independent parts of a federal whole. Might it not be that, whatever happens in respect of judicial review, the Constitution and those of the earlier colonies may, in a sense, have already done their work for the foreseeable future? That is to say they have assisted in the formation of centres of political power which will continue to operate and to be seen, to a degree, as independent units, with a considerable degree of legislative and executive power (Partridge 1952; Wildavsky, 1967).

I am not trying to suggest that in this or any other respect all is well with our governmental system. I should, however, emphasise, as a member of the Constitutional Commission, that I have concentrated on the Constitution as it is and the efforts of the High Court to grapple with it in the light of the concept of federalism. There have been a great many arguments and submissions that the Constitution should be changed in order better to provide for relations between the Commonwealth and the states and the demarcation of powers. The questions whether our federal system would be better served by change, whether the Constitution needs alteration to ensure we retain a federal system or whether the federal system serves any useful purpose are beyond the scope of this chapter.

Judicial decisions

Actors Equity v Fontana (1982) 150 CLR 169.
Attorney-General (Canada) v Attorney-General (Ontario) [1937] AC 326.
Attorney-General for Canada v Cain [1906] AC 542.
Attorney-General (Cth) v Colonial Sugar Refining Co. Ltd [1914] AC 237.
Australian Assistance Plan case: *Victoria v Commonwealth and Hayden* (1975) 134 CLR 338.
Australian Communist Party v Commonwealth (1951) 83 CLR 1.

Australian Railways Union v Victorian Railways Commissioners (1930) 44 CLR 319.
Citizens Insurance Co v Parsons (1881) 7 App. Case. 96.
Commissioners of Taxation (NSW) v Baxter (1907) 4 CLR 1087.
Deakin v Webb (1904) 1 CLR 585.
Engineers' case: *Amalgamated Society of Engineers v Adelaide Steamship Co. Ltd* (1920) 28 CLR 1.
First Uniform Tax case: *South Australia v Commonwealth* (1942) 65 CLR 373.
Franklin Dam case: *Tasmania v Commonwealth* (1983) 46 ALR 625.
Garcia v San Antonio Metropolitan Transit Authority (1985) 469 US 528.
Garnishee case: *New South Wales v Commonwealth* (1932) 46 CLR 155.
Gazzo v Comptroller of Stamps (Vic) (1981) 149 CLR 227.
Hematite Petroleum Pty Ltd v Victoria (1983) 151 CLR 599.
Hodge v The Queen (1883) 9 AC 117.
Huddart Parker & Co. Pty Ltd v Moorehead (1908) 8 CLR 330.
Koowarta v Bjelke-Petersen (1982) 153 CLR 168.
League of Cities v Usery 426 US 833.
Payroll Tax case: *Victoria v Commonwealth* (1971) 122 CLR 353.
Queensland Electricity Commission v Commonwealth (1985) 61 ALR 1.
Railway Servants' case: *Federated Amalgamated Government Railway and Tramway Service Association v New South Wales Railway Traffic Employees Association* (1906) 4 CLR 488.
R v Barger (1908) 6 CLR 41.
Re Duncan; ex parte Australian Iron and Steel (1983) 49 ALR 1.
Re Lee; ex parte Minister for Justice (Qld) (1986) 65 ALR 577
Second Uniform Tax case: *Victoria v Commonwealth* (1957) 99 CLR 575.
State Banking case: *Melbourne Corporation v Commonwealth* (1947) 74 CLR 31.
Steel Rails case: *Attorney-General (NSW) v Collector of Customs* (1908) 5 CLR 818.
Union Label case: *Attorney-General (NSW) v Brewery Employees of New South Wales* (1908) 6 CLR 469.
West v Commissioner of Taxation (NSW) (1937) 56 CLR 657.
Western Australia v Commonwealth (1975) 7 ALR 159.

References

Australian Federal Convention Debates, 1897, 17.
Barrett, E.L. (1985), 'A Parliamentary System of Government in a Federation—The Australian Experience', *University of California Law Review* 19: 153.
Blair, P.M. (1981), *Federalism and Judicial Review in West Germany*, Clarendon Press, Oxford.
Cowen, Z. and Zines, L. (1978), *Federal Jurisdiction in Australia* 2nd edn, Oxford University Press, Melbourne.
Davis, S.R. (1978), *The Federal Principle*, University of California Press, Berkeley.

Galligan, B. (1987), *Politics of the High Court*, University of Queensland Press, St Lucia, Qld.

Grodzins, M. (1964), 'Centralization and Decentralization in the American Federal System', in R.A. Goldwin (ed.), *A Nation of States: Essays on the American Federal System*, Rand McNally, Chicago.

La Nauze, F.A. (ed.) (1968), *Federated Australia*, Melbourne University Press, Melbourne.

—— (1974), *The Making of the Australian Constitution*, Melbourne University Press, Melbourne.

Livingston, W.S. (1967), 'A Note on the Nature of Federalism', in A. Wildavsky (ed.), *American Federalism in Perspective*, Little, Brown & Co., Boston.

Mathews, R.L. (ed.) (1980), *Federalism in Australia and the Federal Republic of Germany*, ANU Press, Canberra.

Mathews, R.L. and W.R.C. Jay, (1972), *Federal Finance: Intergovernmental Financial Relations in Australia Since Federation*, Nelson, Melbourne.

Partridge, P.H. (1952), 'The Politics of Federalism', in G. Sawer (ed.), *Federalism: An Australian Jubilee Study*, Cheshire, Melbourne, 174–210.

Riker, K.H (1964), *Federalism: Origin, Operation, Significance*, Little, Brown & Co., Boston.

Sawer, G. (1962), 'State Statutes and the Commonwealth', *University of Tasmania Law Review*, 580–9.

—— (1976), *Modern Federalism*, 2nd edn, Pitman, Carlton, Vic.

Tribe, L.H. (1978), *American Constitutional Law*, Foundation Press, New York.

Wheare, K.C. (1946), *Federal Government*, Oxford University Press, Oxford.

Wildavsky, A. (1967), 'Party Discipline under Federalism: Implications of Australian Experience', in A. Wildavsky (ed.), *American Federalism in Perspective*, Little, Brown & Co., Boston, 162–81.

Wiltshire, K. (1980), 'Australian State Participation in Federal Decisions', in R.L. Mathews (ed.), *Federalism in Australian and the Federal Republic of Germany*, ANU Press, Canberra.

Zines, L. (1987), *The High Court and the Constitution*, 2nd edn, Butterworths, Sydney.

3

A POLITICAL SCIENCE PERSPECTIVE

Brian Galligan

Introduction: why bother with federalism?

Observers of Australia's political system have been troubled by the basic question of how to explain the continuing vitality of federalism when there are apparently no significant regional differences to sustain it. Or, more simply, why do Australians bother with federalism? If the question is loaded, as it usually is by those who pose it, with the alleged administrative inefficiencies of federalism, the political wastage of multiplying parliaments and politicians, the conservative bias of the system against the implementation of progressive social policies, the federal Labor Party's historical commitment to abolition and its continuing dislike of federalism, the needless tensions and intergovernmental conflicts that federalism entails and promotes, and the sheer complexity it introduces into processes of government, the puzzle about Australian federalism is heightened.

In his provocative book on federalism, William Riker (1964) summed up this abiding concern of generations of scholars. With no intense regional identification in Australia, social and economic divisions were primarily national rather than regional. Australian patriotism was apparently 'unobstructed by loyalties to states'. So much so, concluded Riker (1964: 113), that: 'Indeed, of all the federalisms now in existence, Australia seems less in need of appeasing subordinate patriotisms than any other government. One wonders, indeed, why they bother with federalism in Australia'.

Why bother, indeed, if the conclusions of Riker and other leading authorities on federalism in general and the Australian federal system in particular were true? If federalism were really a function of regional diversities in society (Livingston, 1956), or if it were obsolete (Laski, 1939), or trivial (Riker, 1970), such a structure of government should have little salience for Australia. If federalism in Australia were a transitional form of government naturally inferior to a unitary system (Crisp,

1965, and subsequent edns), if it had outlived its usefulness and was incapable of dealing with Australia's social, political and economic problems in the post-war period (Greenwood, 1946; 2nd edn 1976), if federalism was 'an unfortunate accident of history' to many Australians (Maddox, 1985: 132), if Australian federalism had '*allowed* rather than placed barriers on the emergence of despots' and if Australia 'needs a unitary state' (Brugger and Jaensch, 1985: 194–5), as it clearly would if even some of the above were true, its continued existence would be problematical.

Obviously an explanation of Australian federalism would need to be different from the accounts of any of the above authorities if we are to answer or escape from this dilemma. That is, providing federalism is truly significant for Australian politics. I take for granted that federalism is the central organising principle of Australian government and as such is one of the most significant facts in the whole of Australian political life. Many might wish it to be otherwise, but that does not change reality. In any case the leading critics of Australian federalism attest to its significance, implicitly by their attention and often explicitly by grudging acknowledgement of its continuing vitality.

Crisp (1978: 104–5), for example, affirmed that 'seven decades after federation, a much-transformed and ever-adjusting, yet still recognisably and obstinately federal structure and six busy . . . state units are basic facts of Australian political and governmental life'. Moreover, he insisted, they are likely to remain so short of some great national catastrophe. Sadly, in Crisp's view, Australia's abiding commitment to federalism represented 'a refusal either to confront its development into nationhood or to act as a well-integrated adult'.

Geoff Sawer, a more profound analyst of federalism who nevertheless preferred a unitary system, provided it came with an entrenched bill of rights, acknowledged the continuing strength of federalism:

> Australia, after over seventy years of federalism, shows no signs of adopting a unitary system, though outside observers keep expressing incredulity that the country should still bother with federalism and habitually exaggerate the power and importance of the Australian centre (1976: 147).

This quotation is from the second edition of *Modern Federalism* after the period of the Whitlam government when Sawer thought there had been some centralisation of policy-making despite the countervailing assertion of states' rights. In the first edition of his book Sawer had been more forthright, claiming Australia was rather more federal in 1968 than it had been in 1948 and dismissing the centralist claims out of hand:

> if there is any movement in the Australian federal balance at all, it is not towards but away from organic federalism [Sawer's term for his sort of centralism]; the contrary view common outside Australia is due to the prevalence of journalistic values, which magnify the melodramatic and flashy activities of the Centre and its apparent financial strength, while ignoring the

> inability of the Centre to turn its money power into effective policy control and the dour persistence with which Region governments go their own way (Sawer, 1969; quoted 1976: 148).

Sawer's realistic assessment of the strength of Australian federalism was in no sense influenced by his enthusiasm for the system. In fact his was a rather jaundiced view: among constitutional systems federalism was adjudged 'a prudential system best suited to the relatively stable, satisfied societies of squares' that abound in Australia and other western federal countries. It was definitely 'not a swinging system' that might fire the popular imagination. Nevertheless Sawer admitted that he would sooner live 'in a moderately incompetent affluent federalism than in any centralised system with no entrenched bill of rights at all' (Sawer, 1976: 153).

Whether critics like it or not, Australians appear destined to live under a federal system for as long as can reasonably be predicted. Once put in place in a receptive, liberal, democratic polity like ours, federalism has a self-perpetuating life of its own. Through federalising popular allegiances, political culture, political parties and pressure groups and by providing the constitutional machinery whereby relatively sovereign state governments control the extensive range of social, economic and legal areas that they do, federalism becomes an organic system that shapes political and social life and is in turn reinforced by what it has shaped (Partridge, 1952; Cairns, 1977; Smiley, 1984; Galligan, 1986a). The federal system acts as a living skeleton that shapes the body politic.

The unity-preference tradition in Australian political thinking

Not liking the shape of the Australian political system that federalism produces is no good reason for ignoring federalism in the hope that it might go away, or assuming it is already nearly defunct, or calling it derogatory names and advocating some vague unitary alternative that is dressed up with positive attributes like rational, efficient, mature and modern. Yet this is what many academic commentators on Australian politics and federal Labor Party leaders have indulged in for generations.

While federalism may have dominated much of Australian politics, anti-federalism has enjoyed a strong tradition in political writing and thinking. Despite being the central organising principle of Australian politics, federalism has been dismissed or ignored by leading political scientists during much of the post-war period. The most eminent was L.F. Crisp, whose book *Australian National Government* (1965; subsequent edns: 1970; 1973; 1978; 1983) has been the main text on Australian politics for the last twenty years, going through five editions and a further six reprints. Crisp's superficial and slighting treatment of federalism was based on his assumption that it was a transitory stage of government and inferior to a unitary system.

Crisp's dismissive view of federalism was characteristic of a generation of public figures and intellectuals who experienced firsthand the heady atmosphere of war and post-war reconstruction. To that generation national security, national development, national welfare policies and Keynesian-style economic management all seemed to require, or to be facilitated by, the centralisation of power in Canberra (see Davies and Serle, 1954). Harold Laski's pronouncement of 'The Obsolescence of Federalism' in 1939 after a trip to the USA found fertile ground in Australia among this generation and was popularised during the next decade. Laski argued that federalism was an inappropriate political structure for dealing with modern capitalism because it fragmented and weakened political power whereas capital was being amalgamated into powerful national corporations.

Gordon Greenwood made the definitive application of Laski's thesis to Australia. His classic study *The Future of Australian Federalism* (1946; 2nd edn 1976) argued that federalism had no future in post-war Australia. Greenwood claimed that, despite its earlier achievements for an emerging nation,

> the federal system has outlived its usefulness, that the conditions which made federation a necessary stage in the evolution of Australia's nationhood have largely passed away, and that the retention of the system now operates only as an obstacle to effective government and to a further advance. The problems which are today of greatest urgency are those which can best be solved either by a unified government or by a central government possessed of vastly expanded powers. It is time to recognise that the federation should be replaced by a unified state (xii).

Greenwood even titled the main chapter of his book 'The Evil Effects of the Division of Powers between State and Federal Authorities' (chapter 4).

Two recent texts on Australian politics that are self-consciously theoretical in their approach, Brugger and Jaensch's *Australian Politics: Theory and Practice* (1985) and Maddox's *Australian Democracy: In Theory and Practice* (1985), devote considerable attention to federalism. Both accounts, however, are tendentiously hostile. Brugger and Jaensch rehash the Laski–Greenwood strictures against federalism, concluding that 'the time has come for major change. Australia needs a unitary state' (195). Maddox gives a more sophisticated restatement of the traditional democratic socialist case against federalism (see also Maddox, 1976). These two books indicate that the unity-preference tradition is still a major stream in academic writing on Australian politics.[1]

Similar prejudices and presuppositions about federalism being an immature, transitional, old-fashioned, inefficient, irrational and even perverse form of government have persisted among federal Labor leaders despite the party's formal reconciliation with federalism. The

Labor party's unification plank was modified in the 1960s and formally abandoned in the 1970s. However, while pragmatically working the system, federal Labor leaders have remained hostile in principle or at least unsympathetic to federalism.

Whitlam was instrumental in changing the Labor Party's old hard-line abolitionist stance, but remained at heart a rational centralist (Whitlam, 1982). His 'new federalism' was a heady mixture of Labor's traditional preference for national policy-making plus a humane concern for improving the quality of life in needy local and regional areas through targeting federal money for programmes designed in Canberra (APSA, 1977). This New Federalism was devised to bypass 'existing states with their irrelevant state boundaries and malapportioned electoral boundaries' in favour of 'a meaningful decentralisation of power' at the local and regional level. 'The future of Australian federalism', as Whitlam explained to a seminar at the Australian National University in 1971, lay in cutting out the states:

> The new federalism will rest on a national framework for the establishment of investment priorities and a regional framework for participation in all those decisions which most directly determine the quality of our lives (1971 in Whitlam, 1977: 161).

Alas, Whitlam's attempt at a new federalism foundered on the brute fact of the states that he sought to bypass and was offset by the countervailing federal forces that his roughshod centralist approach aroused.

As befits the most pragmatic leader that the federal Labor Party has ever had, Hawke seems the most reconciled of any Labor prime minister towards working within the established federal system. But as well he has to work with highly competent and stable Labor governments in four of the five main states. In his more speculative reflections before entering politics, however, Hawke strongly asserted an anti-federal view that was typical of federal Labor leaders of old. Using the 1979 Boyer lectures as a platform for a broad-ranging review of Australia's system of government and current affairs, Hawke singled out federalism for special attack. He ran the traditional 'horse-and-buggy' argument but with some colourful embellishments and surprising fervour. State boundaries were depicted as 'representing the meanderings of British explorers some one hundred and fifty years ago as they etched out a new colonial structure'. The founders had embodied the colonial attitudes and aspirations of the 1890s and the vested interests of six separate colonies in the Constitution, Hawke claimed. Australia had since become a nation with a national economy and national problems, but the Constitution had frozen our institutions of government within quasi-national boundaries. Hawke's view was essentially that formulated by Greenwood thirty years before:

> The essential distribution of powers between state and federal governments embodied in the document emerging from the 1898 Convention has not been

> changed in that time. But the nation has changed almost beyond recognition. We are not, and have not been for a long time, six economies, but one . . . The reality is that overwhelmingly the economic influences determining the welfare of the people of Australia are either national in their dimensions or international in their origin and only capable of a sensible response by a national government equipped with appropriate constitutional authority. That authority does not exist (Hawke, 1979: 12).

Hawke used surprisingly strong language to describe federalism and its consequences variously as 'absurd folly', 'anachronistic lunacy', 'an increasingly irrelevant structure', 'irrelevant and inadequate' to deal with the current crisis, and a 'dangerous anachronism'. Australians were 'delinquents' to themselves and their children by not adopting a more appropriate structure of government for modern times, Hawke claimed (1979: 12–18).

How does one explain the continuation and vehemence of such anti-federal sentiment among leading political writers and public figures on the progressive-left-Labor side of Australian politics? The answer is to be found, I think, in the political theory of federalism which has not been sufficiently articulated either in the public debate over federalism or in the more specialised literature on federalism which has been primarily descriptive and technical.[2]

The federalist theory of federalism

The initial points that need emphasis are that federalism is neither a function of societal differences nor primarily a matter of institutional arrangement. These points require some exposition since sociological or institutional explanations of federalism have tended to dominate the political science literature during the post-war period.

The sociological theory of federalism was summed up by its leading proponent in the proposition: 'Federalism is a function not of constitutions but of societies' (Livingston, 1956: 4; 1952). Livingston's thesis was published at a time when political science was recoiling from the overly institutional thrust of the discipline in pre-war America and discovering political sociology. According to this view institutional forms were a function or manifestation of underlying sociological phenomena; in the case of federalism, of societal differences that were regionally based. The sociological account of federalism gained enormous currency in the succeeding decades and still bedevils much writing on federalism (for a critical account, Cairns, 1977).

Besides leaving students of Australian federalism puzzling over the unanswerable 'why bother?' question, this fallacy encouraged the wholesale foisting of federal systems onto genuinely multicultural territories as the European powers withdrew from colonial empires. Needless to say most of these hastily contrived federations failed (listed in Frenkel,

1986: 102–3; select failures discussed in Franck, 1968). That was hardly surprising since federalism is fundamentally unsuited in principle for such situations. Federalism works best for countries like Australia that are uniformly liberal, democratic and have only incidental cultural and sociological differences that are not regionally based. To borrow Sawer's terms, the system is best suited to 'relatively stable, satisfied societies of squares' like Australians. By the same token Canadian federalism has been periodically at risk because of Quebec, rather than being sustained by its volatile francophone province (Smiley, 1980; Black, 1975).

Nor is federalism primarily a matter of institutional arrangements (see Wheare's classic account, 1946; 4th edn 1963); it is not simply a function of constitutions, as Livingston quite rightly pointed out. Obviously a genuinely federal regime will adopt a federal type of constitution in which the essential feature of 'dual sovereignty' is given some concrete institutional form. But it is fallacious to think that the institutional form constitutes the essence of federalism and to expect that by reproducing such institutions in a different country a genuine federal polity will result. This institutional fallacy complemented and accentuated the sociological fallacy during the post-colonial proliferation of federations when well-designed constitutional systems were seen as the solution for creating nations out of disparate linguistic, religious and tribal regions.

What then is federalism if it is not a means of uniting regionally distinct societies, or even primarily a particular set of institutions? According to the American founding fathers who invented it for their Constitution and defended it in the *Federalist Papers*, federalism was a means of ensuring safe and stable democracy, or republican government as they called it. Federalism added the national advantages of largeness to the local advantages of smallness while at the same time ensuring the democratic character of both. It created a strong national government while preserving existing regional state governments. That was a major breakthrough for democratic theory and a considerable achievement for liberal constitutionalism. Each of these points needs some development because together they form the core of federal theory.

Until the founding of the American nation with the adoption of its Constitution in 1789, democracy was considered suitable only for small regimes: tiny city states like Geneva for Rousseau, or the small eastern seaboard states of America for the anti-federalists who opposed the Constitution. Tocqueville summed up the wisdom of the ages in his observation that:

> Small nations have always been the cradle of political liberty; and the fact that many of them have lost their liberty by becoming larger shows that their freedom was more a consequence of their small size than of the character of the people (Tocqueville, 1835; 1945 edn: 166).

Rousseau had argued that the larger the state, the more power had to be concentrated in fewer hands out of administrative necessity. The great nations of Europe like France and Russia, and the empires of the past, seemed to bear out that claim. Even for a champion of democracy like Rousseau, the conditions for a viable democratic regime were so stringent that it was effectively ruled out for all but 'small and poor countries':

> Besides, how many things that are difficult to have at the same time does the democratic form of government not presuppose? First, a very small state, where the people may be readily assembled and where each citizen may easily know all the others. Secondly, a great simplicity of manners and morals, to prevent excessive business and thorny discussions. Thirdly, a large measure of equality in social rank and fortune, without which equality in rights and authority will not last long. Finally, little or no luxury. . . (Rousseau, 1792; 1968 edn: 113).

The second major problem with democratic government, which had been affirmed by political thinkers since Plato, was its volatility and instability. Democracy entailed rule by the many who, it was thought, would invariably be the poor. Reconciling the political claims of the rich and the poor and designing a constitutional framework that would ensure their political harmony were central problems for political science until relatively modern times. Most 'solutions' entailed some balance through a mixed regime that recognised the claims and contributions of both the rich and the poor. The fact that there would always be two such classes, the few who were rich and could contribute disproportionately more and the poor who were many but because of their numbers were necessary for any regime, was taken for granted as a prepolitical given or natural state of affairs. Hence Aristotle's best practical regime was one in which a middle class held the balance of power and moderated the more extreme propensities of the nobles and the people. Machiavelli's preference was for a republic, like Rome after Tarquin and before Caesar, where the nobles and people combined in a dynamic tension and channelled their aggressive tendencies outwards to foreign conquests.

Although there were strong democratic elements in both these constitutional solutions, neither regime was a democracy. Both were mixed regimes in which the democratic part was balanced by a non-democratic or aristocratic element. Mixed regimes were considered to be the best practical polities until early modern times when the English Constitution was widely considered as a practical model. Thus the democratic problem that the American founders faced was not simply how to combine existing small democracies into a larger, viable nation, but how to ensure stable democracy *per se*. That would mean containing the endemic factional strife between the rich few who would be at risk and the many with modest means who would dominate political power.

This lethal problem of faction was squarely faced by Madison, the intellectual father of the American Constitution. In his famous Federalist Paper No. 10, Madison affirmed that the 'violence of faction' was the 'dangerous vice' of popular governments. As a consequence, he claimed, 'instability, injustice, and confusion introduced into their public councils have, in truth, been the mortal diseases under which popular governments have everywhere perished'. It was widely held that in a democracy matters of public interest and conflicts between rival parties were decided 'not according to the rules of justice and the rights of the minor party, but by the superior force of an interested and overbearing majority'. Moreover, the major underlying cause of faction was the age-old tension between rich and poor: 'The most common and durable source of factions has been the various and unequal distribution of property', Madison affirmed. How then was democratic government to be made safe for liberalism and capitalism?

The third main problem that the American founders faced was the one of institutional design: how to overcome the chronic weaknesses of the confederal form of government without surrendering its advantages. According to Montesquieu, the old federal form of government which was essentially confederal combined the virtues of both large-scale and small-scale government:

> As this government is composed of small republics, it enjoys the internal happiness of each; and with respect to its external situation, it is possessed, by means of the association, of all the advantages of great monarchies (Quoted Federalist No. 9: 75).

Having laboured under a confederal form of government in their first Constitution, the Articles of Confederation, leading Americans had assured themselves that the second part of Montesquieu's laudatory tribute was not sustainable. Since a confederation was essentially a league of sovereign states or societies, it was inherently weak, particularly in foreign policy and defence matters. In any case the confederation Montesquieu had in mind was a league of small republics which Hamilton, an avowed supporter of a strong national union, dismissed in contemptuous terms:

> If we therefore take his ideas on this point as the criterion of truth, we shall be driven to the alternative either of taking refuge at once in the arms of monarchy, or of splitting ourselves into an infinity of little, jealous, clashing, tumultuous commonwealths, the wretched nurseries of unceasing discord and the miserable objects of universal pity or contempt (Federalist No. 9: 73).

The Americans invented the modern federal structure as a neat solution to these three interrelated problems of democratic scale, the stability of democratic regimes and national strength in a federation of smaller states (Diamond, 1961).[3] The federalist's theory of federalism was both an ingenious extension of the new principles of political science, and a practical variation of the old federal form of confederation; it was a clever combination of democratic theory and constitutional design that also matched the political compromise that was necessary to federate the American states into a stronger union.

In designing their modern federal Constitution American federalists were self-consciously aware that the 'science of politics' along with most other sciences had 'received great improvement' in recent times:

> The regular distribution of power into distinct departments; the introduction of legislative balances and checks; the institution of courts composed of judges holding their offices during good behaviour; the representation of the people in the legislature by deputies of their own election: these are wholly new discoveries, or have made their principal progress towards perfection in modern times (Federalist No. 9: 72).

The federalists drew heavily on all these new discoveries in devising the American Constitution. In particular the principle of representation had transformed thinking about democracy and allowed great practical expansion of its orbit. By substituting representation for participation, the direct participatory values that Rousseau treasured had been lost, but the liberal values of individual and property rights had been enhanced.

The principle of representation went some considerable way towards alleviating the threat of majority faction. Excluding the turbulent populace from direct participation in government would reduce the scope for demagoguery and remove a public forum for staging 'spectacles of turbulence and contention'. Placing government in the hands of a small number of representatives elected by the body of citizens would 'refine and enhance' public views. By allowing a great increase in territory and population, and thereby multiplying factions and interests, federalism carried this refining process to a new democratic threshold. As Madison explained (in Federalist No. 10: 83), federalism was the structural underpinning of modern pluralist democracy:

> Extend the sphere and you take in a greater variety of parties and interests; you make it less probable that a majority of the whole will have a common motive to invade the rights of other citizens; or if such a common motive exists, it will be more difficult for all who feel it to discover their own strength and to act in unison with each other.

Hence for Madison a federal union was superior to straight representative democracy since it promoted pluralism.

The novelty of the American constitutional design was affirmed by Tocqueville in his authoritative account of *Democracy in America* (1835; 1945 edn: 162): 'This Constitution . . . rests in truth upon a wholly novel theory, which may be considered as a great discovery in modern political science'. The innovation was in making citizens themselves, rather than states or societies, members of the national union. This change had 'the most momentous consequences': the national government became sovereign in its own right, being able to levy taxes, make and enforce its own laws, conduct foreign policy and wage war without first having to win the approval of sovereign constituent states. The new federal government had the means of enforcing and carrying out all that it was empowered to do. The national government represented the will of the people with as much legitimacy and directness as did the states.

In effect the new federal form of government had grafted key aspects of national government onto the old federal form of confederation. That was a sore point with its critics but was acknowledged and defended by the federalists. As Madison concluded his careful exposition in Federalist No. 39 (246), the new federal Constitution was 'in strictness neither a national nor a federal Constitution, but a composition of both'. As I have been arguing, that was not simply an innovation in institutional design but a structural means of implementing a new form of pluralist democracy.

If the endemic problem of democracy was 'majority faction' as Madison put it in the Federalist Papers, or the 'tyranny of the majority' in Tocqueville's terms, federalism was a key part of the solution. For federalism broke up the popular majority in the most fundamental way by dividing the allegiance of each citizen between regional state and national union; it made each person a citizen both of a smaller regional state and of the national union. Besides allowing an enormous expansion in size, and thereby introducing a multiplicity of regional and interest groupings, federalism also multiplied the number of governments. That both enhanced democratic participation by involving more citizens in a multiplicity of governments and as well ensured that centres of government would be checked and restrained by one another. In Tocqueville's (1945: 168, 310) summing up, the federal system was created in order to combine 'the different advantages which result from the magnitude and the littleness of nations'; it was a means of combining the power of a great republic with the enhanced participatory qualities of a smaller democracy.

Federalist theory and the Australian Constitution

Federalist theory has been emphasised in this paper because it remains essentially the political theory of federalism, yet has been largely absent from Australian discussion. A notable recent exception is Brugger and Jaensch's book in which the authors pay tribute to the classic *Federalist Papers* and Madison's 'grand design' of checks and balances of which federalism was an integral part. Unfortunately these authors misunderstand the central purpose of Madison and the federalists. This is evident from the following statement:

> For James Madison, the American federal scheme was part of a grand design in which powers would be separated and interests divided. This would allow the central government to direct policy in *the public interest* by selecting all that was best in the various private and regional interests which were represented at the centre (Brugger and Jaensch, 1985: 166).

The American federal scheme was part of a grand design for fragmenting power and interests; but its purpose was not to allow the central government to direct policy in the public interest by prescribing some overall good. Rather, it was the opposite: to restrict governments from pursuing prescriptive outcomes or imposing 'best' solutions. That was to allow individuals and groups to define and pursue their own happiness and interests. Hence Hamilton could claim that the American Constitution, because of its elaborate system of checks and balances, was 'itself, in every rational sense, and to every useful purpose, A BILL OF RIGHTS' (Federalist No. 84: 555).

Liberal constitutionalism generally and federalist theory in particular are not about prescribing substantive outcomes but rather enshrining institutional processes. Their purpose is to guarantee citizens and groups the right to pursue their own happiness, and to restrict governments from legislating happiness schemes. No public good is presupposed, but rather a multiplicity of private goods; or, put another way, the public good lies in ensuring toleration and pluralism. Hence, liberal constitutionalism, of which federalist theory is a part, is the antithesis both of ancient political philosophy and modern prescriptive ideologies.

A proper appreciation of federal theory resolves Brugger and Jaensch's (1985: 166) puzzle that, despite the role of 'social liberals' like Deakin in its formation,

> the Australian Constitution is remarkably devoid of social liberal concerns. Reading the Australian Constitution, it is difficult to see how such a document could be used effectively in promoting the self-development of citizens towards the common good. The document is merely a set of rules specifying the dimensions of co-ordinate federalism.

Since the federal part of Australia's Constitution was copied from the American model which was designed specifically to prevent governments, and in particular the central government, from prescribing and promoting the common good, it is hardly surprising that it is devoid of social, liberal or radical concerns.

Social or radical liberals like Deakin, Isaacs and Higgins who were prominent at the Federation Conventions favoured institutions that were more compatible with majoritarian democracy and parliamentary responsible government, but they lost out (Galligan and Warden, 1987). However such liberals came to dominate the conservative or Liberal side of Australian politics after the Constitution had been put in place. The lack of enthusiasm of many Liberals for federalism is grounded in a democratic tradition that is alien to that of federalism. This ambivalence of Liberals and the basic duality of Australia's constitutional culture are explored in the next section.

The duality of Australia's constitutional culture

By the time the Australian Constitution was drafted, more than 100 years after the American, representative democracy had triumphed in Anglo-American political thinking and in the Australian colonies. Australia led the world in pioneering the secret ballot and, along with New Zealand, in enfranchising the adult population. Moreover federal systems were well established in North America and Europe. Hence the Australian founders could take for granted both democratic practice and federal theory. The preconditions for American-style federalism were present in Australia's democratic political culture on the one hand and in its well-established states on the other hand. Hence it seemed almost inevitable that the desire for a limited national union that preserved the states should be institutionally embodied in a federal system.

Because of the pragmatic bent of the Australian founders and the practical nature of the task that confronted them, the making of our Constitution can be seen, as it usually is, in terms of political history and institutional design. The constitutional founding of the Australian nation was not an occasion either of great patriotic moment or grand institutional innovation. Rather, it was a more pragmatic piecing together of established parliamentary practices and federal institutional arrangements. The Australian founders' achievement was in hammering out an arrangement that satisfied the diverse interests of the major participants and achieved federation in the absence of momentous events that are usually the occasion for galvanising such national transformations.

The Australian founders had little inclination for political theory, and little apparent need for it. On the one hand they were thoroughly schooled in the practices and traditions of parliamentary responsible government, and on the other hand they had the American and other established federal constitutions like the Canadian and Swiss as working models. The American Constitution in particular dominated their federal thinking. As Sir Owen Dixon (1965: 38, 44) has emphasised:

> The framers of our own federal Commonwealth Constitution . . . found the American instrument of government an incomparable model. They could not escape from its fascination. Its contemplation damped the smouldering fires of their originality.

That is not to say that political and federal theory were absent from the Australian constitutional founding; only that they were taken for granted and not explicitly discussed, perhaps not even realised, by most of the delegates.

Unfortunately, until relatively recently, the work of the Australian founders attracted little attention. Although we have La Nauze's history, *The Making of the Australian Constitution* (1972), there is no systematic exposition of 'the mind of the founders' setting out the theoretical influences and assumptions embodied in the Australian Constitution. Republication of the entire federation debates, together with extensive commentaries and a comprehensive index, as a Bicentenary project (Craven, 1987) should help stimulate such an enterprise.

The 1975 constitutional crisis alerted many of us to the institutional tensions, even contradiction, inherent in the hybrid combination of responsible government and fully blown federal institutions such as an American-style Senate within the Australian Constitution. Subsequent scholarship has probed the origins of this mismatch, but there is still lively debate about what the founders actually did and how they intended such an unlikely institutional arrangement to work (see Browning, 1985; and my critical review, Galligan, 1986b; also Cromelin, 1986; and Rydon, 1985).

What needs emphasising in this context is the theoretical dimension of the institutional mismatch that is at the heart of the Australian Constitution. Responsible government, understood as an umbrella term for the more direct majoritarian practices and institutions entailed in executive dominance of a single, popularly elected chamber that is legislatively superior, presupposes a democratic theory of politics that is at odds with federal theory. The purpose of responsible government is to unify and consolidate political power, whereas that of federalism is to fragment and restrict its exercise. Responsible government presupposes the fundamental principle of undivided sovereignty, is more compatible with a command theory of law that derives from such a sovereign, and is rooted in a direct majoritarian view of democracy that respects the people's will as sovereign. In short, it embodies all the main ingredients of English nineteenth century progressive political thinking and constitutionalism. For responsible government derives from the English tradition of parliamentary sovereignty in which there were considered to be no legal limits on the sovereignty of parliament. In this respect responsible parliamentary government is the antithesis of federalism which fragments political power and checks popular governments in order to break up and restrain democratic majorities. The contrast was forcefully made by that champion of parliamentary sovereignty, A.V. Dicey, in favourably comparing the English Constitution with its American federal counterpart:

> In the principle of the distribution of powers which determines its form, the Constitution of the United States is the exact opposite of the English Constitution, the very essence of which is . . . the unlimited authority of Parliament. . .
> All the power of the English state is concentrated in the imperial parliament, and all departments of government are legally subject to parliamentary despotism (Dicey, 10th edn, 1960: 139, 156).

Underlying these two constitutional structures are radically different views about democracy. Responsible government has basically a positive view of the democratic majority will; federalism a negative view. Hence their institutional mechanisms are quite different. Federalism enshrines complicated procedures and conflicting institutions within the democratic process in order to refine and restrict the majority will. In contrast responsible government relies more directly on the majority will of the people for its efficacy.

Ironically, it was Australia's greatest post-war Liberal prime minister, Sir Robert Menzies, who gave the definitive account of the rationale behind Australian responsible government. Speaking to an American audience after his retirement, Menzies defended 'our steadfast faith in responsible government and in parliamentary legislative powers distributed, but not controlled'. He emphasised that the system of parliamentary government was based on the people's democratic control, through parliament, of ministers and the government:

> With us, a minister is not just a nominee of the head of the government. He is and must be a member of parliament, elected as such, and answerable to members of parliament at every sitting. He is appointed by a prime minister similarly elected and open to regular question. Should a minister do something which is thought to violate fundamental human freedom he can be promptly brought to account in parliament. If his government supports him, the government may be attacked, and if necessary defeated. And if that, as it normally would, leads to a new general election, the people will express their judgment at the polling booths.
>
> In short, government in a democracy is regarded by us as the ultimate guarantee of justice and individual rights (Menzies, 1967: 54).

Menzies argued that such direct popular control of the executive through a parliament of elected representatives obviated the need for a bill of rights. Because the American executive was independent of Congress, Menzies claimed that it had been thought necessary to impose constitutional limits on officials through a bill of rights. Such reasoning must have struck Menzies' American audience as curious.

Of course Menzies was not an anti-federalist, and on other occasions, such as against the centralising drive of the Chifley government in the immediate post-war years, used American federalist-type arguments. For example, in arguing against Evatt's 1944 proposals to greatly expand Commonwealth powers for alleged purposes of national reconstruction after the war, Menzies invoked Jefferson's strictures against centralising power:

> [T]he way to have good and safe government is not to trust it all to one, but to divide it among the many, distributing to every one exactly the functions he is competent to fulfil.
>
> . . . What has destroyed liberty and the rights of men in every government which has ever existed under the sun? The generalising and concentrating all cares and powers into one body . . . (quoted Galligan, 1987: 142).

What I want to emphasise, however, is that Menzies seemed more deeply imbued with the traditions of parliamentary responsible government than with federalism and the division of powers. Other leading Liberals like Malcolm Fraser have expounded the advantages of federalism in constraining Labor's centralist and socialist reformism. In 1975 before ousting the Whitlam government from office, Fraser called on Australians to renew their commitment to federalism 'and return to a federal system of government'. In a perceptive analysis of the ideological dimension of federalism, he argued that 'A federal system of government offers Liberals many protections against those elements of socialism which Liberals abhor' (Fraser, 1975: 29).

For the most part, however, federalism is taken for granted on the Liberal or conservative side of politics and only championed when under perceived threat from federal Labor governments. Most Liberals for most of the time have shown little understanding or appreciation of federalism. Fraser's new federalism rhetoric was not matched with much practical resolution to refurbish Australian federalism when in government. The Fraser government provided no 'tax room' to allow the states to take advantage of the new federalism initiative that was supposed to allow them to re-enter the field of income tax.

Other leading Liberals like Sir Billy Snedden showed surprising ignorance of federalism's powerful restraining force on Australian politics. For several years in the late 1970s, after losing the Liberal leadership and when concentrating his energies on making the speakership of the federal parliament an office of some national significance, Snedden championed the cause against 'elective dictatorship'. This catchy slogan had been popularised by British Conservatives such as Lord Hailsham and used quite effectively to highlight the excessive concentration of power in the House of Commons that was dominated by party and executive. While no doubt concerned that it was the Labour Party that was dominating the Commons at the time, Hailsham made a general attack on the basic English constitutional doctrine of parliamentary supremacy. The 'parliamentary despotism' that Dicey had approvingly articulated had become for Hailsham the root of the problem. The English Constitution was in grave need of major overhaul, Hailsham argued (1976: 14), because:

> Its central defects are gradually coming to outweigh its merits, and its central defects consist in the absolute powers we confer on our sovereign body, and the concentration of those powers in an executive government formed out of one party which may not fairly represent the popular will.

Hailsham recommended federalism as a solution: it provided an effective way of breaking up the elective dictatorship of governments and of protecting individual and corporate rights. Australian Liberals like Snedden who took up the cause against elective dictatorship in Australia failed to appreciate the federal system that was in place.[4] The Whitlam government was hardly an elective dictatorship but had been effectively constrained by a hostile Senate and entrenched state governments.

This is not the place for attempting a full-blown account of the theoretical bases of Australia's dual constitutional culture, nor a history of the uneasy combination of the two traditions in Australia's constitutional history. Both would involve large speculative and historical enterprises. Articulation of the theoretical underpinning of Australia's constitutional culture would entail an extension of the analysis that H.L.A. Hart sketches in his essay contrasting 'Utilitarianism and Natural Rights' (Hart, 1983). So far a couple of Australian authors have used Bentham to throw considerable light on aspects of Australia's political and constitutional culture. Following Hancock (1930), Hugh Collins (1985) has used the broad concept of Benthamite utilitarianism to characterise notable traits of Australia's political culture. Michael James (1982) has shown how Bentham's theories of sovereignty, law and parliamentary democracy fit key parts of Australia's anti-constitutional tradition. These are more in the way of provocative insights, however, than systematic accounts.

There has been even less attention to the theory embodied in the federal part of our Constitution that has been my concern in this chapter. Despite being so deeply entrenched and profoundly significant in shaping Australian politics, federalism has not been much appreciated or respected. The ethos of parliamentary responsible government has tended to dominate the minds and hearts of both Australian federalists and anti-federalists alike. In that respect Menzies had much in common with Whitlam. At the same time, however, because of its basic federal structure, the Constitution has been a major partisan issue dividing the Labor and anti-Labor sides of politics. On this issue Menzies and Fraser were dramatically opposed to Chifley and Whitlam. The analysis of federalism given earlier in the chapter explains why this has been the case: federalism is a structure that promotes liberal or pluralist democracy and frustrates and restrains majoritarian, reformist democracy. Hence the emotive opposition of the anti-federalists presented in the first part of the chapter is well founded, even if it has not been well articulated.

Democratic participatory qualities of federalism

The analysis of federalism presented so far has emphasised its liberal or pluralist qualities of fragmenting political power, checking popularly elected governments and breaking up, in order to restrain and refine, the majority will. In its American federalist origins, federalism was a liberal institution of government, and both in American (Lowi, 1984) and Australian politics (Galligan, 1987) it has been a major structural component in reinforcing decentralised and pluralist politics. The ideological dimension of federalism has been recognised and deeply resented by generations of democratic socialists, radical progressives and Australian Labor Party leaders and supporters. To majoritarian democrats and democratic socialists, federalism is a perverse and anti-democratic system because it hampers centralised reforms and frustrates the majoritarian national will. In Greenwood's terms these are 'evil effects' that flow from the basic federal division of powers.

But if federalism were only that, its ability to withstand the persistent hostility and periodic assaults from the Labor side of politics would be problematical. The resilience of Australian federalism is particularly notable in view of the ambivalence on the Liberal side that is grounded in our dual constitutional culture that tends to favour parliamentary responsible government over federalism. The 1975 crisis might suggest otherwise, but its uneasy accommodation to the established parliamentary order is, in my view, the outstanding consequence of that crisis.

Why then has federalism continued to flourish in Australia? The answer, I think, is to be found in its democratic participatory qualities that were also an important part of the original federalist design. As was pointed out earlier, federalism preserves the states as smaller democratic polities and establishes a system of dual citizenship or double democracy. Federalism combines the national strength of a large nation with the enhanced participatory qualities of smaller democratic states. The average Australian treasures both, while the whole paraphernalia of state and federal governments institutionalises and reinforces this dual system of politics. We have a strong intuitive sense and periodic political reminders of the strength of state identification and loyalty in Australia. Citizens of the various states seem deeply attached to politics and political participation at the state level. In this sense I think that we do have a strong federal culture (Holmes and Sharman, 1977), and that Australians do seem to look primarily to their state governments for recurrent political needs (Hancock, 1930: 64–5; Aitkin, 1982; Sharman, 1988). Canberra is not only geographically distant for most Australians; it is far removed from their sentimental attachments and daily recurrent needs. Canberrans have only to visit the various states, particularly the outlying ones, to be reminded of that.

Because they are quasi-independent political communities, the states can play a major policy role. That they do has been extensively documented in a recent study of *Comparative State Policies* (Galligan (ed.), 1988) by the Federalism Project. The character of the states' policy role varies among policy areas, depending on whether the states have primary jurisdiction, or have a shared input along with the Commonwealth, or are involved in a mediating role of delivering Commonwealth programmes, or have an indirect impact through their control over related programmes. As one might expect given the cultural homogeneity of the Australian people and the fiscal dominance of the Commonwealth, there are striking similarities in the policies of the various states. But there are also notable and persistent differences. While the policy differences are obvious manifestations of the independent character of the states as distinct political communities, the more pervasive similarities are not evidence to the contrary.

For even if the states produced identical policy outcomes, that would not constitute a good reason for not having them, as some might think. For the justification for states does not depend on their producing different policy outcomes. It might simply be that all the state political communities have the same or similar policy preferences. In no way does that derogate from the inherent value of enhanced democratic participation in the political and policy processes of smaller polities. In the same way, just because individuals or groups choose the same thing does not imply that they should not be allowed to choose. The justification for democracy at any level has to be primarily in process rather than outcome terms because democracy itself is defined and justified not in terms of policy results but in terms of the basic values embodied in its political processes. Democracy is essentially rule by the people: it entails popular participation in politics and popular sovereignty over policy outcomes. Since federalism both increases popular participation in politics and allows public goods to be more finely tailored to popular preferences, it can be said to enhance democracy.

This enhancement of democratic participation through dual citizenship and multiple governments is undoubtedly federalism's most positive quality that largely explains its strength and resilience in Australia. Surprisingly this quality has been widely overlooked, particularly by the self-professed champions of democracy on the Labor side of politics. How many times have we been subjected to the tired old slogans of 'Too many parliaments!', 'Too many politicians!' and 'Too many elections!'. The positive side of this is the increased democratic participation and political diversity that federalism allows. It is perhaps ironical that the strong Australian democratic tradition which the anti-federalists so often invoke also sustains the states and the federal system which they attack. One of the most significant developments in Australian political thinking in recent years is that such an appreciation of the states and federalism is gaining ground (Birrell, 1987) and permeating the Labor side of politics, particularly at the state level (Cain, 1987).

Endnotes

1 A contrary positive view of federalism has been strongly put by Rufus Davis, who has written extensively on the federal principle (1952; 1955–56; 1972; 1978) and been a staunch defender of the states (most recently, 1987), and by Campbell Sharman (1975; 1980; 1984; 1987; 1988). Others like Robert Parker (1947; 1949; 1969; 1976; 1977), Joan Rydon (1975), Jean Holmes (1973; 1974; 1976; 1984; and with Sharman, 1977) and Kenneth Wiltshire (1977; 1986; ed. 1977) have made substantial ongoing contributions to the study of Australian federalism.

2 My purpose in this paper is not to review the literature on Australian federalism, which is now quite extensive. There is a common perception that the study of federalism has been dominated by constitutional lawyers and fiscal economists who have concentrated on the more formal legal and fiscal aspects of federalism. Aitkin (1985: 8–9) pointed out in a recent survey of the discipline of political science that 'there has not been much interest in fundamental constitution-making, Parliament, the federal system, legal institutions and the like: these are assumed to be given, or taken to be the province of lawyers'. Since its establishment in 1972 the Centre for Research on Federal Financial Relations has produced an enormous quantity of material, mainly on the fiscal aspects of federalism. The Centre's 1986 Report On Activities lists forty books, forty-seven research monographs, forty occasional papers and seventy-four items in its 'Reprint Series'.

There has been a significant amount of work on Australian federalism by political scientists, with some of the major contributors being cited in the text or referred to in note 1 above. Interest in federalism by political scientists has waxed and waned over the decades, but at present there seems to be a resurgence of interest. A sizeable number of political scientists from most of the state universities have been involved in the Federalism Project co-ordinated in the Department of Political Science of the Research School of Social Sciences at the Australian National University, and have collaborated to produce two major publications (Galligan, 1986; 1988). These are supplemented by a recent book on the states (Birrell, 1987).

Currently I am preparing a bibliography of Australian federalism and have over one thousand items entered on a computerised listing. This does not include the additional thousand or so items in Crisp's (1979) bibliography of *The Later Australian Federal Movement 1883–1901*. In any bibliography of federalism there is of course a major problem in drawing the boundaries so that it does not become simply a bibliography of Australian politics. Excellent select bibliographies are available by Davis and Hughes (1963) and Knight (1981), and federalism is an important part of Jinks' (1985) bibliographical review of Australian 'Political Institutions'.

Finally I should like to pay tribute to the outstanding contribution to the study of Australian federalism that the 'veteran' participants in this seminar have made. The work of Geoffrey Sawer, Russell Mathews, Robert Parker and Rae Else-Mitchell, in various ways all contributors to the mid-century reviews of federalism which were the inspiration for this seminar, constitute a major part of the corpus of work on Australian federalism.

On another occasion and in a more substantial study of Australian federalism I hope to do justice to the work of the authors mentioned above in a way I have not been able to in this more speculative paper.

3 For a recent debate on the Federalist's view of federalism and of Diamond's exposition of that view, see the exchange between Vincent Ostrom (1985) and Paul Petersen (1985) in the *Publius* 'Symposium', vol. 15, no. 1 (Winter 1985).

4 Harry Evans (1983), in an excellent short piece titled 'Questioning the Tyranny', uses Hailsham's arguments to question the British heritage

in Australia's Constitution and to attack the would-be 'reformers' who are intent upon increasing that 'tyranny'. Evans defends the Senate against its post-1975 critics.

References

Aitkin, D. (1982), 'Australian Politics in a Federal Context', in R.L. Mathews (ed.) *Public Policies in Two Federal Countries: Canada and Australia*, Centre for Research on Federal Financial Relations, ANU, Canberra: 47–50.

—— (1985), 'Political Science in Australia: Development and Situation', in D. Aitkin (ed.), *Survey of Australian Political Science*, Allen & Unwin, Sydney: 1–35.

APSA (1977): Australasian Political Studies Association, *The Politics of 'New Federalism'*, Special no. of *Politics* vol. 12, no. 2, by D. Jaensch (ed.).

Birrell, M. (ed.) (1987), *The Australian States: Towards a Renaissance*, Longman Cheshire, Melbourne.

Black, E.R. (1975), *Divided Loyalties: Canadian Concepts of Federalism*, McGill-Queen's University Press, Montreal.

Browning, H.O. *1975 Crisis: An Historical View*, Hale & Iremonger, Sydney.

Brugger, B. and Jaensch, D. (1985), *Australian Politics: Theory and Practice*, Allen & Unwin, Sydney

Cain, J. (1987), 'Towards a federal reformation: the renaissance of the Australian states', in Birrell (ed.): 1–17.

Cairns, A. (1977), 'The Government and Societies of Canadian Federalism', *Canadian Journal of Political Science* 10: 695–725.

Collins, H. (1985), 'Political Ideology in Australia: The Distinctiveness of a Benthamite Society', *Daedalus*, Winter: 147–69.

Craven, G. (ed.) (1987), *The Convention Debates: Commentaries, Indices and Guide*, Legal Books, Sydney.

Crisp, L.F. (1978), *Australian National Government*, Longman Cheshire, Melbourne. 1st edn 1965; 2nd edn 1970; 3rd edn 1973; 4th edn 1978; 5th edn 1983.

—— (1979), *The Later Australian Federation Movement 1883–1901: Outline and Bibliography*, published by the author, Canberra.

Crommelin, M. (1986), 'The Commonwealth Executive: A Deliberate Enigma', Papers on Federalism, no. 9, Intergovernmental Relations in Victoria Programme, Law School, University of Melbourne, in Craven (ed.).

Davies, A. and Serle, G. (eds) (1954), *Policies for Progress: Essays in Australian Politics*, F.W. Cheshire, Melbourne.

Davis, S.R. (1952), 'Co-operative Federalism In Retrospect', *Historical Studies* 5: 212–33.

—— (1955–56), 'The Federal Principle Reconsidered', *Australian Journal of Politics and History* 1: Part I 59–85, Part II 223–44.

—— (1972), 'The Federal Principle Revisited', in D.P. Crook (ed.) *Questioning the Past*, University of Queensland Press, St Lucia.

—— (1978), *The Federal Principle*, University of California Press, Berkeley.
—— (1987), 'The State of the States', in Birrell (ed.): 18–37.
Davis, S.R. and Hughes, C.A. (1963), 'Federalism in Australia', in W.S. Livingston (ed.), *Federalism in the Commonwealth: A Bibliographical Commentary, Cassell, London.*
Diamond, M. (1961), 'The Federalist's View of Federalism', in G.C.S. Benson et al., *Essays in Federalism*, Institute for Studies in Federalism, Claremont Men's College, Claremont.
Dicey, A.V. (1960, 10th edn; 1st edn 1885), *Introduction to the Study of the Law of the Constitution*, Macmillan, London.
Dixon, O. (1965), 'The Law and the Constitution', in O. Dixon, *Jesting Pilate and Other Papers and Addresses*, collected by Judge Woinarski, Law Book Company, Melbourne.
Evans, H. (1983), 'Questioning the Tyranny', *Quadrant*, April 1983: 70–3.
Federalist Papers (1961): A. Hamilton, J. Madison, J. Jay, *The Federalist Papers*, Mentor, New York. First published in 1787.
Franck, T.M. (ed.) (1968), *Why Federations Fail*, University Press, New York.
Frenkel, M. (1986), *Federal Theory*, Centre for Research on Federal Financial Relations, ANU, Canberra.
Fraser, M. (1975), 'National Objectives—Social, Economic and Political Goals', *Australian Quarterly* 42(1): 24–35.
Galligan, B. (1986a), 'The Political Economy of the States', in Galligan (ed.): 244–65.
—— (1986b), 'The Origins of the 1975 Constitutional Crisis Revisited', *Canberra Bulletin of Public Administration*, 13: 158–63.
—— (ed.) (1986c), *Australian State Politics*, Longman Cheshire, Melbourne.
—— (1987), *Politics of the High Court*, University of Queensland Press, St Lucia.
—— (ed.) (1988), *Comparative State Policies*, Longman Cheshire, Melbourne.
Galligan, B. and Warden, J. (1987), 'The Role of the Senate', in Craven (ed.): 89–116.
Greenwood, G. (1976), *The Future of Australian Federalism*, University of Queensland Press, St Lucia. 1st edn 1946.
Hailsham, Lord (1976), 'Elective Dictatorship', The Richard Dimbleby Lecture, British Broadcasting Commission, London.
Hancock, W.K. (1930), *Australia*, E. Benn, London.
Hart, H.L.A. (1983), 'Utilitarianism and Natural Rights', in H.L.A. Hart, *Essays in Jurisprudence and Philosophy*, Clarendon Press, Oxford. First published in 1979.
Hawke, R.J.L. (1979), *The Resolution of Conflict*, 1979 Boyer lectures, Australian Broadcasting Commission, Sydney.
Holmes, J. (1973), 'A Federal Culture', in H. Mayer and H. Nelson (eds), *Australian Politics: A Third Reader*, Cheshire, Melbourne.
—— (1974), 'A Note on Some Aspects of Contemporary Canadian and Australian Federalism', *Politics* 12: 313–22.
—— (1976) 'The Australian Federal Process', in H. Mayer and H. Nelson (eds), *Australian Politics: A Fourth Reader*, Longman

Cheshire, Melbourne.
—— (1984), 'The Australian Federal System', *International Political Science Review* 5: 394–414.
Holmes, J. and Sharman, C. (1977), *The Australian Federal System*, Allen & Unwin, Sydney.
James, M. (1982), 'The Constitution in Australian Political Thought', in M. James (ed.), *The Constitutional Challenge: Essays on the Australian Constitution, Constitutionalism and Parliamentary Practice*, Centre for Independent Studies, St Leonards, NSW.
Jinks, B. (1985), 'Political Institutions', in D. Aitkin (ed.), *Surveys of Australian Political Science*, Allen & Unwin, Sydney: 119–78.
Knight, K.W. (1981), 'The Study of Australian Federalism', in G.R. Curnow and R.L. Wettenhall (eds), *Understanding Public Administration*, Allen & Unwin, Sydney: 319–39.
La Nauze, J.A. (1972), *The Making of the Australian Constitution*, Melbourne University Press, Melbourne.
Laski, H.J. (1939), 'The Obsolescence of Federalism', *New Republic*, 3 May: 367–9.
Livingston, W.S. (1952), 'A Note on the Nature of Federalism', *Political Science Quarterly*, vol. 67: 81–95.
—— (1956), *Federalism and Constitutional Change*, Clarendon Press, Oxford.
Lowi, T.J. (1984), 'Why Is There No Socialism in the United States?' *International Political Science Review* 5: 369–80.
Maddox, G. (1976), 'Federalism: or Government Frustrated', in H. Mayer and H. Nelson (eds), *Australian Politics: A Fourth Reader*, Longman Cheshire, Melbourne: 347–50.
—— (1985), *Australian Democracy: In Theory and Practice*, Longman Cheshire, Melbourne.
Menzies, R.G. (1967), *Central Power in the Australian Constitution*, Cassell, London.
Parker, R.S. (1947), 'The Future of Australian Federalism', *Australian Quarterly* 19(1): 93–7.
—— (1949), 'Australian Federalism', *Journal of Political Science* (Wellington) 1(2): 28–35.
—— (1969), 'Federalism—Australian Brand', in H. Mayer (ed.), *Australian Politics: A Second Reader*, Cheshire, Melbourne.
—— (1976), 'Planning, Federalism and the Australian Labor Party', *Journal of Commonwealth and Comparative Politics* 14(1): 3–18.
—— (1977), 'Political and Administrative Trends in Australian Federalism', *Publius* 7(3): 35–52.
Partridge, P.H. (1952), 'The Politics of Federalism', in G. Sawer (ed.), *Federalism: An Australian Jubilee Study*, F.W. Cheshire, Melbourne: 174–210.
Riker, W.H. (1964), *Federalism: Origin, Operation, Significance*, Little, Brown and Co., Boston.
—— (1970), 'The Triviality of Federalism', *Politics* 5: 239–41.
Rousseau, J.J. (1968), *The Social Contract*, Penguin Books, Middlesex. First published in 1792.
Rydon, J. (1975), 'The Frustrations of Federalism', *Australian Quarterly* 47(4): 94–106.

—— (1985), 'Some Problems of Combining the British and American Elements in the Australian Constitution', *Journal of Commonwealth and Comparative Polities* 23(1): 67–79.

Sawer, G. (1976), *Modern Federalism*, Pitman, Carlton, Vic. 1st edn 1969.

Sharman, C. (1975), 'Federalism and the Study of the Australian Political System', *Australian Journal of Politics and History* 21(3): 11–24.

—— (1980), 'Fraser, the States and Federalism', *Australian Quarterly* 52(1): 9–19.

—— (1984), 'The Commonwealth, the States and Federalism', in A. Parkin et al. (eds), *Government, Politics and Power in Australia*, 3rd edn, Longman Cheshire, Melbourne.

—— (1987), 'Coping with the future: the political apparatus of the states', in Birrell (ed.): 38–52.

—— (1988), 'The Study of the States', in Galligan (ed.): 2–17.

Smiley, D.V. (1980), *Canada in Question: Federalism in the Eighties*, 3rd edn, McGraw-Hill Ryerson, Toronto.

—— (1984), 'Federal States and Federal Societies, with Special Reference to Canada', *International Political Science Review* 5: 443–54.

Tocqueville, A. de (1945), *Democracy in America*, vol. 1, Vintage Books, New York. First published in 1835.

Wheare, K.C. (1963), *Federal Government*, 4th edn, Oxford University Press, London. 1st edn 1946.

Whitlam, E.G. (1971), 'A New Federalism', *Australian Quarterly* 43(3): 6–17; reprinted in E.G. Whitlam (1977), *On Australia's Constitution*, Widescope, Camberwell.

—— (1982), 'The Cost of Federation', in R.L. Mathews (ed.), *Public Policies in Two Federal Countries: Canada and Australia*, Centre for Research on Federal Financial Relations, ANU, Canberra: 281–93.

Wiltshire, K. (ed.) (1977), *Administrative Federalism: Selected Documents in Australian Intergovernmental Relations*, University of Queensland Press, St Lucia.

—— (1979), '"The New Federalism"—the state perspective', *Politics* 12(2): 76–96.

—— (1986), *Planning and Federalism: Australian and Canadian Experience*, University of Queensland Press, St. Lucia, Qld.

4

AN ECONOMIC PERSPECTIVE

Peter Self

Introduction: economic and political views of federalism

There is no single economic perspective to express upon the workings of federalism. For one thing, economists may take either a macro-economic or a micro-economic approach to the subject. The former approach concentrates upon the functions of national economic management or planning and may also concern itself with issues of redistribution and with questions about the efficient production of collective goods such as economies of scale. The theoretical basis of this approach was provided for a long time by Keynesian economics, often linked with theories of the 'welfare state' which have their basis in both economic and political thought. The basic inspiration of macro-economic thought derives from the concept of 'market failures'. Because economic markets produce instability, unemployment and inequality, as well as adverse 'spillovers' such as pollution, it is said to be the responsibility of government to remedy these defects through regulating demand, preventing unemployment, providing adequate social security and welfare services and intervening in other ways with market operations.

A micro-economic approach by contrast takes its inspiration from neo-classical models of competitive markets. The essence of economic markets (in their ideal form) is claimed to be that they achieve an optimum allocation of resources spontaneously, without the need for central planning. Of course actual markets in the modern world are far removed from the ideal model. They are far from being fully competitive because of the influence of large firms and monopolies. The classical market model also paid little attention to economies of scale, assuming that competition would automatically ensure the supply of goods at the lowest possible price. However, the theory of 'allocative efficiency' can be applied to governments as well as markets, and economists of this school are wedded to the concepts of consumers' choice and competition between governments. The ruling idea is to maximise the preferences or utilities of the clients of public goods so that the governmental system can move closer to the market model.

Thus there is a basic dichotomy between the two approaches. One sees government as there to remedy the failures of the market, the other seeks to move government closer to an ideal model of a market system.

Macro-economic thinking takes a top-down approach being concerned with the functioning of the whole economy, whereas micro-thinking takes a bottom-up approach being concerned with the articulation and aggregation of individual preferences for public goods. Failures of macro-economic management have led to criticisms of its theoretical basis. Monetarists give a more restrictive interpretation of its tasks than do neo-Keynesians and seek to move closer to a market-operated rather than state-operated model of the economy. The macro-approach has also been criticised for its apparent assumption that the state is a benevolent entity which can be trusted to remedy market defects. Politics, as the critics rightly say, does not work in this way. A more accurate statement might be that in a democracy the government's general economic goals should be settled by majority choice (although this conclusion would not be palatable to all economists). Micro-thinking on the other hand can be criticised for its frequently weak or unrealistic view of the functioning of modern markets. The problems of instability, inequality etc. have certainly not disappeared, and the regulation of the market is itself a complex public good which may require a considerable degree of state intervention.

This essay therefore utilises two rather than one economic perspectives, and moves from one to the other as required in order to elucidate some balance of economic considerations about the functioning of federalism. As will emerge later, a macro approach will be primarily concerned with the broad responsibilities of the federal government, whereas micro theories of resource efficiency stress the virtues of decentralisation and competition within the framework of government. Thus there are economic arguments on both sides concerning the desirable balance of federal powers.

Before proceeding further it will be helpful to call attention to the linkages which exist between economic, political and legal theories about federalism. All three disciplines are not genuinely 'value-free' and their normative conclusions embody significant value judgments, explicit or tacit. Political values have their counterparts in economic thought, while arguments between economists often resemble those between political scientists or lawyers.

These similarities are disguised by different methodologies. Thus modern economists often view government as a vast market in the demand and supply of public goods[1], and are concerned with predicting and measuring the consequent allocations of costs and benefits. By contrast political scientists concentrate primarily upon the institutions and processes of government, and pay less attention to the measurement or evaluation of government outputs. Constitutional lawyers are primarily concerned with the making and interpretation of rules about the powers of government *vis-à-vis* citizens and in federations about the respective powers of the different governments.

However, it is worth noting that these various disciplines have increasingly moved into each other's traditional zones. This is especially true of economics, the most imperialistic of the social sciences. The public choice school of political economists has transposed the concept of rational economic man into the political arena in order to attempt to explain and predict political behaviour (Self, 1985). Some economists within this school have also concerned themselves with the normative structure of constitutional rules, including those specific to federations. Some political scientists have moved into the evaluation of public goods in the burgeoning field of policy analysis. Lawyers make considerable use of political and economic theories in their justifications for particular interpretations of the law.

Thus we might distinguish three approaches to the subject of federalism as follows.

1 The economic value of maximising consumer choice (utility) can be linked with the political value of maximising citizen participation (the former stresses satisfaction with the provision of public goods, the latter involvement in the political process which supplies them). Both values stress the virtues of decentralised government and therefore are of obvious relevance to an evaluation of federalism
2 The economic value of effective economic planning (for growth, stabilisation and employment goals) is closely linked with the political value of non-authoritarian corporatism (for example, institutionalised forms of co-operation among economic groups and government for agreed national goals). In contrast to the previous position both these values stress the need for centralised government and have difficult or adverse implications for federalism.
3 The need for constitutional rules can be explained economically as a necessary bargain between individuals and governments whereby governments acquire certain coercive powers to provide public goods (such as taxation and regulation) in exchange for certain prescribed constraints (constitutional rules) upon the exercise of coercion. This is of course precisely the problem which concerned the social contract theorists of politics such as Hobbes, Locke and Rousseau, the authors of the Federalist Papers, and modern contract theorists such as Rawls. The subject is important for federalism, which can be seen both as a device to limit the total powers of government and as a method for the equitable allocation of power between two levels of government.

Thus we can discern three different approaches to the analysis of federalism which embody different dominant values and modes of discourse that are both economic and political in character. (The constitutional lawyer's main interest will be in the third subject matter although he or she may utilise arguments derived from the other two approaches.) With the advent of the public choice economists and the resurgence of political economy, political and economic arguments about federalism have become intermixed and this brief map of starting positions may help in the following analysis.

Before proceeding further, however, it is desirable to descend from these theoretical considerations and look briefly at the evolution over recent history of the relationship between economic policy and the functioning of Australian federalism.

Federalism and economic policy

The economic functions of government are often classified as stabilisation, redistribution and allocation (Oates, 1977). Stabilisation refers to the macro-economic task of managing the national economy so as to achieve a satisfactory balance between economic growth, employment, the balance of payments and the control of inflation. Redistribution refers to transfers from the relatively rich to the relatively poor through welfare payments and free or subsidised public services. Allocation refers to the operation of all types of public services.

In federations it has generally been held that the federal government must be primarily responsible for the stabilisation and redistributive functions. Only a national government can manage the economy, although the co-operation of state governments is to some extent necessary or desirable. Redistribution is best performed by the federal government because it usually has much more buoyant and progressive tax revenues than do state governments (this is pre-eminently true of the Australian federation), and also because a national government is in a position (if it so chooses) to reduce inequalities and promote minimum standards of welfare across the whole nation. Moreover, according to micro-economic theory, competition between states over taxation and services will restrict the scope for redistribution within any one state.

The allocative function—the operation of public services—is split in federations between the two levels of government. The theory of co-ordinate powers, where functions were in principle tidily allocated and independently performed by separate governments, and which Wheare (1947) and others saw as the necessary hallmark of a federation, is now almost dead. In modern federations most functions require joint action and co-operation between both levels of government (and often, especially outside Australia, by local government as well). In Grodzin's (1964) well-known simile the layer-cake model of federalism has given way to a marble-cake model.

The bias of micro-economists leans towards the decentralisation of functions which implies a preference for state over federal operation and responsibility—though it can also imply a still stronger preference for local government. This preference derives from the theory of consumers' choice, which implies that there will be more scope for differential treatment of the wishes of consumers and more competition over both service provision and tax levels if functions are decentralised. In terms of decentralisation within the federal system, Australia meets this presumption quite well inasmuch as the great bulk of public services other than defence are state operated and the states account for over 50 per cent of public expenditure. However, Australian states raise a much smaller proportion of taxation for their own purposes than do states in other federations, thus severely weakening the connection between taxes and benefits which economists often commend.

It should be noted that this preference of economists for functional decentralisation is conditional, not absolute. Not only does this goal conflict to some extent with the redistributive goal (about whose importance economists differ in much the same ways as ordinary citizens), but also some functions can only be efficiently performed on a national scale and many functions produce 'spillover' problems, for example, they give rise to appreciable costs (such as pollution) or benefits (such as free use of certain facilities) outside their area of operation. Spillover problems can in principle be compensated for by special grants or taxes levied by a higher level of government, although in the jungle of public finance finely tuned measures of this kind are rarely found. It should be noted that Australian states (like Canadian provinces but unlike US states) are rather well placed to avoid spillover effects because of their large size and sparsely populated border zones.

These principles of economic administration within a federation have to be understood within a shifting context of public policies and priorities. Thus after 1945 the stabilisation and redistributive goals of government were elevated to a prominent position in all the western democracies. This development meant an enhanced role for the federal government. It was expected to manage the economy so as to achieve full employment and economic growth. It was expected to bring about a higher level of social services and minimum standards of economic welfare throughout the nation. In Australia the federal government pursued these goals through its exclusive monopoly of income tax (achieved during wartime) and through section 96 conditional grants to the states for a variety of purposes, as well as through quite extensive market regulation.

Although Liberal–Country Party coalitions governed for most of this period, they accepted to a considerable extent the philosophy of this era. The Labor Party believed far more fervently in national economic planning and redistribution and got its chance with the Whitlam government which greatly stepped up the tempo of federal grants and interventions. The Whitlam period was the climax and almost the end of the post-war philosophy of 'Keynes plus the welfare state'.

Subsequent developments have changed the ways in which these various economic functions are perceived. With the end of the post-war boom and the reappearance of substantial unemployment, the stabilisation goal has seemed to become less attainable and has (for the time being at least) been given a narrower interpretation. The now dominant macro-economic goal is to create the market conditions and industrial restructuring which will enable the economy to become more internationally competitive. One implication of this goal is a tight rein upon public expenditure so that the redistributive goal in turn has to be more narrowly conceived. Financial stringency produces a need to reduce federal grants to the states and, as in other federations, a consequence is reduced scope for federal intervention in the provision of state services. Thus the economic balance of the federation becomes subtly changed, although the durability of this change is more doubtful.

The discrediting of macro-economic management of the economy has been accompanied by a strong revival of micro-economic theories of competitive markets. One implication of this revival is the claimed superiority of markets over governments in the allocation of resources, since markets can be said to reflect consumers' preferences more closely than do voting or other political processes. This conclusion does not invalidate the case for any public good which the market cannot provide in an acceptable form; but it has led the public choice school of economists to concentrate upon improving the capacity of the political system to convey individual preferences for public goods more accurately, and hence to move more closely towards the market model of efficient resource allocation.

This particular economic doctrine has considerable implications for federalism. It stresses the case for functional decentralisation which was noted earlier. If accompanied (as the doctrine often is) with a reduced belief in either the virtue or the possibility of redistribution (for it is often claimed that this policy has only led in practice to 'middle-class welfare' and the dominance of special interests rather than to the relief of poverty and inequality) then a further implication of this position is the desirability of strengthening the tax capacities of state and local governments and of developing effective forms of competition between them.

Therefore it will be logical to consider next the extent to which Australian states satisfy the conditions of allocative efficiency by responding effectively to differential demands for public goods. We can then consider the financial principles of intergovernmental relations, and relate these both to the case for stronger state autonomy and to the future economic role of the federal government.

Economic tests of state efficiency

The USA is the home not only of federalism but of pluralism. Nowhere else is there such a proliferation of general purpose governments and special agencies at federal, state and several local levels (and at intermediate regional levels too). This dizzy array of public bodies is often praised both by political scientists and by economists for replicating within government the virtues of the market system. The variety of agencies, so it is claimed, ensures a multiplicity of responses to differential consumer demands. Agencies bargain, co-operate and compete with each other. True, there are significant differences from the idealised market model: for example, public agencies unlike firms rarely go bankrupt (though New York and some other cities have done so), and in any case—bankrupt or not—they almost never die like commercial firms. However, following the Tiebout (1956) thesis, it is claimed that citizens can vote with their feet by changing their jurisdiction. How far they actually do so is a doubtful question, except for the marked tendency of rich citizens to congregate together in protected local government enclaves, entrenched by zoning and other laws designed to exclude the non-affluent (Self, 1982).

However, this United States governmental pluralism—whether or not it provides a satisfactory model of service delivery—can no longer be equated with the claimed virtues of federalism. In this sense Madison's dictum that federalism is the structural underpinning of pluralist democracy, quoted with approval by Galligan (see page 54), has to be treated with some reserve in respect of Madison's homeland. The state governments have become overshadowed both by the growth and financial powers of federal government and also by the great expansion of local governments which now account for more public expenditure than do the states (a striking difference from Australia where states spend over ten times as much as local government). It is true that the Reagan administration has somewhat strengthened the relative independence of the states through some reduction of federal intervention as the necessary price of cuts in federal aid, and through curtailing the special relationship between Washington and the city governments which grew up in the Kennedy and Johnson years (Milnor, 1985). All the same the multifaceted character of modern United States pluralism, of which the states are but one element, has not been changed basically.

Federalism in the USA is in fact no longer the preoccupation of economists or political scientists that it is in Australia and Canada. The stress (by those who praise the system) is upon the virtues of decentralisation and pluralism more than upon federalism as such. Years ago Carl Friedrich (1968) practically assimilated the concept of federalism to that of decentralisation in general, and was hauled over the coals by Rufus Davis (1978: ch. 6) in Australia for violating the federal ideal. Vincent Ostrom (1973), along with other public choice economists, delivered a blistering attack upon big bureaucracy in Washington, but his chosen remedy was not a return to stronger state autonomy but the creation of numerous representative bodies to run public services in the interests of their respective clienteles. Wallace Oates' (1972) theory of fiscal federalism rests more upon concepts of decentralisation than a constitutional concept of federalism. Nothing has excited more interest among American public choice economists than the 'Lakewood plan', whereby a small (and affluent) local government buys in its services from the most efficient provider, whether public or private. (Many of its services are actually purchased from Los Angeles County.) Here is a model of a small elected body buying in its requirements in a competitive market style which accords well with the predilections of market economists but owes nothing whatever to the theorists of federalism (in Australia a Lakewood, if it could exist at all, would probably be promptly suspended by the state premier).

All this may seem some distance from Australian federalism but it is not really so; for in considering the perspectives of market economists who claim to be apostles of service efficiency it is necessary to look to the logical tendencies of their theories if they are to have relevance to Australia. Not only that, but Australian federalists frequently appeal to American experience, as they do in this volume, so that a glancing look at the fate of federalism within the USA is not without some relevance to its prospects within Australia.

We must now, however, turn from this contemplation of what is actually a very different kind of society to consider the relevance of the economic criterion of 'allocative efficiency' to conditions in the Australian states.

It is a point of logic among economists that the gains to individual consumers of public services from a federal system will be greater where the nation itself is relatively heterogeneous (in respect of patterns of demand) and the states are relatively homogeneous. In other words gains are maximised where the people of each state share similar tastes, demands or preferences, while there are marked differences between states. While such an ideal model is nowhere approximated, Australia would seem to exhibit a more or less converse situation to this preferred arrangement. Australian states do not differ at all markedly, as the world goes, in respect of wealth, incomes, occupational structure, ethnicity, or political affiliations (except for the special situation with the Queensland Liberals, the two main parties are nation-wide and enjoy rather similar levels of support in each state, while the degree of political differentiation by state is markedly less than in Canada). Also each state possesses a relatively heterogeneous population, marked, for example, by appreciable differences of interest and culture between the metropolitan city and its rural hinterland.

If, therefore, these factors provide a guide to popular preferences respecting services and taxes, we would expect to find relatively small differences between the various states at least on this account (for differences can of course be due to other factors, such as swings of party control, the predilictions of individual politicians or bureaucrats or the access of powerful lobbies to state governments). Equally, the existence of more heterogeneity within each state suggests the likelihood of internal conflict over policies and indicates that the preferences of elected local governments (supposing local government were strong enough to transmit such preferences) could be expected to differ considerably.

So much is hypothetical. What does the evidence actually suggest? It is clear that there are many variations between the states in respect of their organisation, processes and legislation, but there is disagreement among commentators about how far there are real and substantive differences over the extent and quality of their public services (Aldred and Wilkes, 1983). One suspects that much depends upon the perspective or bias of the commentator.

The only hard evidence is to be found in the extensive data collected by the Commonwealth Grants Commission for equalisation purposes. The Commission states that its inquiries do reveal a considerable divergence between state policies, although it has also admitted that its inspection of state services at first hand (as opposed to statistical analysis) has been very limited.[2] The Commission estimates for each state the expenditure that would be required for each service if standards were uniform throughout Australia after allowing for cost differences due to different numbers of clients and other inescapable costs. The differences between these standardised costs and the actual expenditure of each state offers some guide to its differential policies and priorities, and the same exercise can be repeated in respect of each state's use of its revenue sources.

Gerritsen's (1987) analysis of these data, to which I am indebted, suggests to me rather limited differences between the states in respect of their tax and expenditure policies.[3] Taking a three-year average (1979–82) so as to try to eliminate such factors as a pre-electoral spending splurge, the one strong result to emerge is that Queensland is almost consistently a low taxer and a low spender compared with the other states. Tasmania emerges as the highest overall spender per head, followed by South Australia, Western Australia and Victoria–New South Wales, which are lumped together by the Commission as its basic standard. (Consequently the differences between Victoria and New South Wales cannot be seen from these data.)

Table 4.1 gives fuller details of relative state expenditures upon the group of 'social services' which together account for about 70 per cent of all state spending. Naturally enough there was more variation over spending upon culture and recreation, welfare, and law and order than upon the much more expensive basic services of education and health (as Gerritsen notes, recreation is also an obvious target for pre-electoral spending). The most obvious variation in the two major services, apart from Queensland's low spending, was the high expenditure of Western Australia upon health, said to be due to its extensive system of regional hospitals (a policy choice, although perhaps a justified one in terms of its widely scattered population) and to higher staff costs than in some other states. As regards the more minor services, Tasmania as well as Queensland was a low spender on welfare, but Tasmania was a very high spender upon culture and recreation and upon law and order. Welfare is an example of a service with considerable policy variations, the actual expenditure per capita on the three-year average being $22.3 in Queensland, $27.5 in Tasmania, $37.0 in South Australia and $37.6 in Western Australia, whereas all four states were assessed as having very similar welfare needs. Another perspective upon the extent of policy differences is that total assessed need for all social services (three-year average) was virtually the same for Queensland ($727 per capita) and Western Australia ($726) but Queensland actually spent $612 and Western Australia $812. However, the clearly deviant behaviour of Queensland means that differences between Western Australia and the other states were much smaller.

Table 4.2 performs the same exercise for revenue sources. There were considerable variations over the utilisation of land and mining revenues but, except for mining in Western Australia and Queensland, these are relatively small revenue sources. Western Australia emerges as a relatively low taxer next to Queensland. South Australia and Tasmania are near average and Victoria–New South Wales somewhat above average.

Table 4.1 State expenditures per capita as ratios of needs-adjusted national standard (= 1.0); three-year average (1979–82)

	Qld	WA	SA	Tas.	NSW –Vic. average	Under spending states[1]	Over spending state[2]
Education	0.81	0.92	1.07	1.14	1.04	Qld	Tas.
Health	0.91	1.35	1.08	1.13	1.03	—	WA, Tas
Culture and recreation	0.90	1.15	1.48	1.51	0.89	NSW–Vic.	Tas., SA & WA
Welfare services	0.69	1.15	1.20	0.84	1.05	Qld Tas.	SA WA
Law, order and public safety	0.88	1.03	1.18	1.56	0.95	Qld	Tas., SA
Total social services	0.84	1.08	1.10	1.17	1.03	Qld	Tas., SA

[1] Variation in excess of −0.10.
[2] Variation in excess of +0.10.

Source: Gerritsen, R. (1987), Tables 1–17 (pp 33–54) and Reports of Commonwealth Grants Commission.

Table 4.2 State revenues per capita as ratios of needs-adjusted national standard (= 1.0); (1979–82) three-year average

	Qld	WA	SA	Tas.	NSW–Vic. average
Taxation	0.79	0.83	0.97	0.98	1.06
Land revenue	0.69	1.35	1.41	1.81	0.95
Mining revenue	0.71	0.99	0.93	0.53	1.24
Total revenue	0.80	0.88	0.99	0.97	1.13

[1] Includes interest earnings (1981–82 only). Figures not closely comparable with the sum of the other three items.
Source: as for Table 4.1

I do not pretend that a great deal can be made of this data which anyhow requires fuller research.[4] However it does at least raise some questions. Are Queensland's low spending and taxing due (as public choice theory might suggest) to the preferences of a relatively large rural and non-metropolitan population? Rural and smalltown people tend to be averse to spending on welfare and social services but keen on roads. The rural and non-metropolitan bias of the Queensland electoral system and government might support this analysis. Tasmania is the other state with an above average rural population and it too is low on welfare, but it is the highest spender overall, which contradicts the above hypothesis. Other possible explanations of Queensland's behaviour are the special features of its recent politics and the possibility that it is or was more administratively economical than other states.

An important factor in this analysis is the operations of the Commonwealth Grants Commission itself. Australia has in principle a far more comprehensive system of equalisation between states than the other federations. The USA has no such system apart from politically balanced weightings of certain federal grants. Canada and West Germany follow the more usual principle of compensating states for disabilities in their revenue-raising capacities, but not for the differential costs incurred in the provision of services. The philosophy behind this arrangement is that it is equitable to provide states with adequate revenues but that their expenditures are tied up with their efficiency, their policy choices and the different economic costs of servicing particular locations. In Australia, however, expenditure disabilities are included in the formula equally with revenue ones and the Commission does its best (which is not easy) to exclude costs due to inefficiency or deliberate policy.

This equalisation philosophy has a considerable influence upon the operation of federalism in Australia. It reflects a certain concept of geographic (not individual) equity which seems in Australia to have widespread support, yet it also reduces the claimed advantages of service diversity based upon local choice. Strong equalisation measures reduce the incentive and the need for states to pursue different policies, while the equalisation philosophy itself may suggest (at least to the popular mind) that the ideal would be the same standards of service and taxation everywhere—in which case why federalism? Equalisation policy can be seen as one way of seeking to approximate federalism to the service conditions of a unitary state and indeed there is little reason to believe that the service variations within Australia are greater (and they may indeed be less) than those between the regions of a unitary state such as the UK or France. Of course, a further factor here is that variations of wealth (and of culture, ethnicity, etc.) among the Australian states are actually less than among the UK and French regions so that the choices of their electorates might produce a relative uniformity of service demands even in the absence of equalisation.

It must be remembered that the role of the Commonwealth Grants Commission is advisory and the final determinations of grants to the states are political. Politically speaking it is difficult to change the relativities between states other than very gradually, and for that and other reasons the distribution of the grants has lagged behind population changes. It may seem a curious fact that, among the states having claims for special assistance, Queensland should emerge as very parsimonious while the other three states (Tasmania, South Australia and Western Australia) are clearly above-average spenders. Part of the explanation is the lagged character of the equalisation system in practice, which has channelled extra funds to the three higher spending states at the expense of the other three states including Queensland, which suffered inadequate compensation for its population growth. These facts help to explain the contrasting behaviour of Tasmania and Queensland which seemed to contradict the hypothesis about the preference of a rural electorate. They also help to explain the relatively high tax levels of Victoria–New South Wales shown in Table 4.2.

Thus if equalisation measures were more accurately implemented, the tax and expenditure differences between the states would probably be less. Of course, one must be careful not to explain too much by financial interest. For example, South Australia's above-average spending levels and its much stronger housing and planning policies do also suggest differential policy preferences (howsoever arising) in that state.

If one is seeking a vehicle for the claimed virtues of localised choice over tax and service levels, the obvious candidate is not state but local government. This conclusion has been demonstrated, consciously or not, by the growth of local government in the USA. Local governments enable a greater variety of individual preferences to be expressed and they offer more scope for competition between localities than is possible between states. This is clearly true in Australia. Local areas within each state differ much more markedly in their social composition, wealth and way of life—for example, between rural and metropolitan areas, and between inner cities and outer suburbs—than the states (taken as complete entities) differ from each other. Individuals might to some extent move from one locality to another so as to enjoy better services or lower taxes—at any rate within metropolitan areas—but, given the size of Australia, mobility between the states for this reason must be rare (a partial exception may be the choice of a retirement home, but climate and other factors will usually be more important). Generally, jobs, family and tradition will be the determinants of choice of state.

However local government also has disadvantages compared to states. It creates many more spillover problems, it cannot utilise some economies of scale and specialisation, and it produces much greater inequalities of revenue capacity and service costs. If local government in Australia were to expand its functions substantially, it would need to be restructured into larger units in order to reduce these defects—although some use might be made of devices like the Lakewood plan for combining local choice with efficient service production. Some of the advantages of the present small scale of Australian local government would be lost in the process. Even with the benefit of restructuring, polarisation and inequality between areas would remain a problem. The federal equalisation grant currently paid to local government (again a feature unique to Australia) would need to be extended to meet this situation, and could of course replace equivalent grants to the states, but this proposal would meet fierce state resistance. Alternatively, state governments could develop their own equalisation system for local government, but history suggests that they might be reluctant to do so—which is why the federal government entered this particular arena in the first place (National Inquiry into Local Government Finance, 1985).

Despite these difficulties, local government is at present so weak in Australia (accounting for less than 6 per cent of public expenditure) that there would be much to be gained (in terms of the economic and political values of individual choice and participation) from extending its coverage and role. The Australian states have been, and in various degrees remain, dominant and dictatorial in their treatment of local government and will concede to its representatives no part of the constitutional rights which they so vehemently claim for themselves. This accords with a frequent Australian assumption that the virtues of constitutionalism and pluralism reside in the states and need not be extended more generally.

This section must end on a sceptical note. If one of the economic rationales for federalism is that of effectively expressing diversity of individual preferences, there is not a lot of evidence of this result in Australia. Insofar as state policies do differ substantively as well as procedurally there are other factors which could largely account for these differences such as the access of particular interests to state governments, the individual preferences of powerful ministers or bureaucrats, and the institutional interest of the state government and its functionaries in protecting their turf. Of course all these other inputs can also be claimed (on a pluralist model) as a virtue of federalism, but the difficulty lies in judging what political activities actually advance or hinder the effective articulation and aggregation of individual preferences.

It will not do to adduce all political activity as evidence for the vitality of federalism. For example, there is much diversity in the decisions reached on land and development decisions in the states, but the major decisions at least usually reflect inside deals between government and business. In such cases the multiple access points of federalism favour strong special interests not majority opinion. There are other cases where a state government does seem responsive to local tastes—public housing in South Australia is one example. Behind this problem lies the vexed question of how far political preferences can in fact be evaluated on the basis of a market model.[5]

Constitutionalism and federal rules

Some economists in the public choice school take a different approach to the emphasis upon welfare maximisation.[6] Their concern, like that of many political scientists, is with appropriate individual rights and constitutional rules. The objective now shifts to processes rather than outcomes. Thus it can be claimed that, even if citizens of state A exhibit much the same preferences as those of state B, it is still a value that they are free to choose differently if they so decide. It can also be claimed that they ought to be able to make such choices in an effective and predictable manner, which may point to a case for constitutional rules which cannot be broken or set aside through the play of political pressures or through the whims or interests of federal politicians and bureaucrats.

But what should be the basis of such constitutional rules? The economists in question do not drop the assumption of self-regarding individuals. Their primary concern is with the protection of individual rights against the coercive power of the state. Their assumption is that individuals will only be willing to accept coercion, as a necessary condition for the provision of collective goods, if this coercive power is controlled and restrained by appropriate rules. This 'social contract' approach has a long history in political science and was reflected in the design of the American Constitution. It was not much of a factor, if present at all, in the design of the Australian Constitution. This can be explained historically by the fact that the American Constitution-makers were deeply distrustful of the power of government, whereas on the whole Australians conceived government as a necessary and beneficent force. However, the Australian Constitution-makers were deeply concerned about the federal division of powers.

Federalism was not introduced into Australia as a check upon the powers of government in general. Nonetheless, it may operate in this way and be supported or strengthened for this reason. Certainly Australian federalism offers considerable impediments to the 'Thatcher effect', whereby the leadership of a party which (in three elections) achieved no more than 45 per cent of the popular vote could effect radical changes such as the abolition of large city governments without encountering any effective institutionalised opposition. In Australia (in addition to the different voting rules) a federal government either of the left or the right must reckon with formidable institutional barriers in both the Senate and the states, linked with the destabilising effect of frequent interlocked elections at both levels of government. However, the veto power of the states does not get a lot of support from the Australian Constitution and hinges upon electoral and political processes.

It should be remembered that state governments can also act in arbitrary ways, as the recent history of Queensland suggests. Federalism on its own can offer no ultimate guarantee against the excessive or arbitrary uses of government power, but it may be assigned a role within a system of constitutional rules designed to control and limit the powers of government.

There is no space here to examine the economic approach to constitutionalism in general, which has been advocated by Buchanan (1975) and by Brennan and Buchanan (1985). However, its relevance to federalism does warrant consideration. In *The Power to Tax* (1980), Brennan and Buchanan make the very strong assumption that government is or anyhow tends to behave as a Leviathan which, unless checked, will maximise its revenue surplus at the expense of the citizen-taxpayer. This thesis stands on its head the earlier macro-economic assumption that government would act as a benevolent reformer of market failures, and I confess (although there is no space to develop the point) that this opposite assumption seems to me as excessive and mistaken as the 'benevolent despot' thesis which the authors reasonably criticise.

However, accepting (as I would) that the revenue-raising powers of government can be exploited for the profit of bureaucrats and politicians, one arrives at federalism as one device for checking this tendency through introducing competition between governments. The monopolistic powers of the central government can be checked through the maximum possible devolution of powers to state governments, and competition between states will deter any state from excessive taxation (since its citizens can move to a lower taxing state). From this standpoint the Australian Constitution is clearly defective, since it does not constrain the tax powers of the federal government (as this theory requires) but instead leaves the states heavily reliant upon federal grants. This arrangement produces a cartel effect whereby the state governments can collectively acquire surplus revenue and are under insufficient pressure to compete with each other over the efficiency of their tax-services packages.

This argument is quite logical and persuasive as far as it goes, but as the authors admit it does not deal with all the factors relevant for the optimum design of a federal Constitution. It leaves out problems about economies of scale and spillovers, while (as the authors agree) mobility of population is much more relevant to competition between local governments than between states—especially given the character of the Australian states. The argument does not deal either with the federal government's macro-economic role. The authors' treatment of issues of redistribution is to be found in their general argument that this matter is better treated through constitutional rules about taxation and entitlements, rather than left to the shifting preferences of an electoral majority. However, failing the adoption of such rules, the effects of promoting strong tax competition between states while tightly restricting the federal tax base would be to undermine the scope for distribution, and could lead to government resource allocations largely replicating market inequalities.

Thus it is difficult to believe that the case for tax and service competition between the states should outweigh other important goals with which it conflicts, while the actual efficacy of such competition is also open to some doubt. However, the criticism of the cartel effect of Australian federal arrangements does need further consideration, because it accords with often stated principles of financial accountability.

It is not clear how far the system whereby the Australian states receive over half their tax revenues without being responsible for raising this money leads to extravagant spending or to excess pay-outs to bureaucrats and politicians, but some effects of this kind are not unlikely. In theory the system could also lead to underspending upon public goods if the federal government were to impose tight financial constraints upon the states—although the balance of political pressures in Australia perhaps makes this unlikely. A further economic criticism is that the system leads to distortions of political choice for public goods because the citizens of each state have their preferences altered by the weight of federal financial influence.

The difficulty with this last argument is that the federal government needs to alter the states' priorities in order to perform its own economic functions. Both the stabilisation and redistributive functions are best served by conceding the bulk of progressive taxation to the federal government. These functions and also other considerations of allocative efficiency (such as compensation for spillovers and economies of scale) can also justify selective federal interventions with state priorities. Thus it is impossible to specify any simple basis for the distribution of financial resources in a federation. Much will depend upon the weight placed upon different values—upon allocative efficiency as against redistribution, for example. Much will depend too upon how federal financial influence actually operates—upon the design of federal grants and their influence upon state priorities.

In this situation recourse is often had to international comparisons. Thus it can be said that the financial dependence of Australian states is excessive and unnecessary when compared with the situation in other federations. This certainly is a strong argument. Offsetting it are the facts that the Australian states account for a high proportion of total public services and expenditure (thus increasing both the need and the rationale for federal grants) and that, unlike the USA for example, they receive a high proportion of federal aid in untied grants which they can spend as they choose. On balance it does seem likely that allocative efficiency could be improved without a serious impairment of federal functions through some transfer of tax powers to the states together with a reform of federal grants. The very narrow revenue basis of the states is not conducive to responsible government, and indeed the states have shown their financial irresponsibility by their own unwillingness to resume income tax powers.

Whatever tax powers can or should be transferred to the states (a subject I leave to other writers), a reform of federal grants seems desirable both in itself and as the condition of such a transfer. Section 96 grants often lack any economic rationale. For example, federal road grants (the oldest of the conditional grants) are clearly justified for interstate highways, not needed for state highways (unless a state has a large proportion of interstate travellers) and not necessary at all for local roads. A frequent justification for many of these grants is the desirability of ensuring satisfactory basic standards of public services throughout Australia. The extent to which financial incentives can achieve this result is limited because the states can to some extent redeploy their own resources elsewhere. But in fact many section 96 grants have been given for specific political and electoral reasons and have not been redistributive in their effects. Mathews (1986) points out that equalisation grants to the states have been necessary to offset the inegalitarian effects of section 96 grants, and concluded that much of this money should be absorbed into general purpose grants.

Federal grants also increase the influence of professional bureaucracies whose tendency is towards more uniform policies and standards. Sam Beer (1977) has shown how in the USA the 'technocrats', led by the Washington bureaucrats, gained ground over the 'topocrats', the state governors and legislators, although this process has been partly reversed in the Reagan years. This technocratic influence grew rapidly in Australia in the Whitlam period, under the influence of expert Commonwealth agencies spending large federal grants. Although such influence has since declined, its continued existence clearly conflicts with the freedom of choice of state electorates.

In fact there is no present way of preventing section 96 grants from reflecting federal political and bureaucratic interests rather than economic grounds for intervention. State interests might theoretically be protected, as Cheryl Saunders suggests, through constitutional rules for co-operative agreement. However it is doubtful whether such rules would produce more economically rational grants or much affect the processes of technocratic influence and co-operation. It should also be recognised that the federal government does have (and perhaps will increasingly have) specific purposes of economic management which could be compromised by the requirements for state co-operation. Thus the wiser policy would seem to be to reduce the need and scope for such grants (through strengthening the states' financial base), and thereby also put pressure upon the federal government to order its interventions more selectively.

Insofar as it is impracticable, on grounds of the efficiency and equity of tax collection, to devolve tax powers to the states, the rational alternative is a system of guaranteed and untied grants allocated according to some known and defensible system of rules. The Australian system of financial assistance grants to the states is rational in intent but has lacked defensible rules. The introduction of revenue sharing by the Fraser government improved matters through giving the states a specified and known share of federal income tax and subsequently (more sensibly) of total tax revenue. However, this principle was soon lost and the system returned to one of *ad hoc* political bargaining.

Much of this bargaining has been due to the political difficulties of implementing the equalisation proposals of the Commonwealth Grants Commission. The Commission's original role of advising upon the needs of the poorer claimant states was undermined by the assimilation of these states into the general system of financial assistance grants through a series of *ad hoc* political agreements, so that only Tasmania was left as a claimant. These developments threw issues of equalisation into a political whirlpool and eroded the Commission's role. In recent years that role has been restored and enlarged through getting the Commission to undertake comprehensive reviews for determining the fair allocation of the total grant between all the states. This is an important step forward. It is not yet certain whether, as Mathews (1986) hopes, the Commission's reviews will become regular triennial affairs or whether its recommendations will be more promptly implemented.

If there is scope for constitutional reform in grant allocation it is surely here. The total of financial allocation grants could be fixed as a proportion of total federal taxation and revised every three years after a federal-state review which would take account of changes in functions and in general financial conditions. This review would be advised by an impartial body, the Commonwealth Grants Commission, but the final determination would almost certainly need to be made by the federal government which after all is the guardian and provider of federal finances. The allocation of the money between the states should be determined every three years by the Commonwealth Grants Commission and here it is reasonable to say that the Commission's decisions ought to be binding, since the federal government's proper interest is in the total size of the grant not its allocation, while the states are not appropriate judges in their own cause. In this situation an umpire is called for. However the umpire's principles and methods should be open to public debate, and it should be possible for the federal government and the states (or a suitable proportion of them) to give instructions to the Commission about its methodology.

The Commission's broad concept of equalisation is open to the economic criticism that it distorts the allocation of resources through discouraging the movement of workers and capital from the poorer to the richer states and also mobility within states. For example, in Australia the high costs of providing public services in rural areas are compensated in the federal grants paid both to states and to local governments, thus shoring up what many economists would see as uneconomic locations.

However this criticism needs further analysis. If subsidies were withdrawn from rural areas, their population would decline further, leading to still higher costs and so on. Further, if the migrants moved to the big coastal cities (as is probable), costs of congestion for services such as transport and housing and the control of pollution would rise there too. If these extra costs were not compensated (as they are now) there would certainly be some incentive for individuals and firms to move to those settlements where service costs are lowest—which are generally agreed by economists to be medium-sized towns of perhaps 50 000 to 250 000 people. Curiously this type of settlement is almost absent in Australia, although some state decentralisation schemes and the policies of the Whitlam government tried to encourage movement to places of this kind. (These schemes were too shortlived and scattered their incentives too widely to be successful except in the case of Albury–Wodonga.)

This economic objection to equalisation is therefore too crude because it does not allow sufficiently for the costs and consequences of population movements. It does not consider the disruption of individual and community life which would occur in many cases from the withdrawal of public subsidies and which can also be seen (even if not quantified) as losses of economic welfare. In other cases—such as congestion in big cities—it can be argued that the removal of subsidies would exert a beneficial stimulus upon state governments to produce more effective schemes of decentralisation to medium-sized towns where service costs are lower. The Commission is currently reviewing the effects of its rules upon resource allocation, and Grewal argues in this volume that subsidies for uneconomic locations should be eliminated. (It might be noted that Victoria would profit from this change.) Some variation of the rules may well be desirable but in some cases at least a full cost-benefit analysis would provide some support for locational subsidies.

Economists disagree about the equalisation principle[7], although as an exercise in redistribution, equalisation between states is clearly less effective than equalisation between individuals, since citizens in the assisted states benefit proportionately to their wealth. Yet geographic equalisation has its own rationale and, up to a point anyway, can be considered a well-established preference of the Australian electorate.

We can conclude that there is a good case for establishing constitutional rules which regulate more closely and predictably the financial relations between the federal government and the states; but the final evaluation of such a reform should depend upon wider considerations about the economic health of the federal system.

Economics and the health of the Australian federation

Writers in this volume such as Brian Galligan and Campbell Sharman have praised Australian federalism as a happy combination of the virtues of big and smaller government. Of course all modern democratic governments are decentralised in varying degrees, and if the distinctive virtue of a political system is the existence of multiple levels of government catering for different popular needs and responsive to different constituencies, then the Australian system would not rank particularly high and would be markedly inferior to American pluralism. However the distinctive feature of effective federalism as such is two levels of government entrenched within a Constitution which ensures to each level an effective degree of independent power and which corresponds well with the pattern of civic interests and loyalties. It is ideally a system that citizens feel comfortable with and from which they can extract efficient responses to their wants or preferences.

Thus stated, few would contend that all is right with Australian federalism. The main critique to be gathered from some writers in this volume, such as Campbell Sharman and Cliff Walsh, is that the states need to be strengthened in order to serve their own constituencies more effectively and to resist intrusions from the federal government. Other writers, such as Brian Head, have pointed to some of the new tasks which need to be tackled through forms of 'co-operative federalism', under the aegis or guidance of the federal government; but of late no strong reasons have been advanced—such as were often heard in earlier discourses upon this subject—for increasing the role or powers of the federal government. The contributions of constitutional lawyers do suggest a lack of legal limits to the continued expansion of federal powers, but this is not necessarily to praise the prospect. Instead one can view these writings as part of the case for entrenching stronger state powers within the Australian Constitution.

A balanced economic perspective upon Australian federalism may suggest much more cautious and qualified conclusions about the health of the system. Any such conclusions should of course take account of present differences within economic thought—between micro approaches and macro approaches to the subject and between different schools of thought about the functioning of markets and the state. Such conclusions cannot be free of value judgments about the scope and relevance of particular economic theories—of what is left out as well as what is assumed by the theory. From this standpoint there is an inevitable tension between theories of efficient resource allocation, as developed by the neo-classical economists, and theories of macro-economic management and redistribution.

Much of this paper has been given over to the analysis of allocative efficiency which is rooted in micro-economic theory. In principle, such efficiency can be improved by the decentralisation of public services to small and homogeneous units of government, but this conclusion is subject to considerable qualifications about the economies of scale and spillovers. It is also subject to criticisms about distributive effects (the tendency to polarisation into rich and poor units) and to questions about the actual preferences and capacities of citizens concerning their system of government. These questions are often remitted to political science, but modern political economy cannot ignore their significance for the preferences of individuals.

Part of this problem derives from a difference between economic and political methodologies. Economists are concerned with the maximum aggregation of individual preferences, whereas political scientists assume that individuals have entrenched loyalties to particular states which constitute viable and desirable political communities. How strong these loyalties are and what is their value to individuals are uncertain issues, and an alternative view is that the states' survival as strong political forces is primarily due to institutional interests.

In Australia considerations of allocative efficiency provide a clear case for stronger delegation of powers to local government, but other considerations suggest that such delegation should be cautiously handled to avoid social and economic polarisation. Under the actual political conditions of Australian federalism the larger issue concerns the balance of powers between federal and state governments. I have argued that while the economic case for strengthening the independent tax base of the states in itself is a cogent one, it has to be weighed against the requirements of the federal government's economic role. Such an examination suggests a need for the reform of federal grants to the states. Conditional (section 96) grants frequently lack any clear economic rationale and it would be preferable for such grants to be targeted more closely to necessary federal interventions although (for the same reason) they should remain fully under federal control. Financial assistance grants should be determined by clear and predictable rules that are periodically reviewed, and they should be allocated according to equalisation principles which also are periodically reviewed.

These suggested reforms would assist a number of desirable economic and political objectives. They would strengthen the financial capacities and responsibilities of the states through providing (by a reduction of total federal grants) some scope for a transfer of tax powers to the states and through introducing greater certainty and predictability into the size and allocation of the untied federal grants. In these ways they would reduce such temptation as exists for extravagant state spending, strengthen the states' responsibilities for raising their own revenue, and give the states more freedom to determine their own priorities. All these developments should reduce political haggling and begging over federal revenues and should go some way to meet the case of those political economists, such as Brennan and Buchanan, who have argued for greater recourse to clear and defensible constitutional rules.

These conclusions also take some account of the macro-economic role of the federal government, but this role has been only lightly sketched. Unfortunately macro-economic thought is currently in a state of confusion. The dominant school of market economists, rooted in micro-economic theories, assumes that the regulatory role of the state should be cut down and the functioning of the economy left in the main to the play of competitive market forces. This view is of necessity qualified. It is usually accepted that federal interventions are necessary for easing the transition to a more competitive Australian economy, for example, through industrial assistance plans, retraining schemes and relief work for redundant workers. However it seems often to be supposed that when (and if) the economy has become adequately competitive in international terms, the need for such interventions will diminish or cease. The federal government's economic role is likened to that of a benevolent colonial power seeking to work itself out of a job.

Such assumptions rest upon a simplified and unrealistic view of the international market economy. Since most national economies are under strong pressure to become more competitive, it is improbable that all can succeed while the rapid movements of international finance and investment will continue to require equally frequent and rapid changes in the Australian economy if it is not shielded from their blast. In fact most economically successful modern governments play a highly active role in both maximising gains from foreign trade and shielding their economies from the ill-effects of rapid economic changes. It seems quite likely that the federal government's function of 'stabilisation' will become more not less important and difficult in the years ahead.

Australia is a relatively small country in economic terms, and the division of powers between federal and state governments is certainly an impediment to national economic policy-making. In a world of giant international firms and conglomerates, of enormous protective states or blocs such as the USA or the EEC, and of powerful interventionist governments such as Japan (conditions that are far removed from the economists' competitive market model), Australia might seem to be in need of a greater concentration and co-ordination of economic powers in such matters as the control of natural resources, the location of major industrial developments, the regulation of industry and trade, the promotion of employment and aid to regions or localities seriously affected by the shifts of international trade. If these arguments are right even in part, and if failure in the international economy should add to their cogency, considerable pressure will be placed upon the federal system in Australia.

In his contribution to this volume Brian Head points out that the institutions of 'co-operative federalism' will need to be expanded to deal with some of these economic problems. Such developments would take the form of joint action in selected fields, but they may also require some transfers of economic powers from the states to the federal government. This stronger federal role could be backed up by a much more selective use of conditional grants. How far such federal interventions will be necessary may be a matter of opinion, especially in a climate of scepticism about the effectiveness of macro-economic management, but their rationale ought to be taken seriously in any reassignment of federal powers. If market deregulation produces unacceptable results, the climate of opinion may again swing back towards government interventions, especially perhaps in the rather fragile economic circumstances of Australia.

The federal government's redistributive role has been mentioned at several points in this essay. This role primarily involves financial redistribution between individuals exerted through progressive taxation and welfare payments. In the future it may need to be extended, as many critics have argued, to a more comprehensive scheme of social security, financed by joint contributions from employers, workers and government.[8] Considerations of economic efficiency as well as equity can be adduced for this proposal, such as the need to assist economic change through more effective protection of individuals and the strong case for broadening Australia's narrow tax base with its heavy dependence upon income tax. Ultimately the desirable extent of redistribution hinges upon political philosophy and preferences—with the awkward rider that effective redistribution must depend upon the choice of the federal rather than the state electorates. From this standpoint the federal government's financial capacity has to be protected against too much erosion through the transfer of tax powers.

The federal government has been much less effective, and often only half-hearted, in its efforts to achieve satisfactory basic standards of public services. In its dealings with the states, geographic equalisation of resources is an easier target and does not interfere with state priorities, but for this very reason it does not necessarily benefit poorer individuals. Despite these limitations, professional and administrative co-operation between two levels of government has possibly had some equalising effect upon public services, but on the whole section 96 grants would need much closer targeting to be effectively redistributional and can be the opposite.

This review of the federal economic role suggests the inevitability of conflict between the goals of co-operative federalism and those of strengthened state autonomy and freedom of choice. The first goal draws upon the likely requirements of macro-economic management in the modern world, together with claims for equitable redistribution which seem likely to gain greater salience under conditions of rapid economic change and instability. The second goal draws upon classical market theory for demonstrating the advantages of a more competitive governmental system geared more closely and directly to the exercise of political choice. This conflict raises the basic question of whether Australia will develop as a corporate state marked by a considerable degree of integration between both economic interests and governments under federal leadership, or whether both the economic system and (to some extent) the government system will develop along more competitive and differentiated lines.

Without stargazing too far it may be hazarded that Australian federalism will have to accommodate both types of pressure and objectives. This conclusion accords with the pragmatic nature of Australian federalism and with its lack of philosophic principles. But within such a framework there is scope—and there is need—for some significant adjustments to be made. Macro-economic management requirements will quite likely compel some transfer of economic powers to the federal government and joint action in other economic fields. The federal government also needs the financial capacity to maintain a redistributive role and quite possibly to initiate developments such as a comprehensive social security scheme. But, in the special circumstances of Australia, these considerations still leave some scope for strengthening the financial basis of the states and for placing federal financial relations upon a firmer and more predictable constitutional basis. Thereby the economic as well as the political health of the system could be improved and the Australian federation moved a little closer to the enthusiastic claims that are sometimes made on its behalf.

Endnotes

1 The phrase 'public goods' is often used in a restrictive sense, for example, 'pure public goods' refer to functions like defence which can not be allocated through the market. Public goods may also refer to all goods where there is some degree of market failure, but market failure is sometimes a matter of opinion. In this chapter public goods is used more broadly to refer to all goods which are or might be provided by government. The term thus covers regulatory activities (such as control of pollution), promotional activities (such as aid to sport) and subsidies as well as public services. By some writers it is extended still more broadly to include any individual preference which can only be satisfied by the state, such as a preference for redistribution or for regional institutions (Head, 1980). An alternative term is 'collective goods' but such goods may be provided by co-operatives, etc.

2 See Commonwealth Grants Commission (1985), *Report on Tax Sharing Relativities*, vol. 1, 2.48 and 8.16 for these statements. Vol. 1, ch. 2 of this report explains the methodology which is used here to examine policy differences between the states. The Commission's account of its first fifty years (*Equality in Diversity*, 1983) recounts the earlier evolution of the Commission's methodology (see also the Commission's 1981 *Report on Tax Sharing Entitlements*, vol. 1, chs 2 and 3 and its 1982 *Report on State Tax Sharing and Health Grants*, Vol. 1, ch. 2).

3 Gerritsen's conclusions differ from mine because in his ranking of the states he accords each function an equal weight which will accentuate the significance of minor services or sources of revenue (whereas I give more weight to major functions and aggregated expenditures and revenues). On this basis Gerritsen reaches the conclusion (26) that 'in the unity-or-diversity debate my interpretation inclines, albeit equivocally, towards the diversity position'.

4 In particular the Commission's calculations deal with recurrent not capital expenditure, do not cover all services (e.g. housing) and do not deal with the use of 'hollow logs' whereby states use profits from their public utilities to subsidise general revenue (or other utilities). The reverse position also occurs—for example, Queensland's low revenue from mining royalties disguises the fact that mining companies strongly subsidise the state rail system through high freight charges.

5 For problems of equalisation in local government finance, see *The Report of the National Inquiry into Local Government Finance* (1985), and Brennan (1987). The strong interest in geographical equalisation in Australia, as opposed to other federations, is shown by the unique existence of a very complex equalisation grant for local government despite its very small expenditure base, and by the detailed analysis of its effects in the National Inquiry Report. These facts perhaps suggest that it should be possible to increase the powers of local government without running into the serious polarisation effects which occur in the USA.

6 The market model would logically fragment government into a large number of elective authorities supplying different public goods to their clients at cost in each local area, together with some overall (and very difficult) arrangements for co-ordination and equalisation; but ordinary citizens would probably not want such a system because it would be so difficult to control. Just because politics cannot work with anything like the precision of markets, individual political evaluations have to be made largely in terms of the expected welfare of some group or the nation rather than of direct individual benefit. Many political philosophers of course have commended this requirement for citizens to consider the welfare of a broader reference group than the individual, provided it is responsibly exercised.

7 See the debates between economists in Part Four of B.S. Grewal, H.G. Brennan and R.L. Mathews (eds), *The Economics of Federalism* (1980).

8 See the debate on future welfare requirements in *The Welfare State*, special issue of *Canberra Bulletin of Public Administration*, no. 51, May 1987.

References

Aldred J. and Wilkes, J. (1983), *A Fractured Federation?*, Allen & Unwin, Sydney.

Beer, S.H. (1977), 'A Political Scientist's View of Fiscal Federalism', in W.E. Oates (ed.), *The Political Economy of Fiscal Federalism*, Lexington Books, Lexington, Mass.

Brennan, H.G. (ed.) (1987), *Local Government Finance*, Occasional paper no. 41, Centre for Research on Federal Financial Relations, ANU, Canberra.

Brennan, H.G. and Buchanan, J.M. (1980), *The Power to Tax*, Cambridge University Press, Cambridge.

—— (1985), *The Reason of Rules*, Cambridge University Press, Cambridge.

Buchanan, J.M. (1975), *The Limits of Liberty*, University of Chicago Press, Chicago.

Commonwealth Grants Commission (1981), *Report on State Tax Sharing Entitlements 1981*, vol. I, *Main Report*; vol. II, *Appendixes*, AGPS, Canberra.

—— (1982), *Report on State Tax Sharing and Health Grants 1982*: vol. I, *Main Report*; vol. II, *Appendixes and Reports of Consultants*, AGPS, Canberra.

—— (1983), *Equality in Diversity: Fifty Years of the Commonwealth Grants Commission*, AGPS, Canberra.

—— (1985), *Report on Tax Sharing Relativities 1985*: vol. I, *Main Report*; vol. II, *Appendixes and Consultants' Reports*, AGPS, Canberra.

Davis, S.R. (1978), *The Federal Principle*, University of California Press, Berkeley.

Friedrich, C.J. (1968), *Trends of Federalism in Theory and Practice* Praeger, New York.

Gerritsen, R. (1987), *What do State Budget Outcomes Tell us About the Australian States?*, Discussion paper no. 6, Public Policy Program, ANU, Canberra.

Grewal, B.S., Brennan, H.G. and Mathews, R.L. (eds) (1980), *The Economics of Federalism*, ANU Press, Canberra.

Grodzins, M. (1964), 'Centralization and Decentralization in the American Federal System', in R.A. Goldwin (ed.), *A Nation of States: Essays on the American Federal System*, Rand McNally, Chicago.

Head, J.G. (1980), 'Public Goods and Multilevel Government', in Grewal et al. (1980): 383–406.

Mathews, R. (1986), *Fiscal Federalism in Australia: Past and Future Tense*, Reprint Series no. 74, Centre for Research on Federal Financial Relations, ANU, Canberra.

Milnor, A. (1985), 'The American Experiment with Intergovernmental Transfers, 1965–84', in *National Inquiry into Local Government Finance; Research and Consultancy Reports*, vol. I, AGPS, Canberra: 242–92.

National Inquiry into Local Government Finance (1985), *Report*, AGPS, Canberra.

Oates, W.E. (1972), *Fiscal Federalism*, Harcourt Brace Jovanovich, New York.

—— (1977), 'An Economist's Perspective on Fiscal Federalism', in W.E. Oates (ed.), *The Political Economy of Fiscal Federalism*, Lexington Books, Lexington Mass.

Ostrom, V. (1973), *The Intellectual Crisis in American Public Administration*, University of Alabama Press, Tuscaloosa, Alabama.

Self, P. (1982), *Planning the Urban Region*, University of Alabama Press, Tuscaloosa, Alabama.

—— (1985) *Political Theories of Modern Government*, Allen & Unwin, Sydney.

The Welfare State (1987), special issue of *Canberra Bulletin of Public Administration*, no. 51 May 1987, Royal Australian Institute of Public Administration, Canberra branch.

Tiebout, C.M. (1956), 'A Pure Theory of Local Expenditures', *Journal of Political Economy* 64: 416–24.

Wheare, K.C. (1947), *Federal Government*, Oxford University Press, Oxford.

Federal Institutions and Processes

5

A POLITICAL SCIENCE PERSPECTIVE

Campbell Sharman

In any study of the evolution of the Australian federal system two preliminary matters must be settled: the first is to choose a starting point, the second to select a style of analysis. The two are related not only because the problems to be explained are heavily dependent on the periods chosen, but because both have a role in the shaping of themes and conclusions. While this may be clear in the choice of methodology, it is perhaps less so in the choice of period. Yet to study Australian federalism from the first of January 1901 is to guarantee that a major theme will be the growth of the Commonwealth government from a single public servant (Garran, 1958: ch. 9) to the national government that we know today. If, however, the date selected were 1943, at the height of wartime regulation, a major theme would be the decline in the scope of Commonwealth powers and the continuing constraints on its jurisdiction (Hasluck, 1970). It could also be added that the point of closure is equally important since the perspective of a commentator in 1931 during the Battle of the Plans (Shann and Copland, 1931) would be very different from someone writing during the excitement of the first months of the Whitlam government early in 1973.

It is not that views of the past are coloured by the assumptions of the present—this is perhaps inevitable—but that the past can be used to illustrate present issues and, by the judicious selection of themes, to support current arguments. Much of the writing on Australia's federal system falls into this category. The concerns of the day have been projected backwards to 1901 from whence current trends are seen to have derived. Such an exercise has the benefit of giving the past coherence and the present the legitimacy of inevitability. But it can do this only by a degree of oversimplification and by inserting into historical analysis current assumptions about the shape and desirability of the governmental system. This has been especially true of those who have argued that federalism in Australia is doomed to be swamped by the growth in economic power of the central government. Such a conclusion can easily be reached by taking a few landmark events dealing with economic issues, tracing a line back to 1901 and projecting it forwards through the present in an ever-rising direction. Variations are to be ignored together with themes and issues running in a contradictory direction.

A similar process can be seen at work in the concepts and styles of analysis used to investigate Australian federalism. Several of these have relied on the notion of a federal balance. While the concept of balance may appear to be a neutral way of approaching the relationship between state and national governments, it brings with it a number of unfortunate presumptions, not least of which is a mechanistic view of political interaction. It assumes that intergovernmental relations are a zero-sum game where the winnings of one party must be matched by losses of others. It also presumes that clear boundaries can be established between functions of government and that some currency can establish the relative standing of the various participants (Sharman, 1976).

Each of these points is contentious, yet the most questionable aspect of the notion of a federal balance is a normative one. It assumes that some equilibrium point ought to exist in the relationship between governments. For some this point entails views about the proper sphere of action and accountability of levels of government (for example, Mathews and Jay, 1972; and note Advisory Council for Intergovernmental Relations, 1981); for others it is simply a description of stability or impasse (for example, Sawer, 1952; Introduction): for both it is a unidimensional measure which the Commonwealth has perennially tipped in its favour.

Taken together, this treatment of history and style of analysis have combined to give an oversimplified and partial view of the federal process in which the dynamics are provided by the growth of central power. This has been reinforced by the attitudes of commentators who have been unsympathetic to federalism as a form of government. Taking as their starting points the strictures of Dicey (1967) on the flawed nature of federal constitutions and the economic determinism of Laski (1939) on the obsolescence of federalism, such commentators have stressed the costs of federalism and the benefits of a strong national government (Greenwood, 1946). Even though such views are not as pervasive as they were, there is still a momentum in this direction. It is as though federalism is a settled issue beyond genuine debate and that it is widely accepted that Australia is saddled with a structure of government with few merits, born out of a utilitarian desire to unite six colonies, continued out of habit and conservatism, but doomed to be dominated by an ever more powerful central government (for example, Maddox 1985: chs 4, 5; and Brugger and Jaensch, 1985: ch. 6).

But federalism in Australia is much more contentious than this. Its history has not been a straight-line evolution on a single theme but a diverse interplay of many factors most of which reflect the continuing political dominance of the states. The growth of central power is no more startling than the growth of state power. Both levels of government and the operation of the federal system have been transformed by the post-war surge of government intervention. And the recent decline in the faith that such intervention can solve major social problems is reflected in a renewed interest in the proper sphere of government action. In such a context there is room for debate over the relationship between a lively federal system and the goals of liberal democracy (Dahl, 1983; Braybrooke, 1983), a debate long overdue in Australia.

In sum, the politics of the federal process is much more subtle and contentious than has often been assumed.

1951 to 1987—from quiescence to quiescence

The period from 1951 to 1987 provides an excellent forum to indicate this diversity in the federal process. Nineteen forty-nine had seen the fall of the Australian Labor Party (ALP) government after its longest period in office at the national level during which it had directed the war effort and supervised the period of post-war reconstruction. It had also presided over the steady decline in the ability of the Commonwealth to make regulations under the defence power of the Constitution to regulate the social and economic life of Australians. This, coupled with the ALP's commitment to central planning and the nationalisation of certain key industries, had led to a number of collisions with the High Court and a series of attempts at constitutional amendment (Galligan, 1987). The Menzies coalition government was elected on the promise of hastening the dismantling of remaining wartime controls and the removal of a government committed to increase central power.

The participants in the Jubilee Conference on Federalism in 1951 clearly reflect the prevailing view that there had been a swing to the political right, a halt in the growth of central power and the likely persistence of a period of consolidation in the relations between state and Commonwealth governments (Sawer, 1952). In this they were largely correct. The 1950s and 1960s saw a preoccupation with the problems of economic growth, the transformation of the population by immigration and a high birth rate, and the maturation of the economy in terms of secondary and service industries. These years saw pragmatic Liberal (LP) and National (NP) parties form a series of coalition governments in Canberra while the ALP suffered from the turmoil of internal divisions over communism, union power, and the goals of the party.

While federal issues did not have the intensity of the 1940s, tension began to emerge as state budgets came under increasing strain. The burden of providing the infrastructure for Australia's burgeoning population fell predominantly on the states even though the bulk of taxation revenue accrued to the Commonwealth. By the end of the 1960s, disputes over federal finance had become very acrimonious and caused severe tensions within the LP. Such state dissatisfactions contributed both to the removal of Gorton as prime minister (Reid, 1971; Solomon, 1971) and to the moves to set up a constitutional convention to achieve, among other things, the limitation of central financial dominance (Ryan and Hewitt, 1977).

In the meantime, the Commonwealth had begun to use its financial surplus to indulge in selected involvement in areas of state jurisdiction. It used the mechanism of the conditional grant, usually at the initiative of the states, to contribute funds to specified projects in return for the ability to influence policy and for information about the policy area in question. This process began tentatively, but by the late 1960s a routine mode of Commonwealth involvement in such areas as transport, education and health had been established. A committee of inquiry would be set up which would hear submissions from the states and interested groups pointing out the need for more funds. The committee would discover a national dimension to the issue under investigation and would recommend Commonwealth financial involvement. The Commonwealth government would accept the report and establish a commission to recommend the level of support and supervise the expenditure of Commonwealth funds. This set the pattern for the enormous growth of intergovernmental relations that reached its peak under Whitlam (Scotton and Ferber, 1978).

The election of the ALP government in 1972 marked a critical point both for what was achieved during its three-year period in office and for the reactions to it. The initiatives of the Whitlam government focussed on a major extension of the scope of Commonwealth influence across a wide range of policy areas including health, education and welfare. This was to be achieved not by modifying the constitutional division of powers or testing existing powers to the limit but by the use of conditional grants and the spending power of the Commonwealth.

This programme had quite contradictory results. While it was successful in involving the Commonwealth in aspects of almost the whole range of state activities, it also strengthened the position of the states in partisan, bureaucratic and financial terms. By 1974, federalism had become a highly contentious topic in a way that had not been seen since the 1940s. The states perceived many Commonwealth actions as a direct attack upon areas of state policy discretion. This state government antagonism was exploited by opposition parties at the national level as a means of attacking the legitimacy of the Whitlam government and the national branch of the ALP became increasingly isolated from its state bases of support.

In bureaucratic terms, the surge of new policies both overextended the capacity of the Commonwealth public service and brought Commonwealth public servants into areas where they had little expertise. The results were intergovernmental confusion and an increasing self-confidence of state public servants in their dealings with Canberra. In addition, the political difficulties of the Whitlam government weakened its bargaining position and forced it to buy state co-operation at a high price. By the end of 1975, this had resulted in the Commonwealth becoming heavily committed to subsidising state programmes in a way which gave considerable discretion to the states but had severe budgetary consequences for the Commonwealth (Sharman, 1985).

All this took place in the context of major realignments in other areas of politics. Both the role of the Senate during the term of the Whitlam government and the manner of that government's removal from office in 1975 radically altered the terms of debate on constitutional politics from a concern with federalism to a concern with the operation of the structures of the national government. To a similar extent, the political salience of economic issues was greatly enhanced by the problems of inflation, unemployment and recession from the mid-1970s. Finally, the political agenda was changing as assumptions about the virtues of ever-growing government regulation came under question.

The tension in the federal system did not immediately subside once the Whitlam government had fallen. The coalition government under Fraser had made strong commitments to the states to withdraw those programmes that impinged too closely upon areas of state political sensitivity. But, once in office, the Fraser government found itself in a dilemma. The states wanted the generous financial transfers to remain and sought only the removal of constraints on how the money should be spent. The Commonwealth, on the other hand, needed to reduce, or at least restrain, the growth of its financial commitments to the states so that some control could be restored to the Commonwealth budget. The reluctance of the states to renegotiate the generous arrangements made under the Whitlam regime in such areas as health and education led the Fraser government to impose stricter guidelines on transfers to the states as the only way of limiting Commonwealth expenditures in these areas. In doing this, Fraser incurred almost as much odium from the states for limiting Commonwealth financial commitments to the states as Whitlam had from making the commitments in the first place (Patience and Head, 1979).

The general shift in resources from the Commonwealth to the states was not reversed, however, and the continuing massive transfers from the Commonwealth to the states have meant that the states have had much greater financial flexibility than they had during the 1950s and 1960s. A half-hearted attempt was made by the Fraser government to force the states to incur more of the political pain of revenue raising by the levying of a state income tax. But the scheme foundered on the political opportunism of both levels of government and a reluctance to couple such a move with a thoroughgoing review of the taxation system (Mathews, 1983). The states have found it easier to exploit other sources of revenue within their jurisdictions while requiring the Commonwealth to maintain its high level of transfer payments.

By the time that the ALP returned to office at the national level under Hawke in 1983, federalism had ceased to be a contentious topic. The new Hawke government had gone to great lengths to distance itself from the Whitlam era in its political goals and style. The new politics of pragmatism and consensus were inconsistent with attempts to make major changes to the relationship between state and Commonwealth governments. Hawke appeared anxious to avoid any entanglements with intergovernmental relations except in those very few cases where the partisan gains were clear and unequivocal and the costs were limited.

The Hawke government also benefitted from the routines that had been established in relations between the various levels of government during the Fraser period. Moreover, the politics of limited expectations and managerial efficiency both in state and Commonwealth spheres have combined to defuse most disagreements before they have moved into the political arena. As in 1951, we are in the midst of a period of consolidation in Commonwealth–state relations and a general swing to the political right.

In general terms, the period 1951 to 1987 has thus gone through a complete cycle from quiescence through a rise in the intensity of conflict in Commonwealth–state relations to a major realignment and reaction, followed by decreasing tension and a return to relative quiescence. But the conclusions to be drawn from this cycle are mixed. From the financial perspective little has changed in the degree to which the states are financially dependent on the Commonwealth. The level of transfers is similar to that of the 1950s except that there is an alteration in the mix of conditional and unconditional grants (Harris, 1979) and that it is the Commonwealth rather than the states that has the more severe budgetary problems. In constitutional terms there has been no return to the collisions between the Commonwealth and the High Court of the 1940s. Indeed, the High Court has produced a line of decisions which remove constraints on Commonwealth legislation in commercial, corporate and financial matters and, more recently, has extended the ability of the Commonwealth to use the external affairs power to influence state policies in selected areas (Galligan, 1987). The use of this power, however, is likely to be heavily constrained by the cumbersome way in which it must be invoked, the limited area of its application and, above all, the high political cost of intervention in areas of settled state influence.

Such financial and legal aspects of the federal process over the period are the subject of more detailed study elsewhere in this collection and it is the intention of this paper to focus on three areas of an explicitly political nature. The first is the change in the focus of debate over the institutional structure and constitutional politics of Australia's federal system. There has been a clear shift away from a concern with the division of powers between the spheres of government and a much greater interest in the operation of the machinery of government at the national and state levels. The second is the enormous growth of intergovernmental relations over the period. This growth precludes any simple isolation of winners and losers but the question remains as to the effect that the proliferation of bureaucratic structures has had on the politics of the federal process.

The third area is that of partisan politics. Of the three, it is in this area that changes have been most marked. The internal structures of the major parties have experienced substantial modifications, new parties have arisen, and the relationship between parties—the party system—is very different now from that of 1951. To the extent that the party system reflects and reinforces the dynamics of the federal system, changes in this area may provide the clearest indication of the nature and direction of federalism in Australia.

It is to these questions we must now turn.

The change in the nature of constitutional politics

In 1951 constitutional politics was largely equated with disputes over the division of powers in the federation. On three occasions during the 1940s six referendum proposals for constitutional change had been submitted to the electorate by the ALP government. The dominant theme of these proposals had been to grant more extensive powers to the Commonwealth to regulate the social and economic life of Australians. All but one of the proposals failed to gain the required majorities, the exception being an amendment removing any doubts about the Commonwealth's power to pay social welfare, health and education benefits to individual citizens (Macmillan, Evans and Storey, 1983: ch. 2).

The change of government in 1949 removed this pressure for formal amendment to the Commonwealth Constitution. Apart from the anomalous issue of the control of communism (Webb, 1954), no proposal for constitutional change was submitted to the people during the seventeen years that Menzies was prime minister. When a referendum was next called in 1967, the proposals were not attempts to transfer broad economic powers to the central government but were the widely supported proposal to remove obstructions to Commonwealth powers over Aborigines, and the procedural question of the breaking of the nexus between the size of the Senate and the House of Representatives. This shift in the content of proposals for constitutional amendment was continued in the twelve referendum proposals submitted between 1973 and 1984. Only two of these concerned economic issues, the prices and incomes referendums of 1973. All the remainder dealt with questions of institutional structure: the Senate (four); representation (two); constitutional amendment (one); local government (one); the judiciary (one); and interchange of powers (one) (*Parliamentary Handbook*).

Part of this alteration in the focus of constitutional politics can be traced to a change in attitude on the part of the ALP. The experience of the 1940s had confirmed the belief that a direct attack on the federal division of powers was doomed to defeat. In addition, the availability of such proven weapons as the conditional grant together with the increasingly broad interpretation of Commonwealth powers by the High Court meant that there was no need for the ALP to embark on the perilous course of constitutional amendment. Constitutional limitations could be sufficiently circumvented to permit the implementation of all but the most doctrinaire ALP policies. This approach was to culminate in the new federalism policies of Whitlam.

While this development may explain the lack of pressure for changes to the federal division of power, it does not explain the upsurge of interest in modifying the institutions of government. The answer to this can be found in changes in the role of the Senate and in the transfer in the initiative for constitutional change from the centre to the states.

The transformation of the Senate involved a number of elements but the most important was the adoption of proportional representation in 1949. This, combined with the split in the ALP in the mid-1950s, provided an opportunity for minor parties and independent senators to gain representation and, by 1967, to hold the balance of power in the chamber. The non-government parties used their majority to amend and block government legislation, to create a powerful committee system and, eventually, to contribute to the factors that forced a government to the polls at a time not of its choosing (on the evolution of the Senate, see Reid, 1973; Emy, 1978; Smiley, 1985; and note Sharman, 1988). Each of these activities was an attack on the executive dominance of the legislature that had been established since the rise of the disciplined mass party in the early years of this century. The fact that it must now share the control of the legislative process has been resented by the executive branch of government whichever of the two major party groupings have been in office and both have sought to reduce this erosion of their power by a number of constitutional amendments. These have been largely unsuccessful in limiting the role of the Senate as an independent element in the legislative process, although recent changes to electoral laws may work to reduce the effectiveness of the Senate in the longer term (Sharman, 1986).

The consequences of this development for the federal system are indirect but significant. There is no question of the Senate's new-found importance being used to revive its role as a states house in the sense of block voting in the Senate on regional lines, but the existence of a lively, powerful and independent component of the national legislature means that state governments and their supporting interests have an additional forum for airing matters of regional concern (Sharman, 1977a). Of greater importance, the way in which the Senate is chosen has meant that the balance of power in the chamber is likely to be held by minor party and independent senators whose support is concentrated in particular states. This gives the Senate the opportunity to express regional concerns and, to some extent, to challenge the claims of state governments to be the sole channel for the articulation of regional interests. This federalising of a national institution (note Gibbins, 1982; Smiley and Watts, 1985) is as yet a minor characteristic of the Senate but it has the potential to be of greater significance.

The change in the role of the Senate has had further effects which, though subtle, are nonetheless important. The active and politically visible role of the Senate in the national legislative process has led to a re-evaluation of bicameralism and has probably hastened the recasting of state upper houses that has occurred since 1970. Since that date, three of the five state upper houses have substantially altered their composition by the adoption of proportional representation and all have the Senate as a model of the influential part such chambers can perform in the process of parliamentary democracy (Reid 1983; note Western Australia, 1984–85). Again, the consequences for the federal process are indirect. At neither level of government have upper houses used their considerable powers to maintain a regular scrutiny of the part their governments play in intergovernmental relations, but the potential exists. Finally, it is arguable that, since legislation at the national level is subject to review and is likely to require the support of one or more non-government parties, this moderating effect may reduce the likelihood of subsequent Commonwealth–state disputes. And if the government of the day gains the endorsement of the Senate for a particular measure, its hand will have been strengthened by the airing of the issues and the broadening of the bases of partisan support.

These effects are, however, largely incidental to the fact that the importance of the Senate has been primarily as part of the political process at the national level. The major alterations to the parliamentary process that have been precipitated by the changing role of the Senate, together with the consequences of the dismissal of the Whitlam government in 1975, have meant that from the perspective of the national government constitutional politics has been concerned with the machinery of the national government, not with federalism and the division of powers.

When there has been pressure for a review of federal processes, it has come from the states and not the Commonwealth. By 1968 the financial difficulties of the states combined with what was seen as a centralising trend in High Court decisions led to a call from the Victorian parliament to set up a Constitutional Convention to review aspects of the Commonwealth Constitution. The motive was to limit the growth of central power that was seen to be occurring without any formal change to the Constitution and to enable the states to regain greater autonomy in a number of contentious areas. This call was supported by the other states but by the time the Convention met in 1973 its composition and agenda had been modified by the election of the Whitlam government. Subsequent meetings were affected by the events of 1975 and the partisan acrimony that they generated. Notwithstanding this, a major review of the most contentious areas of the Commonwealth Constitution was undertaken, supported by working parties on particular topics. By 1985 a number of specific proposals had been arrived at dealing with the issues which had been the original reason for establishing the convention (Australian Constitutional Convention, 1985; Howard, 1985: 145–9).

But, by this stage, the Commonwealth government had gained little success with its own agenda for constitutional change and had never given any indication that it would provide the necessary support for constitutional amendments whose major beneficiaries would be the states. The Commonwealth government had been a supporter of the Convention only as long as it provided a useful forum for its own particular concerns and the direction of the Convention's later proposals was not one that appealed to the Hawke government. In a move both to deny the states a continuing forum for debating constitutional change and to regain control of the agenda of constitutional politics, the Commonwealth government attempted to close down the Convention and establish its own nominated Constitutional Commission. Whatever utility the Commission's deliberations may acquire, the motive for its establishment was primarily that of imposing Commonwealth priorities on the process of constitutional reform (Davis, 1987).

The nature of constitutional politics has, in some respects, returned to pre-1975 concerns except that the Commonwealth is now less interested in substantive change to the federal aspects of the Constitution than are the states. Given the gatekeeping role of the Commonwealth government to any amendment to the Commonwealth Constitution, there is little prospect of change.

Changes in intergovernmental relations

Of all the changes to the federal system to have occurred since 1951, the proliferation of transactions between the various levels of government and of agencies to supervise them would seem to be the most dramatic. One measure of this rapid growth can be found in the number of ministerial councils acting as peak bodies for policy consultations between Commonwealth and state ministers. A recent listing includes thirty-six such councils, twenty-eight of which were created after 1960, and twenty one since 1970 (Advisory Council for Intergovernmental Relations, 1986: App. B). The meetings of these bodies themselves represent only a tiny fraction of transactions between governments which span the range from formal consultations between the relevant departments to informal contacts between officials. These are in addition to the dealings of Commonwealth agencies whose major function is to recommend and supervise expenditure in many areas of state concern, all of which have extensive and continuing transactions with the relevant state instrumentalities.

Before examining in what ways these developments have affected the federal process, some explanations need to be provided for this luxuriant flowering of intergovernmental relations. Some explanations can be found in the changing nature of post-war government. As government involvement in social and economic life has grown, so has the need for government agencies to exchange information and to establish appropriate channels of communication. Secondly, the process of increasing government regulation in a federation has meant a greater likelihood of jurisdictional overlap, requiring the creation of bodies to provide a framework for consultation and the harmonisation of policies. Finally, the extension of central government involvement in the financing of state programmes has implied a corresponding expansion of intergovernmental relations.

These structural explanations provide part of the answer but a vital element is missing—the continuing ambition of the Commonwealth to become involved in a large range of politically salient activities that are outside its jurisdiction. With the bulk of the matters that affect the daily lives of Australians falling within the ambit of the states, the Commonwealth has sought to expand its political influence by the use of two strategies. One, already mentioned, has been to use the conditional grant; the other has been to acquire a stake in the administration of state programmes through the collection of relevant information and technical expertise. By employing these two complementary strategies, the Commonwealth has tried to match the settled political influence of the states with financial resources on one hand and bureaucratic resources on the other.

While these policies can be seen in the selective involvement of the Commonwealth government under Menzies and Gorton in such areas as education and health, they accelerated under the Whitlam government to produce controversy not only over the substance of some policies but over the scale and number of Commonwealth initiatives. Indeed, it took a decade for the momentum generated by the Whitlam initiatives to be digested and translated into settled bureaucratic routines.

Apart from the hostility generated by some of the policies of the Whitlam government, the reaction of the states has been to accept these developments with relative equanimity. This has been partly because the larger part of such joint programmes is initiated by the states themselves, partly because such intergovernmental consultation often generates useful information for all parties, and partly because the exchange of information with the Commonwealth has been an acceptable cost to pay for central government financial transfers. Since their creation as self-governing communities, the states have engaged in interstate consultation and the discussion of common problems. Such practices have been greatly extended to include the Commonwealth and to cover most fields of government activity. The mode of such consultations has also changed from being sporadic exchanges of information to the complex and extensive bureaucratic routines that have come to characterise transactions between governments.

This raises the question of what effect the growth of intergovernmental relations has had on the federal process. There is certainly a greater interpenetration of government activities and it is hard to find an area of state policy without some Commonwealth involvement, or Commonwealth activity without some dependence on state co-operation. The resulting relationship has elements of a shared dependency—the states benefit from additional resources and a broader flow of information, while the Commonwealth can claim involvement in areas of high political importance over which it has little formal power. It is for this reason that to look for some relationship of dominance and dependence as suggested by the notion of federal balance is misplaced since all participants gain. It is also why the analogy favoured by those who describe intergovernmental relations is one of bargaining between actors who have shared and competing interests, a variety of resources and strategies, and a variety of forums to resolve their differences (Simeon, 1972).

In spite of this interlocking of bureaucratic structures, it can be argued that the relationships between spheres of government have not changed in their fundamentals. The fact of executive federalism—that the relations between the two spheres of government are dominated by the officials of the executive branch—remains as the predominant characteristic of dealings between governments. This can be illustrated in the role of the Premiers' Conference. The politics of this annual meeting of heads of government is the same as in the 1950s; the opportunity to publicise regional perspectives on a national stage, to express unvarnished opinions on matters of current political concern, and to assess the nature and resources of the key players in the governmental system (Sharman, 1977a). The administrative context may be more sophisticated, but the basic relationships are unaltered.

If this is correct, what has changed is only the style and scope of intergovernmental relations, not their substance. The complex web of bureaucratic and ministerial interactions is less a comment on the changing nature of federalism than on the current style of government in general.

Federalism and party politics

If lack of structural change is a characteristic of the politics of intergovernmental relations, this cannot be said of the pattern of partisan politics since 1951. It has been argued that only a decentralised party system can maintain the dispersal of political power that characterises a lively federal system. Whether this factor alone can explain the persistence of federalism is not a matter to be discussed in this chapter, but the party system can certainly be used as an indicator of the degree of centralisation in a federation as illustrated by Smiley (1987: ch. 5) in the Canadian case. Patterns of partisan competition may be a crude measure of the disposition of political forces in a system but they provide a useful corrective to assessments based on the flow of economic or legal power, or on bureaucratic interaction.

In general terms, the years since 1951 have shown paradoxical developments. On one hand, the two largest parties, the ALP and the LP, have developed much more substantial central party machines, yet, at the same time, there is a greater degree of differentiation between the party systems at state and national levels.

This paradox can be largely resolved once it is realised that Australia's parties have their centres of gravity in the states and, for many years after federation, had only rudimentary branches of the party machine in Canberra. Until the 1970s, for example, while the parliamentary leader made the policy speech, campaigns for national elections were run by the state branches of the party. Membership of a party is still by joining the appropriate state branch and the preselection of candidates for national office remains a matter for the state machine, although the ALP has been providing a growing number of exceptions. In other words, the structure of Australia's major parties has been confederal, with the national level being superimposed on six largely autonomous state parties, and national politicians being dependent on the respective state party machines (Holmes and Sharman, 1977: ch. 4).

A caveat must be entered for the ALP since the Federal Conference of the party has long had the power not only to set binding policy goals for the whole party but to intervene in and, on occasion, to override the decisions of state branches. But this has not altered the fact that, for most purposes, the party has operated very much as a federation of state parties. Indeed, it has often been noted that, for a party with the ostensible goal of greater central control, its internal structure has been highly federalised (for example, Partridge, 1952).

Since the late 1960s this pattern has been modified in a number of ways. Major changes have been made in the structure of the ALP machine, first by giving the federal parliamentary party direct representation at the Federal Conference, and secondly by supplementary the equal representation of state branches with delegates chosen in proportion to the population of each state (Lloyd, 1983). In addition, the Federal Executive of the party is now endowed with the resources not only to mount national campaigns but to monitor the performance of the national party between elections.

These changes have been reinforced by alterations to the disposition of influence within the party prompted by rules which require the proportional representation of factions within each state branch. This, in turn, has led to the emergence of national factions which compete for influence in the national government (Lloyd and Swan, 1987). Such developments are too recent for firm conclusions to be drawn but it appears that the ALP is evolving so that its party structure more closely mirrors a division between state and national concerns, each having its own administrative machinery and mode of political action.

Similar tendencies are visible in the national branch of the LP although no alteration has been made to the strictly federal nature of state representation at the national level. Since the LP makes no claim to bind its national parliamentary leadership to follow specified policies, some of the tensions present in the ALP structure have not been as apparent in the LP. Nor is there machinery available to the national branch of the LP to influence the selection of candidates for national elections as can occur in the ALP, particularly in the case of recent endorsements of ALP Senate candidates. In this respect the LP is similar to the NP whose party structure has seen least change although it too has seen a trend towards a stronger party apparatus to serve the needs of the national parliamentary party.

This strengthening of party machinery at the national level has made Australia's larger parties less confederal and more federal, although the bulk of partisan activity in all parties is still heavily state-centred. This trend has occurred against the background of substantial changes to the party system as a whole. Several of these can be traced to the adoption of proportional representation for the Senate. The sensitivity of this system to smaller parties has meant that some parties have gained representation in the Senate while being denied it in both the House of Representatives and state lower houses. The Senate, in other words, has helped to induce the creation of a distinctively national party system and the existence of such new parties as the Australian Democrats and the Nuclear Disarmament Party whose focus is primarily national not state politics.

A second effect of proportional representation has been to create safe seats for the major parties at the top of each state list of candidates. Competition for these positions has accentuated tensions between national and state levels of the parties. In the ALP the 1987 election saw this resolved by an almost routine involvement of the national party in the choice of candidates for national office. In the LP the contests are still fought out at state level with the national party watching anxiously from the wings.

What can be concluded from this brief and incomplete review, other than the subtle interaction that occurs between mass politics and the institutions which define the rules for selection to office? The use of party as an indicator of the dispersal of power in the Australian federal system shows that our federation is not merely alive, but bursting with health. The disposition of partisan power indicates that the states are dominant in the sense that they are the locus of critical decisions affecting partisan politics not just at state level but at the national level as well. Our party system is still pre-federal in that there is no duplication of membership and branch structure to match a federal division of power. But there are, nonetheless, clear moves for the establishment of a national party system which is differentiated from state systems both in the pattern of partisan competition and in the internal structure of parties (but note Rydon 1988).

Political institutions and processes

The picture of the federal process provided by the study of political institutions indicates the continuing importance of the states in the political process. This is hardly surprising since they are the home of the great bulk of the population and have existed as self-governing political systems from long before federation. The persistence of these state communities may be explained by the existence of distinctive regional political cultures or by the institutional momentum of state governments or, as is most likely, by a combination of the two. But, whatever the reason, there is no doubt that the critical prerequisite of an effective federal system—the dispersal and institutional entrenchment of power on a regional basis—continues to be a characteristic of the Australian federation.

If the persistence of the political importance of the states is an enduring feature of our system, another is the resilience of the federal institutional structure. In spite of the various pressures for constitutional change, the system has coped well with the radical alteration in the role of government that has occurred since 1901. The institutions created at federation have responded to the changing demands put upon them as the Commonwealth parliament has to the rise of the disciplined mass party. The whole system of intergovernmental relations is a commentary on the ability of the governmental structure to respond to new problems and new expectations of government with little change to its basic dynamics. Federalism is an inherently resilient system, if a little untidy in its operation.

There is no reason to think that this will change. It is possible that there will be even greater untidiness in the sense of change encompassing greater autonomy in the raising of state taxation revenue and the reduction of central involvement in the way in which the states respond to the distinctive preferences of their own state communities. But this untidiness is symptomatic of the greatest virtue of federalism—to accommodate, often in apparent defiance of logic, competing demands of national and regional majorities. The period from 1951 shows how varied these competing demands can be. There is no reason to suppose that the variation will diminish or that the federal system will be any less resilient when it reaches its centenary in 2001.

References

ACIR (1981), Advisory Council for Inter-governmental Relations, *Towards Adaptive Federalism: the Search for Criteria for Responsibility Sharing in a Federal System*, AGPS, Canberra.

—— (1986), *Operational Procedures of Inter-Jurisdictional Ministerial Councils*, Information paper no. 13, AGPS, Canberra.

Aucoin, P. (1985), *Party Government and Regional Representation in Canada*, University of Toronto Press, Toronto.

Australian Constitutional Convention (1985), *Proceedings* vol. II, Standing Committee Reports, Brisbane.

Braybrooke, D. (1983), 'Can democracy be combined with federalism or with liberalism?', in J.R. Pennock and J.W. Chapman (eds), *Liberal Democracy*, New York University Press, New York.

Brugger, B. and Jaensch, D. (1985), *Australian Politics in Theory and Practice*, Allen & Unwin, Sydney.

Dahl, R.A. (1983), 'Federalism and the democratic process', in J.R. Pennock and J.W. Chapman (eds), *Liberal Democracy*, New York University Press, New York.

Davis, S.R. (1987), *The Constitutional Commission: The Inescapable Politics of Constitutional Reform*, Institute of Public Affairs, Melbourne.

Dicey, A.V. (1967), *An Introduction to the Law of the Constitution*, 10th edn, Macmillan, London. First published 1885.

Emy, H.V. (1978), *The Politics of Australian Democracy: Fundamentals in Dispute*, Macmillan, Melbourne.

Galligan, B. (1987), *Politics of the High Court: A Study of the Judicial Branch of Government in Australia*, University of Queensland Press, Brisbane.

Garran, R.R. (1958), *Prosper the Commonwealth*, Angus & Robertson, Sydney.

Gibbins, R. (1982), *Regionalism: Territorial Politics in Canada and the United States*, Butterworths, Toronto.

Greenwood, G. (1946), *The Future of Australian Federalism: A Commentary on the Working of the Constitution*, Melbourne University Press, Melbourne.

Harris, C.P. (1979), *Relationships Between Federal and State Governments in Australia*, ACIR, Information paper no. 6, AGPS, Canberra.

Hasluck, P. (1970), *The Government and the People, 1942–1945*, Australian War Memorial, Canberra.

Holmes, J. and Sharman, C. (1977), *The Australian Federal System*, Allen & Unwin, Sydney.

Howard, C. (1985), *The Constitution: What it Means and How it Works*, revised edn, Penguin, Melbourne.

Laski, H.J. (1939), 'The obsolescence of federalism', *New Republic*, 3 May 1939: 367–9.

Lloyd, C. (1983), 'The Federal ALP: Supreme or Secondary?', in A. Parkin and J. Warhurst (eds), *Machine Politics in the Australian Labor Party*, Allen & Unwin, Sydney.

Lloyd, C. and Swan, W. (1987), 'National factions in the ALP', *Politics* 22: 100–10.

McMillan, J., Evans, G. and Storey, H. (1983), *Australia's Constitution: Time for Change?*, Allen & Unwin, Sydney.

Maddox, G. (1985), *Australian Democracy in Theory and Practice*, Longman Cheshire, Melbourne.

Mathews, R.L. and Jay, W.R.C. (1972), *Federal Finance: Intergovernmental Financial Relations in Australia Since Federation*, Nelson, Melbourne.

Mathews, R.L. (1983), 'The Commonwealth–state financial contract', in J. Aldred and J. Wilkes (eds), *A Fractured Federation?*, Allen & Unwin, Sydney.

Parliamentary Handbook of the Commonwealth of Australia (current edition).

Partridge, P.H. (1952), 'The politics of federalism', in Sawer (1952).

Patience, A. and Head, B. (eds) (1979), *From Whitlam to Fraser: Reform and Reaction in Australian Politics*, Oxford University Press, Melbourne.

Reid, A. (1971), *The Gorton Experiment: The Fall Of John Grey Gorton*, Shakespeare Head Press, Sydney.

Reid, G.S. (1973), 'The trinitarian struggle: parliamentary executive relations', in H. Mayer and H. Nelson (eds), *Australian Politics: A Third Reader*, Cheshire, Melbourne.

—— (ed.) (1983), *The Role of Upper Houses Today*, University of Tasmania, Hobart.

Ryan, R.W. and Hewitt, W.D. (1977), *The Australian Constitutional Convention*, Occasional paper no. 6, Centre for Research on Federal Financial Relations, ANU, Canberra.

Rydon, J. (1988), 'The Federal Structure of Australian Political Parties', *Publius*, 18: 159–71.

Sawer, G. (ed.) (1952), *Federalism: An Australian Jubilee Study*, Cheshire, Melbourne.

Scotton, R.D. and Ferber, H. (eds) (1978), *Public Expenditures and Social Policy in Australia: Volume I—The Whitlam Years 1972–75*, Longman Cheshire, Melbourne.

Shann, E.O.G. and Copland, D.B. (eds) (1931), *The Battle of the Plans: Documents Relating to the Premiers' Conference, May 25th to June 11th, 1931*, Angus & Robertson, Sydney.

Sharman, C. (1976), 'The bargaining analogy and federal state relations', in R.M. Burns et al., *Political and Administrative Federalism*, Centre for Research on Federal Financial Relations, ANU, Research monograph no. 14 ANU Press, Canberra.

—— (1977a), 'The Australian Senate as a States house', *Politics* 12(2): 64–75.

—— (1977b), *The Premiers' Conference: An Essay in Federal–State Interaction*, Occasional paper no. 13, Political Science Department, Research School of Social Sciences, ANU, Canberra.

—— (1985), 'The Commonwealth, the states and federalism', in D.Woodward, A. Parkin and J. Summers (eds), *Government, Politics and Power in Australia*, 3rd edn, Longman Cheshire, Melbourne.

—— (1986), 'The Senate, Small Parties and the Balance of Power', *Politics* 21(2): 20–31.

—— (1988), 'Constitutional politics in Australia', in V. Bogdanor (ed.), *Constitutions in Democratic Politics*, Gower, London.

Simeon, R (1972), *Federal Provincial Diplomacy: The Making of Recent Policy in Canada*, University of Toronto Press, Toronto.

Smiley, D.V. (1985), *An Elected Senate for Canada? Clues from the Australian Experience*, Institute for Intergovernmental Relations, Queen's University, Kingston, Ontario.

—— (1987), *The Federal Condition in Canada*, McGraw-Hill Ryerson, Toronto.

Smiley, D.V. and Watts, R.L. (1985), *Intrastate Federalism in Canada*, University of Toronto Press, Toronto.

Solomon, D. (1971), 'Commonwealth–state relations', in M. Harris and G. Dutton (eds), *Sir Henry, Bjelke, Don baby and friends*, Sun Books, Melbourne.

Webb, L. (1954), *Communism and Democracy in Australia: A Survey of the 1951 Referendum*, Cheshire, Melbourne.

Western Australia, Royal Commission into Parliamentary Deadlocks (1984–85), *Report*, Perth.

6

AN ECONOMIC PERSPECTIVE

Bhajan Grewal

Introduction

A satisfactory framework of fiscal arrangements between the different levels of government is vital to the proper functioning of a federal system. It is essential that the institutions comprising such a framework should be flexible and able to adapt to the changing requirements of their economic environment. In Australia, such a framework consists largely of the Premiers' Conference, Australian Loan Council and the Commonwealth Grants Commission. Together, these institutions determine the flow of financial resources from the Commonwealth to the states and influence economic co-ordination between the two levels of government. Unlike the other two institutions, the Commonwealth Grants Commission does not have a policy co-ordinating role. However, its inclusion in this list is justified by its recently extended role in determining the distribution of the largest component of federal transfers—the general revenue grants—among the states. Some other institutions could also have been included, such as the Interstate Commission, the Economic Planning Advisory Council, or the now abolished Advisory Council on Intergovernmental Relations. However, due to limitations of space only those that affect the flow of budgetary resources between governments are considered here.

In this chapter it is argued that at present the agenda of the Premiers' Conference and the Loan Council is dominated directly or indirectly by the existence of a high level of vertical fiscal imbalance in Australia. Consequently the more fundamental issues of intergovernmental co-ordination of policies remain largely neglected or relegated to the background. The extended role of the Grants Commission also raises important issues in relation to the opportunity costs of fiscal equalisation as practised in Australia. It is argued that the restoration of a balance between the revenue-raising powers and the expenditure functions at the two levels of government would remove the major impediment of the current operation of the Australian fiscal institutions. Then the institutions could address the real tasks of policy co-ordination and economic stability. Comments are also made on the processes of these institutions and some gaps in the institutional framework.

This chapter devotes considerable space to the issue of vertical fiscal imbalance and its consequences for efficiency and accountability. This is considered relevant for two reasons. Firstly, as suggested above, issues arising from the high level of vertical fiscal imbalance have pushed into the background the more fundamental issues of intergovernmental co-ordination. Secondly, it is widely recognised that such a vertical imbalance is not necessary for the functioning of a federal system. Rather, it reduces the overall efficiency of the public sector and has a stifling effect on the subnational tiers of government. It is not essential for the effective management of the national economy or for an equitable distribution of income and wealth. In other words, the vertical imbalance is an unnecessary, avoidable and harmful feature of the Australian federation that has adversely affected the roles of major intergovernmental fiscal institutions.

The fiscal institutions: a background

The Premiers' Conference

The Premiers' Conference, the oldest of the three institutions considered in this chapter, emerged as a natural and spontaneous response to the creation of a federation by the aggregation process—to use Professor Wheare's classification (Wheare, 1967). As the previously separate colonial governments agreed to the creation of a federal structure, there were numerous issues requiring consultation and agreement between them. In the first few years after federation, the meetings of government leaders were irregular and without formal records of their proceedings. The first Conference for which a formal transcript exists was held in Hobart in February 1905 (Groenewegen, 1982). The financial clauses of the Constitution left a large number of questions to be resolved, and these became the agenda of the Premiers' Conference in the early years.

Despite its irregular beginnings, and thanks to the significant issues it dealt with, the Premiers' Conference quickly gained the status of an indispensable institution. As early as 1910 it was acknowledged that 'the exigencies of the situation forced frequent conferences between states' governments and between the Commonwealth and the states' governments and . . . the interstate conference, in one form or another, . . . passed from an event to an institution . . .' (Moore, quoted in Groenewegen, 1982: xi).

However, reflecting the high degree of fiscal dependence of the states on the Commonwealth since the Second World War, the Premiers' Conference has become too narrowly concerned with determining general revenue payments to the states. Consequently, intergovernmental co-ordination on issues of economic and social policy has been given a low priority on its agenda, if it is considered at all. It is argued here that in future, with the removal of the vertical fiscal imbalance, greater opportunities would become available for the Premiers' Conference to play a genuine role in the co-ordination of these policies.

Australian Loan Council

Established under the Financial Agreement of 1927, the Loan Council represented the formalisation of voluntary co-ordination of borrowings between the states and the Commonwealth over the previous few years. Even before a voluntary Loan Council was formed in May 1923, the Commonwealth and the states, except New South Wales, had entered into an agreement that all loans between 1915–19 would be raised by the Commonwealth (Headford, 1954). The purpose of the formalised Loan Council was to co-ordinate the borrowings of all governments by way of an orderly approach to the loan markets, and to promote efficiency and economy by preventing undesirable competition between the governments. Borrowings by local and semi-government authorities were also brought into this framework under the Gentlemen's Agreement in 1936.

In subsequent years, when total demand for borrowed funds started to increase rapidly, the Loan Council started to apply quantitative controls over the states' 'bids' for funds. The Commonwealth, in a better financial position than the states, also started to underwrite the states' borrowings. Although the facility of underwriting undoubtedly meant better terms and conditions for the loans, the states had to pay a price by accepting in exchange the Commonwealth's control over the volume of their borrowings. In spite of some significant changes that have occurred in its processes in recent years (see Groenewegen, 1984, Mathews 1984), the Loan Council plays a vital role in the financing of public investment in the country. Under the Global Limit applied first in 1984–85, it determines the aggregate amount of borrowings by the state governments and their authorities. In the process, the Loan Council also determines the amount of overseas borrowings and the overseas markets which may be accessed for this purpose.

The Commonwealth Grants Commission

During the first three decades after federation the claims of the smaller states for special grants had become particularly strong. In April 1933, in Western Australia even a referendum was passed favouring secession from federation. In other states special committees or commissions had made strong pleas for special assistance (Commonwealth Grants Commission, 1983). The establishment of a board (such as the Tariff Board), a commission (such as the Interstate Commission) or an independent committee were among the several alternatives proposed to deal with special assistance to the financially disadvantaged states before the establishment of the Commonwealth Grants Commission in 1933.

Long before the special problem of horizontal equity in a federation was recognised by the economic profession (see Buchanan, 1950), the Commonwealth Grants Commission had started to formulate principles underlying the determination of special grants. Indeed one commentator on the Commission's First Report even suggested 'the Commission [had] . . . advanced the subject almost to the limits of practicability with the information and co-operation so far available to it' (Brigden, 1934). Although it must have appeared that way to some at the time, significant refinements were subsequently made to the methodology of the Commission in its Third Report and then in the 1970s and early 1980s by the current membership of the Commission.

The centrepiece of the Commission's work at present consists of the six-state relativities reviews. In addition, the Commission has also assessed needs for special assistance to the Northern Territory. It has also conducted inquiries into the financing of the Australian Capital Territory. Furthermore, the Commission has conducted an inquiry into the Cocos (Keeling) Islands in order to determine the principles, methodology and procedures for a review to be undertaken in 1989 of the needs of the residents of the Cocos (Keeling) Islands having regard to the broad commitment of the Australian government to raise, within ten years, their services and standard of living to equal those of the Australian population.

Comments in this chapter are restricted only to the state relativities reviews, not only because of their significance for state finances, but also because the methodology of these reviews underpins much of the Commission's other work.

The critique

Contrary to the original Constitutional division of powers and responsibilities, the financial balance between the two levels of government in Australia has remained, particularly since the Second World War, heavily in favour of the Commonwealth.

Figures in Table 6.1 show the huge shift in the relative financial positions of the two levels. Thus, the Commonwealth's share of 'own purpose outlays' increased from 5 per cent in 1901–02, and 13 per cent in 1909–10, to 66 per cent in the post-war year of 1946–47. It declined

Table 6.1 Commonwealth, state and local government finances 1901–02 to 1985–86: outlays and revenues ($m)

Year	*Commonwealth*[1]	*% of total*	*Six states plus local government*[1]	*% of total*	*total*
Own purpose outlays					
1901–02	3	5	62	95	65
1909–10	10	13	66	87	76
1938–39	134	34	262	66	396
1942–43	1 242	85	218	15	1 460
1946–47	636	66	330	34	966
1948–49	641	56	502	44	1 143
1958–59	1 642	49	1 705	51	3 347
1967–68	3 966	50	3 934	50	7 900
1975–76	12 923	46	15 130	54	28 053
1979–80	20 165	45	24 165	55	44 330
1980–81	23 387	45	28 039	55	51 426
1981–82	27 757	46	32 789	54	60 546
1982–83	32 684	46	38 636	54	71 320
1983–84	38 514	47	42 774	53	81 288
1984–85	44 203	49	46 362	51	90 565
1985–86	49 657	49	51 609	51	101 266
Own revenues					
1901–02	18	41	26	59	44
1909–10	25	41	36	59	61
1938–39	162	47	186	53	348
1942–43	574	77	170	23	744
1946–47	776	85	138	15	914
1948–49	958	85	173	15	1 131
1958–59	2 372	77	723	23	3 095
1967–68	5 252	76	1 703	24	6 955
1975–76	17 554	74	6 085	26	23 639
1979–80	28 775	74	9 985	26	38 760
1980–81	34 008	75	11 476	25	45 484
1981–82	39 763	75	13 426	25	53 189
1982–83	43·027	73	15 884	27	58 911
1983–84	47 460	73	17 668	27	65 128
1984–85	56 431	74	20 155	26	76 586
1985–86	63 421	73	22 918	27	86 339

[1] Includes public authorities outside the budget sector

Source: 1901–02 to 1967–68, R.L. Mathews and W.R.C. Jay (1972), *Federal Finance*, Nelson, Melbourne.
1975–76 to 1985–86, ABS Catalogue 5501.0, 'Government Financial Estimates'.

to 49 per cent in 1958–59 but that is where it has remained since then. On the revenue side, once again, the contribution of the Commonwealth's own revenues increased from 41 per cent in 1901–02 and 1909–10 to 85 per cent after the war and 77 per cent in 1958–59. Since then it has only declined marginally to the current figure of 73 per cent.

This shift has occurred mainly due to the virtual monopoly of the Commonwealth over the major growth taxes. Consequently, about twice as much of own purpose outlays of the states and local government are now funded through Commonwealth payments as was the case just prior to the Second World War. This shift in the fiscal balance has also dictated the agenda of the major fiscal institutions. Thus, instead of co-ordinating the economic policies of different levels, the primary role of the Premiers' Conference in the post-war years has been to determine the amounts of general revenue grants to the states. Similarly, the Loan Council has become in the post-war years, although it was never meant to be, an instrument of the Commonwealth's control over capital resources of the states and their authorities.

The role of the Commonwealth Grants Commission has also changed significantly in recent years. As noted earlier, the Commission was established in 1933 in recognition of the special needs of the less populous states. The Commission's function for some forty-five years remained to determine special assistance for those smaller states that applied for such assistance. However, since 1979 its role has been extended to the determination of per capita relativities among the states for the distribution of general revenue grants. Consequently, the Commission's work now has considerable influence on the budgetary resources of all states, not just the less populous ones. Not only is the principle of fiscal equalisation applied to the distribution of practically all recurrent grants, but the new arrangements have meant that the cost of equalisation is borne by the two more populous states, New South Wales and Victoria (through lower per capita shares of federal revenue grants), instead of by the Commonwealth as was the case before 1979.

Vertical fiscal imbalance and revenue transfers

The shift in the financial balance between the Commonwealth and the states was noted in Table 6.1. Comparisons with other developed federations show that Australia has the highest level of imbalance between the fiscal responsibilities and the revenue-raising powers of the states. Excluding local government and non-budget authorities (that are included in figures in Table 6.1), figures in Table 6.2 show that the states in Australia are responsible for the highest percentage of own purpose outlays in the group (43.4 per cent) but raise the lowest share of taxation revenue (14.9 per cent). The Commonwealth, on the other hand, raises 81 per cent of tax revenue—the highest level for a national government in this group—but is responsible for about 51 per cent of own purpose outlays—third ranking in the group. The result is the high level of imbalance that requires an unduly heavy dependence of the states on payments from the Commonwealth. These payments consist mainly of general purpose grants, largely in the form of tax sharing grants or formula grants, and specific purpose payments.

A major consequence of the vertical fiscal imbalance is the centralisation of budgetary decisions, and economic and social policies. Whatever policy co-ordination occurs is to a large degree dominated by the Commonwealth due to its superior financial position.

Table 6.2 Percentage of total taxation and expenditure for own purposes by level of government

	Federal	*State*	*Local*	*Total*
Percentage of total taxation				
Australia	81.3	14.9	3.8	100.0
Canada	56.4	34.4	9.2	100.0
Germany[1]	68.3	23.1	8.6	100.0
Switzerland	59.5	23.0	17.4	100.0
USA	67.3	20.1[2]	12.7[2]	100.0
Percentages of outlays for own purposes				
Australia	50.9	43.4	5.7	100.0
Canada	40.6	38.8	20.6	100.0
Germany	57.1	23.1	19.8	100.0
Switzerland	47.2	29.7	23.1	100.0
USA	59.5	17.2	23.3	100.0

[1] Federal sector includes customs duties and share of VAT given to the European Community.

[2] Includes 3 and 19 per cent, for state and local government respectively, being the estimated contribution of social security levies.

Sources: OECD Revenue Statistics 1965–1982.
IMF, Government Finance Statistics Yearbook, vol. vi, 1982.

Another consequence of the vertical fiscal imbalance is the loss of accountability and efficiency due to the heavy reliance on revenue transfers. Revenue sharing of any description severs the link between spending and revenue-raising decisions at *both* levels of government and thereby causes these decisions to be made without full accountability. Thus, for the states, revenue-sharing arrangements may generate a temptation for additional expenditure, as the necessary revenue comes largely from the Commonwealth. At the same time, the Commonwealth could have a strong temptation to reduce payments to the states without due regard to the economic and other costs generated by such reductions. In recent years the Commonwealth has shown a strong tendency to regard payments to the states as easier targets for fiscal restraint than outlays for its own purposes. For example, between 1976–77 and 1986–87, payments to the states have increased at the average annual rate of 9.4 per cent while Commonwealth own purpose outlays have increased at the annual rate of 13.6 per cent. For 1987–88, the payments to the states are estimated to increase by only 2.9 per cent whereas outlays for the Commonwealth's own purposes are estimated to increase at 5.0 per cent over the previous year.

It is widely recognised that the accountability and efficiency of decisions at both levels of government would be improved if the dependence of one level of government over another was reduced. For example, the fiscal powers sub-committee of the Australian Constitutional Convention strongly supported the principle that 'each unit of government in a federal system should have revenue-raising powers that are roughly commensurate with its expenditure obligations', and emphasised that this principle should be accepted 'as a goal to be approached as nearly as practicable' (1984: 12).

The situation is made worse by the high degree of arbitrariness and uncertainty in determining the level of Commonwealth payments. In 1985–86, the tax sharing arrangement of the previous three years was abandoned in favour of formula funding grants for the following three years. While this allowed the Commonwealth to avoid passing onto the states the high growth that had occurred in its taxation revenue, the new arrangement was regarded by some states as also providing greater certainty in their grants. Under the new arrangement in 1985–86 the states received the same real level of grants as in 1984–85, on the condition that in each of the following two years their financial assistance grants would be increased by 2 per cent in real terms. This guarantee was incorporated in the *State Grants (General Assistance) Act 1985*. In 1986–87, the 2 per cent real increase in financial assistance grants was retained, although not without considerably larger cuts to the capital payments for the states. However, the guarantee has been abandoned for 1987–88 and financial assistance grants this year will increase by an amount roughly equivalent to a zero real increase over the previous year. The lesson of this experience is that even legislated guarantees have failed to provide the desired degree of certainty in the financial transfers to the states.

By way of reforming the current system it has been suggested that the Commonwealth payments to the states should be made under a financial contract the basic framework of which should be enshrined in the Commonwealth Constitution (Mathews, 1983). Examples of similar constitutionally determined revenue-sharing arrangements can be found in some other federations such as the Federal Republic of Germany (Spahn, 1978) and India (Grewal, 1975). Provided that the necessary constitutional amendment could be made, a financial contract would go a long way to reducing the current uncertainty of Commonwealth payments to the states. However, unless the precise shares of each shared tax base are prescribed in the Constitution, each level of government would continue to seek to minimise the relative share of the other level. To that extent the issue of relative shares would remain at the forefront of the Premiers' Conference agenda. And the problems of uncertainty and lack of accountability would also remain, although to a lesser extent than at present.

Co-ordination of public sector borrowings

The Loan Council, originally concerned with enhancing the efficiency of states' borrowings through co-ordination, subsequently became heavily involved in a system of rationing the capital funds for the states. Its function reflects another facet of the vertical fiscal imbalance, as the Commonwealth has successfully used its financial dominance through the Loan Council to control the volume, allocation and (until recently) the terms and conditions of states' borrowings.

During the period following the Second World War, the financial dominance of the Commonwealth started to be reflected in the operation of the Loan Council. The lack of adequate taxable capacity at the state level meant increasing reliance on loan funds to finance their works expenditures. By the 1950s their borrowing demand had increased to an extent that the states were unable to raise sufficient funds without the so-called special loans from the Commonwealth. Regular reliance on special loans throughout the 1950s meant that by the end of the 1960s while the Commonwealth had become a net creditor, the states were becoming increasingly indebted to the Commonwealth (see Mathews, 1984). In the 1970s a portion of the states' Loan Council programme started to be given by the Commonwealth as a capital grant (generally one-third of the total programme) and the Loan Council programme started to be put through the Commonwealth budget. The servicing of the loans remains the responsibility of the states. However, the fact that these amounts appear as Commonwealth budget outlays has motivated the Commonwealth in recent years to impose stricter restrictions on aggregate loans with a view to reducing its budgetary deficits.

During the last five years, the borrowings of the states' semi-government authorities have been progressively freed from the Loan Council controls and left to be determined in accordance with market forces. This process started with the liberalisation in 1982 of domestic borrowings of state electricity authorities and was extended to the other authorities in the following year. When the concept of 'Global Limit' was adopted for 1984–85 on a voluntary basis for one year, the Gentlemen's Agreement was suspended on 21 June 1984. At the 1985 Loan Council meeting, the Gentlemen's Agreement was terminated and the Global Limit adopted as the ongoing framework to deal with the borrowings of the state authorities.

In spite of these changes the Loan Council still remains primarily concerned with strict quantitative controls of the overall borrowings of the public sector. A major weakness of this approach is that insufficient distinction is made between the purposes of the various demands for loan funds, or their contribution to national infrastructure, or their other economic and social merits.

The Loan Council's fixation with quantitative controls on a yearly basis also means that insufficient account is taken of the ongoing commitments for investment and state policies that influence the demand for infrastructure. Furthermore, the uncertainty of year-to-year allocations undermines the ability of the states to undertake forward planning for major investment development, particularly given the typically long lead times involved in bringing major initiatives to the implementation stage. The uncertainty also adversely affects the efficient management of major capital projects. Capital budgeting for major projects needs to be on a multi-year basis, and funding arrangements need to be flexible enough to enable funds to flow to projects in accordance with project development. However, the present process makes the project development dependent upon year-to-year determination of funds.

Economists are well aware of the futility of quantitative controls which rarely work in the highly sophisticated financial and capital markets such as are available to the borrowing authorities today. Progressively more sophisticated instruments of debt are likely to emerge to undermine the effectiveness of volume controls in much the same way as lease financing proliferated in the early 1980s. The counterproductive nature of the Loan Council controls was demonstrated by the fact that quantitative controls were being avoided by resorting to more expensive and administratively complex forms of finance.

There are a number of sensible initiatives which could be taken to improve the process. One specific example concerns public authorities. Where authorities are operating under guidelines of the type in operation in Victoria (rate of return-based pricing, investment evaluation, etc.), it is unnecessary and inconsistent to impose a further restrictive layer in the form of a ceiling on borrowings. Rather, it would be sensible to free such authorities from Loan Council controls, provided they are operating within a broadly agreed set of guidelines.

A similar approach is possible for other public sector borrowings. A broad set of guidelines should be developed and implemented as a way of ensuring that borrowed funds be directed towards projects with higher economic and social merit. Here again the emphasis should be on quality and flexibility, rather than quantity and the preservation of historical shares.

Fiscal equalisation

The process of fiscal equalisation raises certain issues that relate to the relationship of such equalisation with horizontal equity and allocative efficiency. These are discussed in this section. The process of fiscal equalisation is briefly described first.

The process of fiscal equalisation

The financial assistance grant is by far the largest single grant received by the states; in 1986–87 the total amount for six states was $10 885.3 million out of total payments to the states of $22 211 million. This grant is distributed among the states according to the principle of fiscal equalisation as applied by the Commonwealth Grants Commission (CGC).

Table 6.3 The distribution of financial assistance grants between the states, 1986–87

	NSW	Vic.	Qld	WA	SA	Tas.	Six-state total
1 Estimated population at 31.12.86 ('000 persons)	5573.1	4185.7	2613.7	1450.8	1379.7	448.9	15 651.9
2 Per capita relativities	1.008	1.000	1.416	1.455	1.397	1.605	
3 Row 1 weighted by row 2	5617.7	4185.7	3701.0	2110.9	1927.4	720.5	18 263.2
4 Percentage distribution of row 3 among states	30.8	22.9	20.3	11.6	10.6	3.9	100.0
5 Estimated distribution of financial assistance grants ($m)	3322.2	2475.3	2188.7	1248.4	1139.8	426.1	10 800.5
6 Estimated distribution of financial assistance grants ($ per capita)	596.11	591.38	837.39	860.46	826.16	949.16	
7 Financial assistance grants based on equal per capita payments ($m)	3845.7	2888.3	1803.6	1001.1	952.1	309.8	10 800.5

Source: Commonwealth Budget Paper no. 7, 1986–87

The Commission determines per capita relativities that are expressed as factors—based on Victoria's factor being the numeraire—and are then used as weights for the state populations to determine their respective percentage shares of the total amount. This procedure is illustrated in Table 6.3.

The relativities are determined by the Commission so as to enable each state to provide, without having to impose taxes and charges at levels appreciably different from the levels imposed by the other states, government services at standards not appreciably different from the standards provided by the other states.

The effect of these relativities is to redistribute a large amount of grant money from New South Wales and Victoria to the other four states, as each state receives a share that is different from its respective share of the six-state population. In 1986–87, for example, a total of $936.5 million was distributed away from the two larger states to the other four. The departures from an equal per capita distribution are shown in Figure 6.1, where the origin of the chart represents equal per capita distribution among the states.

Figure 6.1 Consequences of fiscal equalisation: financial assistance grants, 1986–87

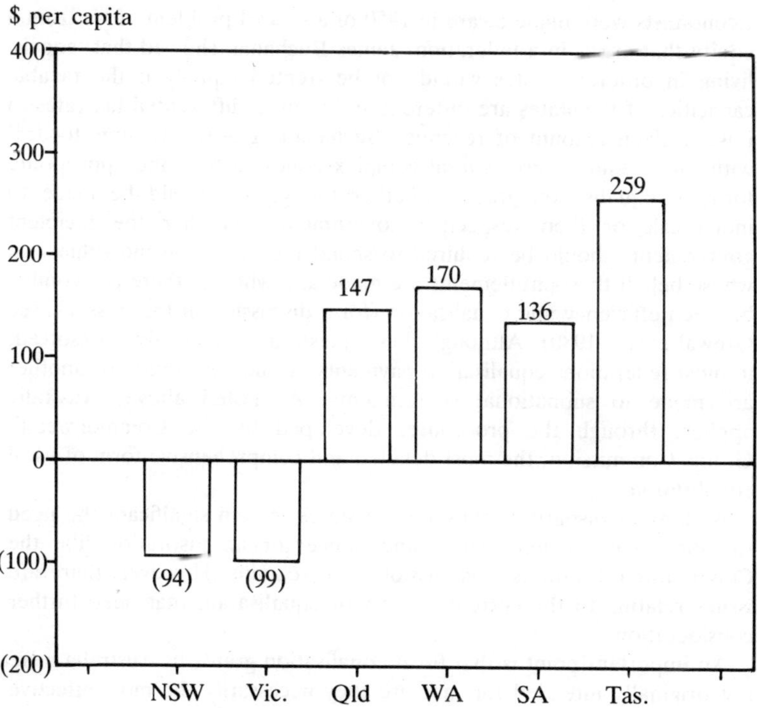

The differences in the states' per capita shares are caused essentially by the Commission's assessment of the following two factors:

1 differences (above and below standard) in the states' revenue-raising capacities;

2 differences in unit costs of services—caused by the size and spatial distribution of populations, i.e. diseconomies of small-scale operations, additional costs of dispersion, isolation or urbanisation, and special characteristics of state populations (for example, Aboriginality).

The Commission assesses separate needs for each of the revenue sources and major expenditure categories. These needs are then summed into aggregate entitlements and are expressed as relativities for the states. Separate needs are also assessed in respect of selected business undertakings of the states (at present these undertakings include metropolitan transit, non-metropolitan railway passenger and freight services, country water supply and sewerage, irrigation and associated drainage, and coastal shipping). Adjustments are also made for the differential amounts of a large number of specific purpose grants received by the states that are regarded by the Commission to be equivalent to general revenues. The contributions of the various components of the equalisation process for 1986–87 are shown in Table 6.4.

Equity and equalisation

Economists were made aware in 1950 of a special problem of horizontal equity that arises in a federation. James Buchanan showed that 'equals' living in different states would not be treated equally if the taxable capacities of the states are different and require differential tax rates to raise a given amount of revenue (Buchanan, 1950). Attempts to deal with this inequity raise several complex issues such as the appropriate form of equalisation grants, whether the grants should be made to individuals or their respective governments, whether the recipient governments should be required to spend the grants on individuals on whose behalf their entitlements are made and whether there is a conflict between efficiency and equalisation (for a discussion of these issues, see Grewal et al., 1980). Although these questions still remain unresolved, in most federations equalisation payments of one description or another are made to subnational governments. As noted above, Australia applies, through the procedures developed by the Commonwealth Grants Commission, the most detailed and comprehensive form of fiscal equalisation.

As long as disparities between the states remain significant the need for some equalisation grants, and hence for an institution like the Commonwealth Grants Commission, also remains. However, there are issues relating to the current process of equalisation that need further consideration.

An important point is that fiscal equalisation grants in Australia were not originally intended for, nor are they necessarily the most effective

Table 6.4 Financial assistance grants, 1986–87 ($m) (est.)

	Per capita allocation	*Recommended grant*	*Total equalisation*	*Revenue equalisation*	*Recurrent expenditure equalisation*	*Equalisation for business undertakings*	*Equalisation for specific purpose payments*	*Rounding adjustment*
NSW	3845.7	3322.2	−523.5	−233.5	−426.7	136.1	3.4	−2.8
Vic.	2888.3	2475.3	−413.0	−76.9	−350.7	16.0	0.3	−1.7
Qld	1803.6	2188.7	385.1	38.5	232.8	−33.4	145.6	1.6
WA	1001.1	1248.4	247.3	−1.6	276.3	38.8	−68.3	2.1
SA	952.1	1139.8	187.7	196.1	154.2	−99.9	−62.8	0.1
Tas.	309.8	426.1	116.3	77.4	114.2	−57.7	−18.3	0.7
NT[1]	104.6	525.3	420.7	15.7	482.1	14.3	−88.7	−2.7

[1]NT is receiving a financial assistance grant in 1986–87 equivalent to $597.1 m implying that it is receiving a payment of $72.8 m in excess of that required for equalisation.

Source: Department of Management and Budget, Victoria.

means of, meeting the requirements of horizontal equity. In seeking to put each state in a position of potential budgetary equality, these grants perhaps create a necessary condition for horizontal equity across the states. But in the absence of a direct focus on the fiscal treatment of individuals in each state, and due to the unconditional nature of the grants, sufficient conditions for horizontal equity are not met. Therefore, although the objective of fiscal equalisation is similar to that of horizontal equity, the two are not identical.

Fiscal equalisation and allocative efficiency

A major issue before the Commission at present is whether the principle of fiscal equalisation as currently applied has significant consequences for efficient allocation of resources in the country. In the letter transmitting the terms of reference of the current review, the Commonwealth has asked the Commission for the first time in the context of the six-state reviews to report on this issue.

In their submissions to the Commission some states argued that the equalisation of expenditure costs, particularly on account of location-based factors such as scale of operations, dispersion and isolation, drives a wedge between the true economic costs and effective tax prices faced by the state governments and their respective taxpayers. This in turn distorts the price signals on which expenditure decisions are based and thereby leads to a loss of allocative efficiency (submission by Government of Victoria, December 1986, chs 2 and 3). It has also been argued that the current approach to revenue-capacity assessment 'provides an incentive for governments to order their revenue-raising activities contrary to the principles of comparative advantage' (Submission by New South Wales, December 1986, ch. 2).

Another issue is the extent to which the Commission's treatment of specific purpose payments received by the states overrides and neutralises the original allocation of these grants among the states. It is argued in the following section that, in principle, specific purpose payments have quite definite roles to play as instruments of co-ordination between levels of government. Insofar as the process of fiscal equalisation neutralises their interstate allocation, their effectiveness in regard to their specific objectives is likely to be compromised.

Specific purpose payments

In 1986–87, some 38 per cent of total payments to the states were in the form of specific purpose payments. During the Whitlam administration in 1975–76 specific purpose payments reached 46 per cent of total Commonwealth payments. Despite such a heavy reliance on them, there is no institutional overview and scrutiny of the specific purpose payments.

These payments are determined by a multitude of organisations including statutory bodies (such as the Schools Commission), various ministerial councils and Commonwealth departments. However, no particular institution has the overall responsibility of reviewing the operation of these payments, their complementarity to or conflict with one another, their effectiveness in achieving specific objectives and, above all, their overall impact on the budgetary processes at both levels of government.

In every federation, there is a role for specific purpose payments. These payments can be used to improve the efficiency of allocation of resources by allowing for the inter-jurisdictional spillovers. Further, in some cases specific purpose payments also help to ensure that national priorities or standards are observed by the state governments.

It follows therefore that proper application of specific purpose grants can play a useful role in policy co-ordination. However, this requires that there should be an institutional mechanism to ensure that the assisted programmes are not selected unilaterally by the financially dominant level but reflect the views of all concerned governments (Commonwealth and states).

The Australian experience of using the specific purpose grants as an instrument of intergovernmental co-ordination has not been a great success. There has been, and continues to exist, a lack of communication and consultation between the governments in the development of the assisted programmes. Programmes have for the most part been unilaterally determined by the Commonwealth, often even without sufficient co-ordination or planning within its own departments (see Harris, 1979).

It has also been suggested that during the mid-1970s the decisions made by a large number of statutory bodies regarding specific purpose grants in isolation from one another and without regard to budgetary constraints contributed to the expansion of the budgetary outlays and inflation (Mathews, 1977). An equally serious problem was that the statutory bodies did not function as intergovernmental co-ordinating agencies—allowing little or limited state involvement in their decisions (Mathews, 1986).

Although the process has improved in recent years with the reduction in the number of statutory bodies involved in this process, the lack of proper intergovernmental co-ordination remains. Due to the absence of an institution that takes an overview of the operation of these payments, each grant continues to operate in a vacuum without being a part of an integrated strategy. The compliance costs of these programmes for the states are often high as most of the payments are accompanied by fairly detailed, but often unnecessary conditions including auditing and accounting procedures.

In its report entitled *Inquiry into Aspects of State-Federal Financial Relations* (October 1986), the Economic and Budgetary Review Committee of the Victorian parliament also criticised the inadequacy of existing intergovernmental consultative processes covering the introduction and review of specific purpose payments. The Committee emphasised the need for a 'truly consultative process which permits full discussion of "national interest" considerations *before* they are unilaterally invoked by the Commonwealth to justify a new tied grant programme' (81).

The fiscal powers sub-committee of the Australian Constitutional Convention also examined the operation of section 96 and made the following recommendations regarding specific purpose payments:

(a) conditions attached to specific purpose grants should relate only to the purpose of the grant and not to matters extraneous to it;
(b) the nature and extent of the conditions attached to a grant should be determined by negotiation between the Commonwealth and the states concerned having regard to the need to strike a balance between the responsibilities of both levels of government involved;
(c) administrative procedures for the purposes of a grant should be established by the Commonwealth only through the relevant state government or department or a state agency nominated by the state.

These recommendations were adopted by the Convention in July 1985. These requirements cannot be met so long as the responsibility for specific purpose payments remains fragmented.

An alternative model

It has been argued above that in the past:

1 the Premiers' Conference has been chiefly involved in dealing with vertical fiscal imbalance, whereas it could play the role of co-ordinating economic policies and strategies of various governments into a cohesive national strategy;
2 the Loan Council is still excessively concerned with strict controls over the volume of borrowings instead of their purposes and merits in the interests of national growth;
3 the process of fiscal equalisation in Australia is more comprehensive than in any other federation, but the implications of fiscal equalisation for allocative efficiency need to be taken into account; and
4 despite a heavy reliance on specific purpose payments, no institution exists to take an overview of their objectives, their operation, and their implications for the budgetary processes.

At the Bicentenary it is useful to stand up and look at an alternative rational model for the federation, without being constrained by the detailed realities of the transition from one situation to another. The alternative model presented aims at providing an institutional framework that facilitates and encourages efficiency at all levels of public sector decision-making. In this model the fiscal institutions play a forward-looking role in making the national economy more competitive and responsive to the economic environment of the next century.

Objectives of fiscal federalism

In the alternative model, the overall aim of fiscal federalism is to provide a structure of the public sector that is responsive to the needs of its citizens and enhances efficiency, social justice and competitiveness of the national economy. In other words, the federalised public sector becomes an integral part of and a motive force for a dynamic, efficient and equitable economy. More specific objectives of fiscal federalism in this setting are:

1 a distribution of taxing powers and expenditure functions that is consistent with efficient and responsible operation of governments and is conducive to decentralisation and public accountability; and

2 co-ordination of economic and social policies of the various governments into medium-term and longer-term strategies aimed at a stable and competitive national economy and an equitable society.

Fiscal institutions and processes

In this model, each of the three major fiscal institutions of Australia would play a crucial role in the achievement of the economic and social objectives of federation. However, their focus will shift from dealing with the financial transfers from the Commonwealth to the states to becoming the primary vehicles for intergovernmental co-ordination and stability.

Premiers' Conference

In this model, the distribution of taxing powers and expenditure functions would be such as to obviate the need for large revenue transfers from the Commonwealth to the states. Such transfers would ideally be limited to equalisation grants to the less populous states (see page 135) and certain specific purpose payments. The role of these payments would be limited to cost-sharing arrangements that have two objectives, namely to internalise spillover effects between jurisdictions, and to ensure that national priorities or standards are observed in those cases where this is considered necessary.

The primary role of the Premiers' Conference in a setting like this would be to co-ordinate economic policies of the states and the Commonwealth with a view to ensuring that they complement one another and are consistent with the medium-term and long-term economic strategies. This task would require the Premiers' Conference to regularly determine and review the medium-term and long-term targets of economic policies and set broad limits within which individual policies are formulated.

Although it is not part of the experience of Australian federal institutions, examples of such co-ordination of policies exist in other federations. The Federal Republic of Germany, under the Stability and Growth Act, has since 1966 adopted a sophisticated legislative and institutional apparatus to achieve policy co-ordination (see Spahn, 1978), a glimpse of which is provided in the Appendix to this chapter. Similarly, through the Planning Commission and the National Development Council, considerable success has been achieved in the co-ordination of economic plans of the centre and states in India (see Grewal, 1975).

It was noted earlier that in Australia there is an institutional vacuum in relation to the specific purpose payments. The Premiers' Conference is an ideal forum to determine the functional areas in which the observance of national standards or priorities is necessary. It would also be the appropriate body to periodically review the effectivenesses of and the need for individual grants.

In order to perform these tasks properly, the Premiers' Conference would need to be served by a secretariat of professional staff and a number of standing committees of ministers with special expertise in such matters as taxation, finance and industrial relations.

Australian Loan Council

As noted, the present processes of the Loan Council place far too much emphasis on controlling the total amount of borrowings by the governments and their semi-government authorities. It has been argued that this largely ignores the qualitative aspects of capital investment. What is needed is a process that determines public investment according to its economic and social merits and encourages efficient management of capital projects. The objective of the Loan Council's co-ordination should be to provide, within broad guidelines, flexible conditions that facilitate and encourage an optimal allocation of resources. This would require, among other things, that historical shares of the states may not be maintained. Rather, the allocation among the states would be made on the basis of merits of their programmes.

Accordingly, in the alternative model the Loan Council would, on the one hand, provide an outline of a broad strategy for public sector investment over the medium-term and long-term and, on the other, provide agreed methods of assessment of investment demands and their performance. In the case of commercial authorities this would mean setting out the agreed principles on which they should operate and the performance criteria such as the rate of return and proper pricing policy. For the non-commercial authorities, this would require agreement on the evaluation processes and criteria such as cost-benefit analyses based on agreed limits and assumptions. Once these arrangements are adopted quantitative controls would become altogether unnecessary.

Fiscal equalisation

It was argued earlier that equalisation of costs of government services due to location-based factors (for example, isolation, dispersion, diseconomies of small scale and urbanisation) is likely to cause loss of allocative efficiency. In the alternative model, therefore, the processes of fiscal equalisation would need to be restricted to interstate differences in revenue-raising capacities and relevant features of state populations such as aboriginality, ethnic background and age or sex composition. (For further detail, see Victoria's submission to the CGC, December 1986.)

At present, revenue equalisation is based on separate assessment of needs for more than twenty-five categories of state taxes and charges. If a particular state does not impose a certain tax (for example, business franchises licence fees in the case of Queensland) or abolishes a certain tax that is still levied in most other states, notional needs are assessed for that state in respect of that tax based on a notional estimate of the revenue-raising capacity. It has been argued by some states that although this procedure may be consistent with the objective of policy neutral needs assessment, it is likely to influence the choice of tax instruments by the states (New South Wales submission to CGC, December 1986). Further, the determination of notional tax bases, necessary for the current procedure, involves subjective judgments in many cases. Accordingly, there is merit in considering whether revenue equalisation could be based on a broad measure of state taxable capacity such as per capita or household income. Although such a measure would not totally dispense with subjective judgments (for example, imputations may still be necessary for some items such as the undistributed corporate income), the process would become considerably simpler and more objective. At the same time, the objective of policy neutrality would be better achieved, as the structure of taxation in a state and the assessment of its revenue needs would have no bearing on each other.

A number of states and the Commonwealth Treasury have also suggested exclusion of business undertakings from the process of fiscal equalisation. They have argued that business undertakings ought to be run, to the extent possible, on commercial criteria, and their demands on state budgets should not be included in the assessment of needs. In the alternative model, fiscal equalisation would, for these reasons, not include assessment of needs for business undertakings.

Finally, as noted above, most of the specific purpose payments are currently treated by the CGC in a manner (the so-called inclusion method) that their original allocation among the states is overridden by the needs assessment made by the Commission. Thus, for example, the allocation of school grants as determined by the Schools Commission is effectively neutralised by the CGC. The Commission's argument appears to be based on the premises that (1) such grants are similar in their effect to general revenue grants and (2) their allocation is often arbitrary or is not based on proper assessment of needs (CGC, 1983; Mathews, 1986).

Once again, this is a matter on which opinions differ. In the alternative model, given that specific purpose grants are based on clearly defined criteria, it would be necessary to restrict fiscal equalisation to the state-funded expenditures only—net of the specific purpose payments (i.e. the application of the so-called deduction method). This would preserve the original allocation of these grants and the criteria on which they are allocated.

Conclusion

Australia has a unique framework of fiscal institutions that should be used effectively to achieve the objectives of efficiency and equity in the nation's economy. The current economic realities facing Australia further underline the need for rationalising the roles of these institutions. The existence of an extreme degree of vertical fiscal imbalance has, in addition to causing losses of efficiency and accountability, distracted the major fiscal institutions from undertaking real policy co-ordination. The alternative model presented in this paper provides a direction for future improvements.

References

Australian Constitutional Convention (1984), *Fiscal Powers Sub-Committee Report to Standing Committee July 1984,* Melbourne.

Brigden, J.B. (1934), 'Grants to States: The Report of the Commonwealth Grants Commission and some of its Implications', *Economic Record,* Supplement XI, reproduced in Prest and Mathews (1980).

Buchanan, J.M. (1950), 'Federalism and Fiscal Equity', *The American Economic Review* 40, reproduced in Grewal et al. (eds) (1980).

CGC (1983), Commonwealth Grants Commission, *Equality in Diversity,* Canberra.

Grewal, B.S. (1975), *Centre-State Financial Relations in India,* Punjabi University Press, Patiala.

—— et al. (eds) (1980), *The Economics of Federalism*, ANU Press, Canberra.

Groenewegen, P.D. (1982), *The Premiers' Conference 1905: Report of Proceedings*, Centre for Research on Federal Financial Relations, ANU, Canberra.

—— (1984), *Public Finance in Australia: Theory and Practice*, 2nd edn, Prentice-Hall, Sydney.

Harris, C.P. (1979), *Relationships Between Federal and State Governments in Australia*, ACIR Information paper 6, AGPS, Canberra.

Harrison, M.W. (1910), *The Constitution of the Commonwealth of Australia*, 2nd edn, Charles F. Maxwell, Melbourne.

Headford, C.G. (1954), 'The Australian Loan Council: Its Origin, Operation and Significance in the Federal Structure', *Public Administration*, reproduced in Prest and Mathews (1980).

Mathews, R.L (1977), 'Innovations and Developments in Australian Federalism', *Publius* 7, 3: 9–19.

—— (1983), 'The Commonwealth–State Financial Contract', in Aldred and Wilkes, *A Fractured Federation,* Allen & Unwin: 37–62.

—— (1984), *The Australian Loan Council: Co-ordination of Public Debt Policies in a Federation*, Reprint no. 62, Centre for Research on Federal Financial Relations, ANU, Canberra.

—— (1986), *Fiscal Federalism in Australia: Past and Future Tense*, Reprint no. 74. Centre for Research on Federal Financial Relations, ANU, Canberra.

Prest, W. and Mathews, R.L. (eds) (1980), *The Development of Australian Fiscal Federalism: Selected Readings,* ANU Press, Canberra.

Spahn, B. (ed.) (1983), *Principlies of Federal Policy Co-ordination in the Federal Republic of Germany*, Centre for Research on Federal Financial Relations, ANU, Canberra.

Wheare, K.C. (1967), *Federal Government*, 4th edn, Oxford University Press, Oxford.

Appendix

Table IV–1 Co-ordination and the West German Stability and Growth Act

Targets	Policy criteria and their development	Co-ordination	
1 *General* Para. 1 → Generation and maintenance of (1) general macroeconomic equilibrium (2) within the order of a market economy 2 *Special* (1) price stability (2) high level of employment (3) balance-of-payments equilibrium (4) steady and adequate economic growth	1 *General* Para. 2 → The Federal government puts forward: (1) annual economic report outlining (2) its judgment regarding the annual report of the Council of Economic advisers and their recommendations (3) annual macroeconomic forecast (national Budget) and exposition of intended economic and fiscal policies 2 *Traditional criteria* (1) deflator of GNP < 5–6 per cent (2) > 99.2 per cent of work force employed	1 *Co-ordinating institutions* (a) Defined by the Act: (1) The Federal government as the ultimately responsible unit (2) Financial Planning Council (Para. 17[1]) as a co-ordinating body in budgetary planning of all levels of government (3) Business Cycle Council (Paras. 18 & 22) (including Capital Market Committee or *Kapital-marktausschuss*) as a permanent body: (a) to assess the current economic situation, to investigate appropriate policy measures and to	(b) Not defined by the Act: (1) integrating State Institutions consulting on concurrent issues, for instance, education (*Kultuaminister-Konferenz*) (2) Municipal Top Associations, *Städtetage* on problems of urbanisation, *Gemeindetage* on problems of rural areas; also on financial matters of communities (3) Top Associations and interest groups of the private sector: (a) employers associations (BDI,

1.5 per cent of GNP (4) minimal oscillations in the development of GNP; about 4–5 per cent growth in real terms	for fiscal policies; and (b) to evaluate the situation in the capital market and to help provide orientation for credit policies; it develops a time schedule for placing public debentures onto the market (4) concerted action (Para. 3) as a body to reconcile public policy actions with private economic agents (labour unions and industry associations) (a) combined evaluation of the overall economic situation; (b) explanation of the government's assessment and orientation on intended government policies; (c) moral suasion	(b) labour unions (DGB, DAG etc.) (c) agricultural organisations (DVB) (d) others 2 *Co-ordinating mechanisms* (1) medium-term financial planning (Para. 9) (2) multi-period investment programs for the public sector (Para. 10) (3) government report on subsidies (*Subventionsbericht*) and evaluation of efficiency (Para. 12)

Note: [1] Para. 51 *Haushaltsgrundsätzegesetz*.
Source: K. Mackscheidt and J. Steinhausen, *Finanzpolitik, Grundfragen fiskalpolitischer Lenkung*, Mohr, Tübingen, 1973, pp. 98–9.

7

A LEGAL PERSPECTIVE

Geoffrey Lindell

As the title of this chapter suggests, its aim is to discuss continuity and change in Australia's federal legal institutions and processes. The institutions referred to have been taken to mean the courts, with a special emphasis on the High Court and the new federal courts, and also the federal parliament. The chapter will attempt to discuss the extent to which continuity and change have occurred in the legal nature of the roles played by those institutions, as well as the way in which those roles are exercised. In particular the chapter will seek to deal with the effect of such developments on Australia's federal system of government. Inevitably some selection has been necessary, for example, in relation to the institutions to be studied. The period chosen for the study will, for the most part, concentrate on that which began in the early 1970s and continues to the present time.

The effect of judicial review on the scope of federal legislative powers

From its inception the High Court has always exercised, and was intended to exercise, a pre-eminent role in the interpretation of the Commonwealth Constitution, particularly as regards those provisions which defined the powers *inter se* of the Commonwealth and the state parliaments. To the Court, at least, it has seemed natural that it should be given the responsibility for ensuring that the Commonwealth and the states observe the limits placed on the legislative powers distributed between them. In *R v Kirby; ex parte Boilermakers' Society of Australia* (267–8) it was said:

> In a federal form of government a part is necessarily assigned to the judicature which places it in a position unknown in a unitary system or under a flexible constitution where parliament is supreme. A federal constitution must be rigid. The government it establishes must be one of defined powers;

> within those powers it must be paramount, but it must be incompetent to go beyond them. The conception of independent governments existing in the one area and exercising powers in different fields of action carefully defined by law could not be carried into practical effect unless the ultimate responsibility of deciding upon the limits of the respective powers of the governments were placed in the federal judicature.

Given the obvious significance of this role for the scope and exercise of federal legislative power something needs to be said about the principles which have governed the exercise of judicial review of legislation under the Constitution. At the outset the observation may be made that those principles contain features which, while remaining constant, have, paradoxically, operated to produce change, or at least the potential for change, by expanding the perceived scope of federal legislative powers.

Literalism and federal implications

Perhaps the most important of those features has been an adherence to a more literal tradition of interpretation and an associated reluctance of the Court to espouse federal implications which would have had the effect of limiting the potential reach of national legislative powers. Two such implications stand out. The first was known generally as the doctrine of the 'implied immunity of instrumentalities' or 'intergovernmental immunity' and the other was that of the doctrine of 'reserved powers'.

As is well known, the *Engineers'* case was to see the High Court's rejection of the first of those doctrines, at least in its original wide form. The same case is also taken to have decisively rejected the reserved powers doctrine even if it may not have been directly in issue in the case. While a more limited notion of state governmental immunity has been accepted by the Court notwithstanding the *Engineers'* case (see, for example, *Melbourne Corporation v The Commonwealth*; *Queensland Electricity Commission v The Commonwealth*; the *Franklin Dam* case, 128 per Mason J), the Court has not shown any willingness to revive the reserved powers doctrine. A majority of the Court during the period under study have also rejected what some may see as a variant of that doctrine, namely, the notion of 'federal balance'. The question has been raised elsewhere whether this concept does in fact mark a return to the 'heresy' of reserved powers (Zines, 1983: 277, 289–90).

It suffices for present purposes to observe that the last twenty or so years have witnessed a dramatic expansion of national legislative power as a result of the Court's continued rejection of federal implications and the need to give full effect to the provisions which confer upon the Commonwealth parliament legislative powers 'irrespective', it has been said, 'of what effect the construction (of those provisions) may have upon the residue of power which the states may enjoy' (*Strickland v*

Rocla Concrete Pipes Ltd, 489 per Barwick CJ.).

An outstanding illustration of this trend is provided by the developments which have occurred in the judicial interpretation of the corporations power in section 51(xx) of the Constitution. (The power of the Parliament to enact laws with respect to: 'Foreign corporations and trading and financial corporations formed within the limits of the Commonwealth'.) These developments have had the effect of recognising that the Commonwealth parliament now has the power to make laws to:

1 regulate and prohibit trading activities carried on by the kind of corporations referred to in section 51(xx), in particular, the intrastate trading activities of those corporations (*Strickland v Rocla Concrete Pipes Ltd*; *Franklin Dam* case);

2 protect the business of a trading corporation from the activities of others (including ordinary individuals and trade unions) which are calculated to cause substantial loss or damage to the business of that corporation, for example, secondary boycotts: (*Actors and Announcers' Equity Association v Fontana Films Pty Ltd*); and

3 regulate and prohibit acts done for the purpose of enabling section 51(xx) corporations from carrying on trading activities including, in particular, intrastate trading activities (*Franklin Dam* case).

These developments complement what was once referred to as the Commonwealth's 'first and most general power' over trade namely the power to make laws with respect to overseas and interstate trade and commerce under section 51(i) of the Constitution. They also go a long way towards filling the gap created by that power as regards the national control of intrastate trade especially given the fact that most business and commercial operations conducted in Australia are conducted by section 51(xx) corporations. As a result, the Commonwealth parliament may not only regulate the intrastate trading activities of those corporations, such as the sales of their products and the terms of such sales, for example, as to price, but also acts which are preliminary to those sales, for example, the manufacture, production and mining of those products where they are sold by section 51(xx) corporations.

The writer has had occasion to discuss these developments in more detail elsewhere where it was concluded that the corporations power has been given an interpretation which rivals the scope of the American Commerce Power except that the latter power is of course not confined to corporations. (Lindell, 1984: 219, 252 and see generally 218–43 on the scope of the corporations power.) The High Court, it was said, had reached the same results as those reached by the United States Supreme Court but by a different and more literal approach to characterisation and constitutional interpretation. It was suggested that the foundations for this process were laid in the *Concrete Pipes* case (485) and especially the willingness of the High Court in this case to uphold the power of the parliament to reach into and control the intrastate trading activities of the relevant corporations. The essential obstacle in the way was the earlier decision of the Court in *Huddart Parker & Co. Pty Ltd v Moorehead* (per Griffith CJ., Barton, O'Connor and Higgins JJ.; Isaacs J. dissenting. Higgins J. did not rely on the reserved powers doctrine) where it was held that the power in section 51(xx) did not extend to control the external and trading activities of the corporations referred to in that section. In the *Concrete Pipes* case (485) the Court was unanimous in rejecting the authority of the *Moorehead* case because it was seen as essentially based on the discarded reserved powers doctrine under which it was presumed that the Commonwealth parliament was not empowered to control the intrastate or domestic trade of a state. In the words of Barwick CJ., however, that doctrine was 'exploded and unambiguously rejected' by the Court in the *Engineers'* case (*Concrete Pipes* case, 485). In effect the failure of the power in section 51(i) to refer to intrastate trade did not mean that such trade could not be controlled under section 51(xx).

If the reluctance of the Court to espouse implications based on federal considerations was the main reason why the Court chose to give the corporations power a wide interpretation, such a reluctance cannot be said to be the only reason why a majority of the Court refused to give the external affairs power a restricted interpretation in relation to the legislative implementation of international treaty obligations. It was held in the *Franklin Dam* case that, subject to certain limitations, the national parliament possesses the power to pass laws for the implementation of any international obligation contained in a treaty to which Australia is a party. The majority of the Court in that case refused to restrict such a power to treaties which dealt with matters of international concern or which were indisputably international in character. The majority view was that the mere existence of the treaty is itself sufficient evidence of an 'external affair' under section 51(xxix) of the Constitution.

Although other factors are given by the majority to support their conclusion, such as, for example, the difficulty of interpreting and applying a test of international concern and other policy considerations, the absence of any federal implication to limit the scope of the external affairs power is reaffirmed in the judgments. Thus Mason J. said:

> . . . it is well settled that it is wrong to construe a constitutional power by reference to (1) an assumption that there is some content reserved to the states . . . ; and (2) imaginary abuses of legislative power (*Franklin Dam* case, 128).

A further reason given for supporting the wide view of the external affairs power is the need for the judicial interpretation of the Constitution to have regard to the dynamic and broad character of the provisions conferring legislative power on the federal parliament. Thus Mason J. also quoted with approval the following well-known remarks from an earlier case:

> . . . it must always be remembered that we are interpreting a Constitution broad and general in its terms, intended to apply to the varying conditions which the development of our community must involve.
>
> For that reason, where the question is whether the Constitution has used an expression in the wider or in the narrower sense, the Court should, in my opinion, always lean to the broader interpretation unless there is something in the context or in the rest of the Constitution to indicate that the narrower interpretation will best carry out its object and purpose (*Franklin Dam* case, 128—the remarks were those of O'Connor J. in *Jumbunna Coal Mine N L v Victorian Coal Miners' Association*, 367–8).

For some, the decision on the external affairs power will only be seen as a reiteration of the view adopted by a majority in the *R v Burgess; ex parte Henry* (per Latham CJ., Evatt and McTiernan JJ.), thus denying any element of change. The fact remains however that only a few months earlier the Court as then composed would have reached a different decision and furthermore there was considerable authority for the contrary view. (See *Koowarta v Bjelke-Petersen* per Gibbs CJ., Stephen, Wilson and Dawson JJ. as regards the view of a majority a few months earlier, and also *R v Burgess; ex parte Henry* 669 per Dixon J., 658 per Starke J. and *Airlines of NSW Pty Ltd v New South Wales* [*No. 2*], 85 per Barwick CJ., 136 per Menzies J.)

The impact of the Court's decision has attracted much attention. The case has been taken as suggesting that there are now no areas of legislative authority which are exclusively reserved to the states since there is no limit placed on the kind of international treaty obligations which can be implemented at the national level. To the writer such a possibility also existed as a result of the width of the defence power in time of hostilities but the significance of the possibility under the external affairs power presumably lies in the fact that that power can be invoked in time of peace and without the need to point to any supreme emergency. To illustrate the width of the matters which could become the subject of federal legislation Wilson J. said in *Koowarta v Bjelke-Petersen* after indicating that 'the entire field of human rights and fundamental freedoms would come within the reach of paramount Commonwealth legislative power':

> The effect of investing the parliament with power through section 51(xxix) in all these areas would be to transfer to the Commonwealth virtually unlimited power in almost every conceivable aspect of life in Australia, including health and hospitals, the workplace, law and order, the economy, education, and recreational and cultural activity, to mention but a few general heads. In *New South Wales v The Commonwealth* (1975) 135 CLR at 503, Murphy J. asserted the impracticability of dealing, at an executive level, with many aspects of Australia's internal affairs other than in the context of international arrangements. He referred specifically to the subjects of minerals and energy, primary industry, the environment and the general management of the economy. That assertion may well be correct, but can it be supposed, consistently with the federal nature of the Constitution, that the power of

> the parliament with respect to external affairs extends to support any laws operating within Australia which have the purpose and effect of carrying out the obligations which form part of these arrangements? So broad a power, if exercised, may leave the existence of the states as constitutional units intact but it would deny to them any significant legislative role in the federation (*Koowarta*, 251–2).

Gibbs CJ. also saw the possibility of the federal parliament being able to enact a bill of rights:

> To understand the power as becoming available merely because Australia enters into an international agreement, or merely because a subject matter excites international concern, would be to ignore the federal nature of the Constitution. It would be to allow the Commonwealth, under a power expressed to be with respect to external affairs, to enact a bill of rights entirely domestic in its effect—a bill of rights to which state legislation and administrative actions would be subject, but which would of course not necessarily have the same effect on Commonwealth legislation or administrative action (*Koowarta*, 207).

Whether the qualified view of the external affairs power as regards the legislative implementation of international treaty obligations would have marked a return to the reserved powers doctrine under a different guise is a matter that has been raised elsewhere. (Zines, 1983: 277, 285–6).

Professor Zines discusses in his chapter the present nature of the immunity enjoyed by the states and their public authorities from the operation of otherwise valid federal legislation. That discussion shows that in the main the Court adhered to the general rule established in the *Engineers*' case, namely that the Commonwealth can make its laws validly apply to the states if they can otherwise be characterised as laws with respect to the matters over which the Commonwealth is given legislative powers.

The adherence of the Court to the general rule referred to above is also apparent in a more indirect sense in the more recent judicial developments regarding the interpretation of the Commonwealth's industrial relations power under section 51(xxxv) of the Constitution. (The power of the Parliament to make laws with respect to: 'Conciliation and arbitration for the prevention and settlement of industrial disputes extending beyond the limits of any one state'.) The Court has now taken the view that the phrase 'industrial disputes' in that section includes all disputes between employers and employees about terms of employment and conditions of work. It is not confined to disputes in productive industry and organised business carried on for the purpose of profit. This was decided in the *CYSS* case (the dispute in this case involved the pay and conditions of project officers employed by the Community Youth Support Scheme Committees) where the Court overruled *Federated State School Teachers' Association of Australia v Victoria*. That case had failed to accept what was seen as the accepted popular meaning of industrial dispute at the turn of the century—a meaning which was not confined to work connected directly or indirectly with production and manufacture. In this and a number of succeeding cases, the Court was seen as preoccupied with questions of state immunity since the adoption of a wide meaning of the relevant phrase would have had a special impact on disputes involving the state as an employer following the overthrow of the earlier doctrine of intergovernmental immunity in the *Engineers'* case. Thus the rejection of that doctrine was seen as resulting in 'an apparent contraction' of the industrial relations power, 'as members of the Court based their exclusion of disputes involving certain categories of state employees on different interpretations of the term 'industrial disputes' (*CYSS* case, 311). For the present Court the correct approach was to adopt the popular and wider view of industrial disputes 'shorn of its association with the doctrine of intergovernmental immunities.' This was in fact the meaning adopted by a number of the justices of the Court before the *Engineers'* case was decided (*CYSS* case, 305–7, 311–12).

The result of the Court's decision is that the power will now be available as regards disputes involving further areas of state employment, for example, school teaching, fire brigades and nursing. (The availability of the power as regards school teachers was confirmed in *Re Lee; ex parte Harper*.) It is true that the Court was careful to leave open the question whether disputes between a state or a state authority and employees engaged in the administrative services of the state come within the power because of the implied immunity referred to above. Even as regards that immunity, however, three out of six members of the Court had difficulty in seeing how it could be attracted under the industrial relations power in the absence of discrimination. (*Re Lee*, 449 per Mason, Brennan and Deane JJ. The remaining justices refused to be drawn on this issue: see *Re Lee* 445 per Gibbs CJ., 455 per Wilson J. and 458 per Dawson J.)

Finally, in regard to the *CYSS* case, it will be noted that the Court thought that the conclusion reached by it was in conformity with the remarks referred to earlier and taken from the judgment of O'Connor J. in the *Jumbunna* case. Those remarks which stress the broad and dynamic nature of the Constitution were seen as part of the accepted canons of constitutional interpretation. (*CYSS* case, 314. The remarks of O'Connor J. are on page 144.)

Characterisation and the relevance of purpose

Reference was made at the outset to the principles of judicial review containing features which, while they have remained constant, have, paradoxically, operated to produce change, or at least the potential for change, by expanding the perceived scope of federal legislative powers. A further feature which falls in this category relates to the relevance of purpose to the characterisation of federal legislation for the purpose of determining its validity.

A number of cases had decided that laws could be enacted by the Commonwealth parliament in the exercise of its legislative powers in order to further objects or purposes which are not relevant to those powers providing the powers in question are not purposive in character. Once a law could be seen to operate upon the subject matter referred to in the provisions defining the power, the law could be characterised as one with respect to the power even if:

1 the law sought to further a purpose which was not relevant to the power; or

2 the law could also be characterised as one with respect to matters over which the Commonwealth was not otherwise given legislative power.

A law could be seen as operating upon the subject matter, such as overseas trade under section 51(i) by prohibiting export—an activity which is treated as falling within the heart of that power. Associated with these principles of characterisation is the principle upheld in *Herald and Weekly Times Ltd v The Commonwealth*, namely, that once a law prohibiting an activity which is within the subject matter of a power is valid, any condition which relaxes that prohibition must of necessity also be valid. Thus it was said in that case:

> A law which qualifies an existing statutory power to relax a prohibition is necessarily a law with respect to the subject of the prohibition. Even if the qualification gives it the additional character of a law upon some other topic—even, indeed, if that other topic be not a subject of federal legislative power—it is still a law with respect to the subject of the prohibition, and is valid if that subject be within federal power (434 per Kitto J.).

This principle enables the Commonwealth to exert considerable influence in areas over which it is not given express or implied legislative powers.

Essentially, however, those principles can be seen to be based on a number of factors, in particular the non-purposive nature of the powers involved; the difficulties involved in a court undertaking the task of choosing what is the sole or dominant character of a law in order to determine whether it comes within power; the failure of the Constitution to expressly define the powers exclusively reserved to the states; and also, last but not least, the practical problems which can arise if authority over a subject matter such as, for example, export was to be fragmented between the federal and state governments (*Actors and Announcers' Equity Association of Australia v Fontana Films Pty Ltd*, 190–4 per Stephen J.; Zines, 1987: 27–32; *Constitutional Commission: Advisory Committee on the Distribution of Powers—Issues paper* 1986, paras 11–13, 21–27).

The case of *Murphyores Incorporated Pty Ltd v The Commonwealth* was to mark the Court's adherence to this approach to characterisation with all members of the Court upholding the ability of the Commonwealth to use its powers to prohibit the export of mineral sands by reference to whether the mining of such minerals would have harmed the environment on Fraser Island. The Constitution does not of course grant the federal parliament any express power over the environment and its protection.

In the *Franklin Dam* case the Court upheld the validity of provisions which prohibited trading corporations from engaging in acts for the purpose of trading even though those acts may have had little or no relevance to the subject matter of the corporations power (other than the fact that the prohibitions actually applied to a trading corporation). As in the *Murphyores* case the prohibitions were concerned with questions of environmental protection. The *Franklin Dam* case would seem to mark the first application of the principles of characterisation which hitherto had been applied to powers defined by reference to activities in relation to a power that is defined by reference to particular legal institutions or bodies (the corporations described in section 51(xx)). The Court seemed to treat the doing of an act by a trading corporation, at least when it is done for the purposes of its trading activities, as coming within the subject matter of the corporations power. This suggests that the same approach will be taken in relation to trading activities undertaken by the same corporations.

It was suggested elsewhere by the writer that the decision in the *Franklin Dam* case gives rise to the strong possibility of the Court applying the principle in the *Herald and Weekly Times* case to the corporations power (Lindell, 1984: 226, 232). As indicated there, the possibility therefore now exists of the Commonwealth parliament prohibiting a trading corporation from carrying on

1 a trading activity, or
2 an act done for the purpose of enabling the corporation to carry on its trading activity

by reference to compliance with conditions which do not have to be relevant to the power. An example of such a law might be one which prohibited a trading corporation from selling its products unless it offered to its employees prescribed terms and conditions of employment. The potential significance of such a law is easy enough to grasp since it could provide a more direct and comprehensive means of controlling wages and conditions of employment than is at present available under the conciliation and arbitration power in section 51(xxxv).[1] As has been seen, the corporations power is now taken as being available as a source of direct power to control intrastate trading activities and acts done for the purpose of such activities, where section 51(xx) corporations are involved.

As a result, it now seems clear that the ability of the Commonwealth to ban the export of mineral sands by reference to whether the mining of such minerals would have harmed the environment on Fraser Island can be supplemented by its ability to ban the sale or the mining of the same minerals for sale within the state in which it was mined. In other words, the corporations power is available as long as the mining was for the purpose of sale and the body mining is a trading corporation.[2]

Principles of progressive interpretation and the relationship of powers to each other

Frequent reference is made to the fact that the Court is required to interpret 'a Constitution . . . [as] as instrument of government meant to endure and conferring powers expressed in general propositions wide enough to be capable of flexible application to changing circumstances' (*Australian National Airways Pty Ltd v The Commonwealth*, 81 per Dixon J.). The *Herald and Weekly Times* case concerned the power of the Commonwealth to control television in the exercise of the legislative power to make laws with respect to 'postal, telegraphic, telephonic, and other like services' under section 51(v). This power has been held to be wide enough to accommodate the control of radio and television even though those services may not have been foreseen at the time the Constitution was framed. (See as regards radio, *R v Brislan: ex parte Williams*, per Latham CJ., Starke, Rich, Evatt and McTiernan JJ.; Dixon J. dissenting; and television, *Jones v Commonwealth* [No.2]). The reason for this was foreshadowed many years ago when it was said:

> The meaning of the terms used in that instrument must be ascertained by their signification in 1900. The parliament cannot enlarge its powers by calling a matter with which it is not competent to deal by the name of something else which is within its competence. On the other hand, it must be remembered that with advancing civilisation new developments, now unthought of, may arise with respect to many subject matters. So long as those new developments relate to the same subject matter the powers of the parliament will continue to extend to them.[3]

This has obviated the necessity to amend section 51(v) so as to cover the control of radio and television as had been proposed by bodies appointed to review the Constitution. (See *Report of Royal Commission on the Constitution* (1929), 262 as regards radio broadcasting and *Report of the Joint Committee on Constitutional Review* (1959), para. 624, 86 as regards television.)

Associated with this approach was the willingness of the High Court to treat the reference to 'naval and military defence of the Commonwealth and the several states' in section 51(vi) of the Constitution as words of extension and not words of limitation. This opened the way for the enactment of laws to provide for all forms of defence including wide-ranging economic measures which may reasonably be thought to assist in the successful prosecution of a war during a period of military hostilities.[4]

The rejection of the reserved powers doctrine and the refusal of the Court to restrict the scope of the corporations power by reference to the failure of the commerce power to refer to intrastate trade and commerce illustrates the usual approach adopted by it in regard to the relationship of Commonwealth legislative powers to each other, i.e. that the powers are normally regarded as adding and supplementing each other and are not exhaustive of each other. A further example of this approach can be found in the ability of the Commonwealth to deal with industrial matters arising in the course of overseas and interstate trade under the commerce power without having to adhere to the limitations created by the conciliation and arbitration power. Another relates to the unwillingness of the Court to restrict the scope of the external affairs power in section 51(xxix) by reference to the power with respect to the 'relations of the Commonwealth with the islands of the Pacific' in section 51(xxx) even if this results in the section 51(xxx) power becoming largely redundant.[5]

The marriage and divorce powers: the failure of judicial techniques to accommodate social and other change?

At the turn of the century marriage was seen as the only socially acceptable family unit. By contrast the last two decades or so have witnessed dramatic changes in social attitudes and also medical technology which have had a serious impact on the composition of families. The question arises whether the record of the High Court in interpreting the scope of the legislative powers over marriage and divorce has proved adequate in the face of those changes. Has the Court indeed been consistent in its willingness to apply and use the judicial techniques to accommodate change?[6]

The effect of at least some of the recent family law cases decided by the High Court appears to demonstrate the application of one technique identified ealier for expanding the scope of federal legislative power. Thus in *Russell v Russell* the Court accepted that the divorce power in section 51(xxii) should not be used to restrict the scope of the marriage power in section 51(xxi). Previously the Court had decided that the section 51(xxi) power was not confined to defining the conditions governing the celebration of a valid marriage but extends to cover the mutual rights and duties flowing from the marriage relationship (the *Marriage Act* case. In *Russell's* case the Court accepted, admittedly by a narrow majority (the majority consisted of Stephen, Mason and McTiernan JJ.; Barwick CJ. and Gibbs J. dissenting), that the marriage power was available to deal with disputes about the maintenance and custody of children of a marriage in cases where the parents had not commenced proceedings in 'divorce' or 'matrimonial causes' against each other, i.e. independently of proceedings for annulment or dissolution of marriage. The contrary view was described by Mason J. as paying:

> . . . insufficient attention to the circumstance that it is a Constitution that we are construing and that the legislative powers that it confers should be construed liberally. There are substantial reasons for thinking that an individual grant of power under the Constitution should be accorded a full operation according to its terms, unrestricted by dubious implications drawn from the existence of another grant of legislative power touching an associated subject matter. There is no inherent reason for supposing that the legislative powers conferred by the Constitution are mutually exclusive; indeed, many instances may be given of overlapping operation. Yet the argument against validity in the present case not only denies this approach to construction but advances to a more extreme conclusion by subtracting from the content of the marriage power, not only what is contained within section 51(xxii), but the entire topic of enforcement of the rights, duties and obligations created in the exercise of the marriage power. (*Russell v Russell* 539.

Jacobs J. had occasion to remark: '[i]t is a fragile argument when the subject is the extent of constitutional power . . .', 550.)

Subsequently, an attempt to reopen the correctness of the view which prevailed in *Russell's* case was rejected even by the justices who dissented in that case essentially because of the undesirable results which would have flowed from the invalidation of custody orders made with respect to children following the Court's decision in *Russell's* case (*R v Lambert; ex parte Plummer* 451 per Barwick CJ., 455 per Gibbs J.). It was accepted in the *Lambert* case that the marriage power also enabled the Commonwealth to deal with disputes between the parties to a marriage as regards their duty to maintain each other and also over property matters directly referrable to the marriage relationship.

The judicial developments referred to were to provide the vehicle for testing the outer limits of the marriage and divorce powers in numerous cases decided by the High Court. In *Russell's* case Jacobs J. delivered a significant warning regarding the judicial interpretation of those powers:

> But because these subject matters enter so deeply into the field of personal and private rights, a field largely left within the legislative power of the states, it is difficult to resist the tendency in oneself to regard the Commonwealth power as an intrusion into an area solidly filled by state laws on a variety of subject matters which govern personal and private rights. The tendency to minimise the unique intrusion by a narrow characterisation of the subject matters so that as far as possible the framework of state laws governing personal and private rights is preserved must be resisted (*Russell v Russell*, 546–7).

It remains to be seen whether the warning was heeded.

Subsequently the Court was to make it clear that the parliament had the power to define the rights and obligations of the parties to a marriage with respect to the children of the marriage, not only as between themselves, but also as against third parties as well (*Dowal v Murray; R v Lambert; ex parte Plummer*; *Vitzdamm-Jones v Vitzdamm-Jones*; *In the Marriage of Cormick*, 176 per Gibbs CJ.; *V v V*, especially 232–3). However, this does not go as far as to authorise the Family Court to make a custody order which interferes with the custody or possession of a child of a marriage in respect of whom an order was made under state law placing the child under the guardianship, custody and control of a state authority (*R v Lambert; ex parte Plummer* per Barwick CJ., Gibbs, Aickin, and Wilson JJ.; Stephen, Mason and Murphy JJ. dissenting). This means that, to that extent at least, the parliament cannot define and enforce the rights and obligations of parties to a marriage in relation to the children of the marriage as against a third party, in this instance the state.

As is mentioned in the chapter written by Professor Zines. in *Gazzo v Comptroller of Stamps* (*Vic.*) (per Gibbs CJ., Stephen and Aickin JJ.; Mason and Murphy JJ. dissenting) the Court held invalid federal statutory provisions which purported to exempt from state stamp duty a transfer of land executed in accordance with an order made by the Family Court. The provisions were not regarded as a law on the subject matter of the marriage and divorce powers or as being reasonably incidental to the execution and furtherance of those powers.

Not surprisingly, questions have been raised regarding whether the developments mark a revival of the reserved powers doctrine. In his dissenting judgment in the *Gazzo* case Murphy J. said:

> The once-discredited doctrine of reserved powers of the states is having a triumphant, if unacknowledged, resurgence, at least in the areas of marriage and divorce . . . (*Gazzo*, 255. The writer is not clear in his mind as to whether the *Lambert* and *Gazzo* cases more accurately involve questions of intergovernmental immunity rather than the reserved powers of the states. However, it is not necessary to pursue this point here.)

Serious doubts have been raised about the correctness of the *Gazzo* case for other reasons apart from any alleged reliance placed on the reserved powers doctrine (Zines, 1983: 277, 280–2).

Some of the provisions of the Commonwealth *Family Law Act 1975* which were challenged in the *Russell* case did not survive the attack mounted against their validity. Other provisions of the same Act were found to be valid only after they were read down in order to ensure that they did not exceed the marriage and divorce powers. The reading-down process was still thought to have left open a considerable scope or potential for using those powers to support the enactment of new provisions. In 1983 the parliament amended the Family Law Act following the recommendations made by the Parliamentary Joint Select Committee on the Family Law Act to the effect that the Act should be:

> amended to the fullest extent possible within the jurisdictional limits of the powers of the Commonwealth to ensure that the Family Court has jurisdiction in all matters affecting custody, guardianship and access to a child. (Report of the Parliamentary Joint Select Committee on the Family Law Act, 1980: vol.1, 62. The amendments were effected by the enactment of the Commonwealth *Family Law Amendment Act 1983*.)

In a series of cases the Court adopted a view of Commonwealth power in this area which had the effect of negating the validity of a number of the 1983 provisions (*Cormick* case: *R v Cook: ex parte C*; *Re F: ex parte F*; and see generally Jessep and Chisholm, 1985: 152). The cases also had the effect, it has been said, of negating the validity of provisions which had been included in the *Matrimonial Causes Act 1959* but which were not challenged during the life of that Act (1959–75). The provisions purported to bring within federal jurisdiction a wide class of children provided that the children were at the relevant time members of the household of a husband and wife (Jessep and Chisholm, 1985: 153).

The Court held invalid *In the Marriage of Cormick*, the provisions of section 5(1)(f) of the *Family Law Act 1975*, as amended, which purported to deem 'a child . . . who . . . was at the relevant time, treated by the husband and wife as a child of their family, if, at the relevant time, the child was ordinarily a member of the household of the husband and wife' to be a child of the marriage. The provision could not be justified as a law with respect to marriage under section 51(xxi) since it purported to treat as children of the marriage children who were not the natural, legitimate or adopted children of the marriage. Accordingly, it was not possible to vest the Family Court with jurisdiction to deal with a dispute between a mother and her daughter concerning the custody of the daughter's ex-nuptial child even though the child had lived most of its life with the mother and her husband (who was not related to the daughter). The mother (who was the grandmother of the child) claimed that she had reared the child with her husband as if the child was one of her own children.

In *R v Cook; ex parte C* the Court held invalid the provisions of section 5(1)(e)(i) of the *Family Law Act 1975*. Those provisions stated that:

> for the purposes of each application of this Act in relation to a marriage—(e) a child of either the husband or the wife, including—(i) an ex-nuptial child of either of them . . . if, at the relevant time, the child was ordinarily a member of the household of the husband and wife . . . shall be deemed to be a child of the marriage.

These provisions could also not be justified as a law with respect to marriage under section 51(xxi). Accordingly, it was not possible to rely on them as a means of authorising the Family Court to deal with a dispute between a married couple and a third party over the custody of an ex-nuptial child of one spouse born before the marriage and living in the marital household. In this particular case the dispute was between a married couple (Mr and Mrs T) over the custody of the child of their daughter (Mrs C). The daughter (Mrs C) was married (to Mr C) but the child in question was born before the marriage and Mr C was not the father. Since her mother's marriage (i.e. Mrs C's), the child had lived with Mr and Mrs C, but the child subsequently ran away from home to live with her grandparents (Mr and Mrs T). The relevant provisions were seen as attempting to deal with the rights of the parties to a marriage with respect to the custody of ex-nuptial children as against strangers to the marriage (or vice versa). Because of the ex-nuptial status of the children, the rights in question were not seen as arising from or having a sufficient connection with the marriage relationship.

Shortly afterwards the invalidity of the provisions of section 5(1)(e)(i) was reaffirmed in *Re F; ex parte F* in a case involving a dispute between a husband and wife over the custody of a child born to the wife as a result of an extra-marital relationship. The majority judges in this case rejected, even if only implicitly, the possibility of reading down those provisions so that they could validly apply to circumstances of this kind despite the common law presumption in favour of the legitimacy of children born during the subsistence of a marriage. This was the view taken by the dissentients.

Two factors combine to explain the analytical legal grounds used to support the conclusions reached in those cases. First, the absence of a sufficient connection between the subject matter of the marriage power, namely, 'marriage' and the ex-nuptial status of the children involved. Thus, for example, in the view of Brennan J.:

> the rights and duties of husband and wife in respect of children who do not enjoy the status of children of their marriage—whether by birth, by legitimation or by adoption—are not, in my opinion, amenable to regulation by a law for which the marriage power alone provides support (*Cormick* case. 183).

The difficulty of bringing within the marriage power ex-nuptial children is then that as their very name indicates the truth of the situation (is) that the child is outside the marriage relationship (*R v Cook; ex parte C*, 253 per Gibbs CJ.).

The second factor lies in the acknowledged inability of the parliament to recite itself into power by deeming certain matters to come within the subject matter of Commonwealth legislative power—in this case deeming children to be children of a marriage when they otherwise lack the necessary or sufficient connection with a marriage relationship.

Nevertheless, the fact that these cases were not the result of a unanimous view reached by all members of the Court is probably sufficient in itself to indicate that the conclusions reached were not inevitable. In the view of the writer there is much to be said in favour of the view expressed by Murphy J. in the *Cormick* case when he upheld the validity of section 5(1)(f) of the *Family Law Act 1975*. In his view:

> Parliament correctly considered that its legislative power with respect to marriage extended to the protection of all children who became part of the family which arose from the marriage . . . This reflects the realities of our society, that such a family often includes children who are not strictly born of the marriage, but are absorbed into it. (*Cormick* case, 180. See also the remarks of Mason and Deane JJ. in their dissenting judgments in *Re F; ex parte F*, 600.)

Even so, however, the approach of Murphy J. would probably not bring within Commonwealth power the adjudication of disputes between persons who are not and never have been married when the children whose custody is in issue are not children of any marriage. (As to which, see *Cormick* case, 176 per Gibbs J. See also Blackshield, 1986: 244 where it is stated that the view expressed by Murphy J. would only 'ameliorate' the 'appalling jurisdictional tangle' which exists at present where in one household disputes over some children may come under Commonwealth law while disputes over others come under state law).

The result of judicial review in this area has been to draw a sharp distinction between the Commonwealth's powers over children of a marriage and children born outside the marriage relationship. A similar distinction flows in regard to the Commonwealth's powers over maintenance and property disputes between partners in a marriage relationship and partners who are not married. This has led, not only to the separate application of Commonwealth and state laws on those matters, but also to the adjudication of disputes in separate Commonwealth and state courts. It requires little evidence to show that social developments have rendered such constitutional divisions of power and jurisdiction somewhat unreal, inconvenient and unfitted to present conditions. It is true that jurisdictional problems can to an extent be overcome by vesting state courts with jurisdiction over all family law matters including those matters arising under federal law, but this will not overcome differences in the law to be applied to those matters. There is no assurance that the relevant state laws can become uniform either with those of the other states or with those of the Commonwealth. In essence the law governing a family dispute will turn on whether the family is based on marriage or some other relationship which is now found to be socially acceptable. Only the family based on marriage appears to come within the Commonwealth's legislative power over marriage.

The constitutional distinctions discussed may also prove to be inadequate in the face of modern medical technological developments especially in view of the absence of any general Commonwealth power to determine who, in law, will be recognised as a child's parents. The *Family Law Act 1975* contains provisions which purport to bring within its scope children born to a married woman as a result of medical procedures which involve the use of donor sperm. (See sections 5(1)(c), 5(1)(d) and 5A, inserted in the Act by the *Family Law Amendment Act* 1983.) However, the validity of these provisions can be doubted insofar as they deem a child to be the child of a marriage notwithstanding that the husband is not the biological father. (See Jessep and Chisholm, 1985: 169. See also generally Constitutional Commission: Distribution of Powers *Issues Paper*, 1986: para. 69, 29–30.)

At the political level recommendations have been made over a number of years to increase Commonwealth powers in the family law area. The Australian Constitutional Conventions held in 1975 and 1976 recommended that the Commonwealth should be given power over 'illegitimacy', 'adoption' and 'maintenance (other than in divorce proceedings)'. (Australian Constitutional Convention, Proceedings, Melbourne 1975, 172 (Resolution 8); Hobart 1976: 203–4 (Resolution 4). The Commonwealth Parliamentary Joint Select Committee on the Family Law Act in 1980 (16–17, 23–4) recommended, among other things, that the states should, as a matter of urgency, refer power to the Commonwealth over the custody, guardianship and maintenance of ex-nuptial children and legitimate children of a previous marriage. The constitutional aspects of family law were widely debated without any recommendations being made at the meetings of the Australian Constitutional Convention held in Adelaide (1983) and Brisbane (1985). (Australian Constitutional Convention, Proceedings, Adelaide 1983, vol. 1, 207–22; Brisbane 1985, vol. 1, 170–205, debate not confined to family law.)

After a period of negotiations which lasted for ten years agreement was reached between four states and the Commonwealth under which the states concerned referred to the Commonwealth legislative power over:

1 the maintenance of children and the payment of expenses in relation to children or child rearing; and

2 the custody and guardianship of, and access to, children.

The referral of power does not cover children who are under the custody, guardianship, care or control of the state. (In other words the four states will retain their welfare or protective jurisdiction in relation to children in need of care.) (See *Commonwealth Powers (Family Law—Children) Act 1986* (NSW); *Commonwealth Powers (Family Law) Act 1986* (SA); *Commonwealth Powers (Family Law) Act 1987* (Tas.); *Commonwealth Powers (Family Law—Children) Act 1986 (Vic.).)*

The reference of power also does not include a reference of power over adoption, the determination of the parentage of children created with the help of modern medical technology or disputes between parties to a de facto relationship over financial and property matters. Nor is the reference going to be effective in the two remaining states which have not been prepared to refer powers to the Commonwealth. (Those states are Queensland and Western Australia. In Western Australia a state court is empowered to exercise federal jurisdiction over family law matters governed by federal law.) This shifts the focus of attention back to the judicial response to the problems in this area.

It is true that there are as yet unresolved doubts about whether the marriage power will support the enactment of laws dealing with disputes:

1 in relation to 'de facto adopted children' (as being 'children of a marriage' of the adopting married parents) (see, for example, *R v Cook; ex parte C*, 255 Gibbs CJ., 255–6 per Mason J. See also *Cormick* case, 177 per Gibbs CJ.); and

2 as between married persons, as among themselves, regarding children who are not children of the marriage (*Cormick* case, 176 per Gibbs CJ., and also *Re F; ex parte F*, 596 per Gibbs CJ.).

There is, however, no assurance that such disputes will be held to come within the marriage power. (Some members of the present Court have either already taken the view, or adopted reasoning which suggests they will take the view, that Commonwealth power does not cover those disputes : see, for example, *Re F; ex parte F*, 603–4 per Brennan J., 606–7 per Dawson J. and *R v Cook; ex parte C*, 256–7 per Wilson J. As to the 'de facto adopted' child possibility, see Jessep and Chisholm, 1985: 172.) Even if such disputes do come within the marriage power the possibility referred to in para. 2 does not cover disputes between the married partners, on the one hand, and strangers to the marriage, on the other, as regards the custody of children who are not children of the marriage (*Cormick* case, 176 per Gibbs CJ.). This problem also exists as regards the availability of the divorce power even if the Court is prepared to construe the reference to 'parental rights, and the custody and guardianship of infants' as covering the same kind of children in 'divorce and matrimonial causes' proceedings—an issue which is also unresolved at the present time. (See *Re F; ex parte F*, 597 per Gibbs CJ. who indicated that his 'present opinion' was that the word 'infant' in the concluding part of section 51(xxii) did 'not refer to children other than those who are children of the marriage'. Wilson, Brennan and Deane JJ. were more definite in their acceptance of that view: at 602, 605, 607–8.)

It can be argued that even if reliance on the reserved powers doctrine was avoided, the Commonwealth's powers over marriage and divorce are by their very nature incapable of accommodating the social and other changes which have occurred since the Constitution was framed. The provisions of section 51(xxi) in particular do not refer to the concept of a family or of marriage as an example of a family unit, although arguably this may have been implicit or assumed by the framers of the Constitution. Accordingly it is not, on balance, possible to interpret the provisions referring to marriage as words of extension rather than restriction or limitation, i.e. as only a form of family known in 1900. Marriage remains as the essential subject matter of the power so that it cannot be treated as the mere denotation or illustration of the wider concept of a family.

Not without some hesitation, the writer has formed the view that the argument advanced above is soundly based. If that view is correct it will mean that if constitutional change is to come about it will have to take place by a formal amendment of the Constitution approved by the voters at a referendum or by a reference of powers. What form such an amendment or reference of powers should take and how far it should extend in transferring power to the Commonwealth are, however, difficult issues which lie beyond the scope of this chapter.

The effect of judical review on the composition and functioning of the federal parliament

The double dissolution of the Commonwealth parliament in 1974 and other events which occurred during the life of the Whitlam Labor government provided the occasion for testing the scope of judicial review in relation to a number of matters affecting the composition and operation of the Commonwealth parliament.

On the one hand the Court affirmed, by what was to prove only a narrow majority, the justiciability of questions concerning compliance with the provisions in the Constitution which deal with the resolution of deadlocks between the House of Representatives and the Senate over the enactment of ordinary legislation (section 57). The scope of judicial review in this area was however confined to the question of compliance with section 57 for the purpose of determining the validity of laws enacted without the assent of the Senate at a joint sitting of the parliament. The ability of the Court to consider the question of compliance with section 57 for the purpose of determining the validity of a double dissolution of the parliament was denied even though the double dissolution forms an essential step in the enactment of proposed laws at a joint sitting of both Houses.[7]

On the other hand, however, the Court's adherence to a literal approach seemed to play a significant role in giving section 57 an interpretation which may minimise the scope of judicial review in regard to that section. The literal approach referred to here is one which eschews the drawing of implications. This can be seen in the cases in which the Court affirmed that:

1 the third paragraph of section 57 did not limit the number of proposed laws which could be enacted at a joint sitting, with the section being read distributively to apply to each proposed law which otherwise satisfies the conditions prescribed by section 57 (*Cormack v Cope*);

2 the absence of a need to establish a temporal connection in time between the occurrence of the conditions which give rise to the power to dissolve and the actual exercise of the same power; (*First Territory Representation* case, Barwick CJ. was the only member of the Court to accept such a connection but he thought it was satisfied in this case. All other justices rejected the connection);

3 the power to dissolve is not confined to disagreements between the Senate and the House of Representatives in relation to vital legislative measures or measures that are likely to bring parliamentary or government business to a halt;[8]

4 the three-month interval referred to in the first paragraph of section 57 commences from the date of the Senate's rejection or failure to pass a proposed law passed by the House of Representatives (*Petroleum and Minerals Authority* case, per Barwick CJ., Stephen, Gibbs and Mason JJ.; Jacobs J. dissenting); and

5 the prorogation of the session of parliament during which the conditions of a double dissolution occurred does not put an end to the power of the Governor-General to dissolve both Houses (*First Territory Representatives* case).

In a number of these cases the attempt to persuade the Court to interpret section 57 as requiring compliance with requirements which were not stated on the face of the section was based on the threat which would otherwise arise as a result of the 'wholesale impairment of the legislature's bicameral character'. Thus the rejection of the restrictions referred to in 1 and 2 could be seen as opening the way to the use of the double dissolution process as a means of building a storehouse or stockpile of bills which could be enacted without the assent of the Senate. The Court's rejection of those restrictions can probably be justified on other grounds apart from the reliance placed on purely literal considerations—in particular, the difficulty of interpreting and applying them to concrete cases.

Associated with the matters referred to is the failure of the Court to read down the provisions of section 122 of the Constitution in such a way as to deprive the Commonwealth parliament of the power to create senators with full voting rights to represent the Territories. (*First Territory Representation* case per McTiernan, Mason, Jacobs and Murphy JJ.; Barwick CJ., Gibbs and Stephen JJ. dissenting. See also *Second Territories Representation* case per Gibbs, Stephen, Mason, Jacobs and Murphy JJ.; Barwick CJ. and Aickin J. dissenting where the Court reaffirmed the earlier decision and also upheld territory representation in the House of Representatives with full voting rights.) The legislation providing for the creation of such senators was one of the six legislative measures enacted without the Senate's assent in the joint sitting of the parliament held in 1974. The power to pass the legislation was justified by reference to the power of the parliament to 'allow the representation of such territory in either house of the parliament to the extent and on the terms which it thinks fit'.

The contrary view was based on an apparent conflict between the provisions of section 122 quoted earlier and section 7 of the Constitution, and also the federal nature of the Constitution. A further illustration of the Court's reliance on literal considerations can be seen in the remarks of a majority of the justices in the *Petroleum and Minerals Authority* case which affirm the power of the Senate to reject money bills especially having regard to the provisions of section 53 which state: 'Except as provided in this section, the Senate shall have equal power with the House of Representatives in respect of all proposed laws'. The restrictions contained in the preceding provisions of section 53 are confined to the initiation and amendment of money bills by the Senate. (*Petroleum and Minerals Authority* case, 121 per Barwick CJ., 143 per Gibbs J., 168 per Stephen J., 185 per Mason J.)

The one aspect of section 57 which did not lend itself to determination by reference to purely literal considerations concerned the difficult question of interpreting the meaning of a 'failure to pass' a proposed law by the Senate. On one approach the phrase could simply mean that the Senate *did not pass* a proposed law. (This view was adopted by Jacobs J in *Petroleum and Minerals Authority* case, 192–8. It has considerable attractions in view of the difficulties involved in applying the view accepted by the majority.) While this approach would avoid a good deal of uncertainty it does have the consequence that the Senate would fail to pass a proposed law almost immediately after it receives the law from the House of Representatives. A majority of the Court preferred to interpret the phrase as meaning in effect that the Senate does not pass a proposed law *until after the expiration of a reasonable time* has been allowed for the consideration of the law by the Senate. (*Petroleum and Minerals Authority* case, 122 per Barwick CJ., 148 per Gibbs J., 171 per Stephen J. and 186 per Mason J.) This view was preferred despite obvious difficulties that could be encountered in the future in determining what constitutes 'reasonable time' in this context. The importance of the position of the Senate in the Australian bicameral parliamentary system and the fixed nature of the terms of office enjoyed by its members were undoubtedly important factors which either did or would have influenced the majority in rejecting the first of the two interpretations referred to above.

The literalism inherent in the Court's approach on matters affecting the composition of the parliament is also illustrated by what was decided in *Attorney-General for the Commonwealth (Ex rel. McKinlay) v The Commonwealth*. On the one hand the Court, with only one dissentient, refused to imply from the provisions of paragraph 1 in section 24 a constitutional obligation that electoral divisions for the House of Representatives should be equal in size as had occurred with very similar provisions in the United States Constitution. (Although some limits on the disparity of electoral divisions were recognised by Stephen, Mason, McTiernan and Jacobs JJ.: see Hanks, 1977: 169–77 and also 205–7. The dissentient was Murphy J.) On the other hand, however, the Court did decide that certain long-standing provisions in the Commonwealth *Representation Act 1905* were invalid because they failed to comply with the express requirements created by paragraph 2 of section 24. (Sections 3,4 and 12(a). Section 24 of the Constitution states :

> **24** The House of Representatives shall be composed of members directly chosen by the people of the Commonwealth, and the number of such members shall be, as nearly as practicable, twice the number of the senators.
>
> The number of members chosen in the several states shall be in proportion to the respective numbers of their people, and shall, until the Parliament otherwise provides, be determined, whenever necessary, in the following manner:
>
> (i) A quota shall be ascertained by dividing the number of the people of the Commonwealth, as shown by the latest statistics of the Commonwealth, by twice the number of the senators:

(ii) The number of members to be chosen in each state shall be determined by dividing the number of the people of the state, as shown by the latest statistics of the Commonwealth, by the quota; and if on such division there is a remainder greater than one-half of the quota, one more member shall be chosen in the state.

But notwithstanding anything in the section, five members at least shall be chosen in each original state.)

This requires that the number of members of the House of Representatives chosen in the several states shall be in proportion to the respective numbers of the people in those states, i.e. the proportionate representation of states requirement. According to a majority of the Court section 24 requires that the number of members to be chosen from each state should be determined and given effect to in time for each ordinary general election of the House of Representatives. An alternative and less stringent view accepted by two members of the Court was that fresh determinations need only be made every five years, thus allowing a determination to operate during the life of two instead of one House of Representatives (Assuming those Houses run for their normal terms envisaged by section 28 of the Constitution. Those members were McTiernan and Jacobs JJ.: see *McKinlay's* case, 40–1.) It remains to be seen whether the majority view proves to be too stringent given the consequential need for electoral redistributions to take place once the number of members chosen from a state is altered to comply with the proportionate representation of states requirement.

It has been said that the requirement is a 'curious one' and that it arises 'from the use of states, even in the so-called "national" or popular lower chamber, as forms of electoral unit, a use which reflects the essentially federal nature of the Constitution' (*Attorney-General* (*New South Wales*) *Ex.rel.McKellar v The Commonwealth*, 552 per Stephen J.). It is, in any event, this requirement which has been applied and enforced by the Court leading to important changes being made to the Commonwealth's electoral legislation.[9] Ironically, the same requirement has not received the same attention of the United States Supreme Court which has been preoccupied with the implied guarantee of one person one vote—a guarantee which only one member of the High Court would have been prepared to imply from the Australian Constitution based partly on the 'democratic theme' said to be seen as pervading that document. (*McKinlay's* case, 71 per Murphy J. Among other things he also relied on the prohibition against multiple voting in section 30 of the Constitution: 72.)

To an Australian lawyer schooled in the traditions of British 'principles' of statutory interpretation there should be little cause for surprise in the Court's reliance on a literal approach to constitutional interpretation. As the choices facing the Court in the *First Territory Representation* case show, however, this does not mean that a literal approach will solve many of the problems that come before the Court. Nevertheless, the writer believes it is still a significant feature of the Court's approach to constitutional interpretation. In that sense there is an element of continuity evident in the Court's approach to the interpretation of the provisions governing the operation and composition of the federal parliament. What is new, by contrast, is the fact that the Court found itself having to deal with provisions of that nature thus increasing the scope of its role in regard to the structure and functioning of the parliamentary and electoral processes.

Some time ago the writer had occasion to foreshadow that the consequences of judicial review in these areas are more fundamental and different to the judicial review of ordinary legislation passed by the parliament. They involve the potential for a court to review the legal existence of that body. While it may be one thing to find that an Act is invalid, it is quite another to find that there is no parliament in existence to pass any Acts at all if, for example, it is alleged that the composition of the parliament does not comply with the requirements of section 24 (Lindell, 1974: 89–90, 99, 104–5).

It would also be quite different and much more far-reaching for a court to entertain a dispute about which parliament was in existence following a double dissolution and the election of a new parliament where it was alleged that the double dissolution was invalid for a failure to comply with section 57. The Court has avoided such results by asserting its authority to review:

1 the validity of legislation passed at a joint sitting under section 57, but not the validity of the dissolution even though the failure to comply with the provisions dealing with the dissolution would invalidate the same legislation (as indicated on page 158 and in endnote 7); and
2 compliance with the proportionate representation of states requirement under section 24, but without accepting that the effect of such non-compliance would be to invalidate elections and the consequent membership of the House of Representatives if the elections were held for the House when its composition failed to satisfy section 24 (*McKinlay's* case 34–5 per Barwick C.J., 50, 53 per Gibbs J., 60 per Stephen J., 63 per Mason J.).

The reasoning used by the Court to arrive at those conclusions has not escaped criticism (Zines, 1977b: 230–3). They are conclusions which are doubtless reached on pragmatic grounds based on the necessity to avoid constitutional uncertainty and confusion arising out of the existence and non-existence of a legislative body.

Something should now be said about the effect of the changes that have occurred to the composition and functioning of the federal parliament. To a lawyer, at least, it is difficult to see that the inclusion of territorial senators has had any major impact on the working of the Senate. Neither has there been any move to 'swamp' that body with territory senators as could potentially occur given the Court's view of section 122. The potential referred to has, however, been thought to be great enough to warrant recommendations for altering the Constitution.[10]

There have now been six double dissolutions of the parliaments—with the last four having occurred in 1974, 1975, 1983 and 1987. This suggests that the double dissolution is becoming a much regular means of holding elections than was the case for the first seventy years of federation. As is illustrated by what occurred in 1975 (and possibly, also, 1974), its use as an option for seeking early elections is not confined to governments but can be exploited by political opposition parties as well when they control the Senate.

Clearly the deadlocks which occurred between the Senate and the House of Representatives over the enactment of twenty-one bills and which gave rise to the double dissolution in 1975 were merely used as a vehicle for resolving a much more important conflict. That was, of course, the failure of the Senate to pass supply even though that particular deadlock did not itself come within section 57. Moreover, the Fraser opposition which advised the granting of the dissolution had no intention of seeking the enactment of the twenty-one bills at a joint sitting. Arguably the deadlock which gave rise to the double dissolution in 1983 was also used only as a vehicle to bring about elections for reasons not strictly connected with the deadlock. The Fraser opposition did not seem to press the legislation rejected by the Senate as a campaign issue.

To what extent can the recent flurry of double dissolutions be laid at the door of the High Court? The series of High Court cases on section 57 and the resulting interpretation given to that section have, at most, *not obstructed* the increasing use made of the double dissolution option. This is so, particularly as regards the failure of the Court to imply requirements additional to those expressly provided for on the face of section 57, for example, the need to show that the disagreement between both Houses continues to exist and has not become stale.

One question that the High Court may not have resolved is whether it is legally permissible to rely on disagreements between both Houses over the enactment of legislation as grounds for a double dissolution even if the purpose of invoking that option is extraneous to the disagreement over the same legislation. This issue arose in regard to the legality of the 1975 double dissolution (Zines, 1977b: 236–7 and compare P. Bayne's commentary at 246–50) and might possibly have been raised even in relation to the 1914 double dissolution (Sawer, 1956: 121–4, especially on page 123 where reference is made to the suggestion that the exercise of the power might have constituted a 'fraud on the power'). It may now be more difficult for the High Court to assert that such a purpose cannot be made the subject of judicial review where the validity of a law passed at a joint sitting is in issue. Modern developments now suggest that the good faith of the Governor-General can be judicially reviewed in relation to *statutory* powers exercised by the same person (*R v Toohey : ex parte Northern Land Council; FAI Insurance Ltd v Winneke; South Australia v O'Shea*; see also *CCSU v Minister for Civil Service* as regards *prerogative* powers). Those developments probably mean that reliance can no longer be placed on earlier authority to the effect that the principles which govern the exercise of 'discretionary powers confided to subordinate administrative officers or bodies' are not applicable to those of a vice-regal representative (Zines, 1977b: 237 n. 88).

However, the modern developments probably only mean that merely because a power is vested in a Governor-General it will not for that reason alone operate to immunise that officer from judicial review. Even if the modern developments are applied to *constitutional* powers there may still be some powers (and *prerogatives*) which do not lend themselves to judicial review. As was said recently by Lord Roskil in *CCSU v Minister for Civil Service* (at 418):

> But I do not think that that right of challenge can be unqualified. It must, I think, depend upon the subject matter of the prerogative power which is exercised. Many examples were given during the argument of prerogative powers which as at present advised I do not think could properly be made the subject of judicial review. Prerogative powers such as those relating to the making of treaties, the defence of the realm, the prerogative of mercy, the grant of honours, the dissolution of parliament and the appointment of ministers as well as others are not, I think, susceptible to judicial review because their nature and subject matter are such as not to be amenable to the judicial process. The courts are not the place wherein to determine whether a treaty should be concluded or the armed forces disposed in a particular manner or parliament dissolved on one date rather than another. (See also the remarks of Mason J. in *R v Toohey; ex parte Northern Land Council* 220–1 and compare in relation to treaties *Minister for Arts, Heritage and Environment v Peko Wallsend Ltd*)

The difficulty of the Court being required to ascertain the existence of the extraneous purpose not apparent on the face of the documents used to dissolve the parliament should not be underestimated. The writer therefore continues to believe that the Court will not insist that as a matter of law the power to dissolve must only be used for the purpose of resolving the deadlock which attracts the operation of section 57.

If the use of the double dissolution power has become more common in recent times, the same can hardly be said of joint sittings to enact laws without the assent of the Senate. Only six laws have ever been passed in this fashion and of course one of those was declared invalid because the conditions of section 57 were not met in relation to that law. Obviously the enactment of a law without the approval of the Senate forms an important exception to the bicameral system of parliament but at the moment its main significance lies in its potential use in the future rather than the actual use made of it in the past. The possibility of a government lacking a majority in the Senate storing a stockpile of rejected bills will no doubt be important in that regard. Furthermore, the timing of the double dissolution (1987) may have set an example for the future since it illustrates how a government may still be able to ensure the availability of the joint sitting procedure if it is prepared to cut short its maximum term of office by a little more than six months.

Nevertheless, it needs to be recalled that this still remains a somewhat cumbersome way of enacting legislation.[11] The developments which transpired over the proposed legislation for the establishment of an identity card underline the point. The rejection of the legislation by the Senate provided the grounds for the double dissolution which took place in 1987 ('The Sixth Double Dissolution, June 1987' (1987), 61 ALJ 677; *Hansard (House of Representatives), 27 May 1987*: 3431). After the double dissolution the federal government was forced to abandon its proposal to have the legislation enacted without the approval of the Senate and at a joint sitting of both Houses when it was found that the Senate could have disallowed regulations required to bring the legislation into operation (*Hansard (House of Representatives), 6 October 1987*: 749 and see also *Hansard (Senate), 23 September 1987*: 565 and 566–7). An alternative method of bringing the legislation into operation without the co-operation of the Senate would probably have involved the enactment of new legislation with the possibility of having to recommence the lengthy procedures prescribed by section 57 if the Senate continued to oppose the passage of the legislation.

The High Court and the development of a dual system of federal and state courts

The High Court

Two developments during the period under review have helped to strengthen the role of the High Court as a constitutional court and a final national court of appeal in all cases decided in Australia. The enactment of the Commonwealth *Australia Act 1986* was to see the final step taken to abolish all appeals to the Privy Council (Section 11. See also the UK *Australia Act 1986*, s. 11). Appeals from the High Court to the Privy Council were abolished as a result of Commonwealth legislation enacted in 1968 and 1975 (*Privy Council (Limitation of Appeals) Act 1968*; *Privy Council (Appeals from the High Court) Act 1975)*. Secondly, the ability of the High Court to concentrate on questions of law of general importance in the exercise of its appellate jurisdication was facilitated by the abolition of appeals lying as of right and replacing these with appeals only lying by the grant of special leave—a measure eagerly sought by the justices of the Court but opposed by the legal profession (*Judiciary Amendment Act (No. 2) 1984*; *Federal Court of Australia Act 1984*).

A number of significant developments also took place in relation to the appointment and tenure of High Court (and Federal Court) justices. As a result of a referendum held in 1977 the life tenure of federal justices (a requirement which was once described as a 'self-regarding act of judicial legislation') was removed and replaced with tenure expiring on the attainment of seventy years of age in the case of High Court justices and an age fixed by parliament not exceeding the same age in the case of other federal court judges. (See section 72 as amended by the *Constitution Alteration (Retirement of Judges) Act* 1977. With the elevation of Sir Anthony Mason as Chief Justice of the High Court all current members of the Court are subject to the new tenure provisions.

The constitutional provisions governing the appointment of High Court justices vest their appointment in the hand of the federal government without enabling the states to participate in that process. As a result of growing criticism voiced by state politicians at the meetings of the Australian Constitutional Convention, the Commonwealth parliament was persuaded in 1979 to enact provisions which require the Attorney-General of the Commonwealth to consult with the Attorneys-General of the states in relation to High Court appointments (*High Court of Australia Act 1979*, s. 6). The procedure was applied to each of the current members of the Court. There is evidence, however, that not all of the states are happy with the present procedure (see generally, Australian Constitutional Convention, Judicature Sub-Committee: *Second Report to Standing Committee*, May 1985: ch. 3 and Appendices B–D; Australian Constitutional Convention: *Proceedings, Brisbane 1985*, vol. 1: 170–205 [discussion of agenda item no. 5 which, however, was not confined to the issue discussed in the text]). The dissatisfaction was either because of the level of consultations presently conducted by the Commonwealth[12] or more fundamentally because of the belief that the states should have a greater role in the appointment of members to a body which determines disputes between the states and the Commonwealth—a role which should therefore receive constitutional recognition by some kind of a state veto. That argument gains some support from the fact that judicial appointments in other comparable federal systems are said to allow, in varying degrees, state or provincial influence on judicial appointments. (Australian Constitutional Convention, Judicature Sub-Committee Report, 1985, Appendix C, especially paras 9, 19 and Appendix D. A proposal of this kind was defeated at the Brisbane meeting of the Australian Constitutional Convention in 1985: see *Proceedings*, Brisbane 1985, vol. 1, 178–80, 205). For its part the Commonwealth government has resisted further change because the adoption of a veto could lead to the appointment of lesser qualified candidates with the claims of those best qualified for appointment being 'submerged by the demands of the lowest common denominator'; and also because it could result 'in an open public and political debate about the merits of a particular person'. (Australian Constitutional Convention, Judicature Sub-Committee Report, 1985, Appendix B, especially paras 14–15. It appears that the consultations under the present position take the form of private discussions: see Appendix C, para. 5.)

The unhappy events surrounding the allegations of misconduct against Murphy J. brought to light the nature of the process created by the Constitution for removing a member of the Court on grounds of 'proved misbehaviour or incapacity'. The incident exposed a number of uncertain aspects of that process which were left unresolved by the death of the judge as a result of a terminal illness. These will no doubt require attention in the future. On a happier note, 1986 saw the appointment of the High Court's first female member, Justice Mary Gaudron, a former New South Wales Solicitor-General.

Federal and state courts—a dual system of courts

Section 71 of the Constitution contemplates that the judicial power of the Commonwealth will be exercised by the High Court, federal courts created by the Commonwealth parliament and in such other courts as the parliament invests with federal jurisdiction. ('Federal jurisdiction' is taken to mean the 'matters' referred to in sections 75 and 76 of the Constitution as falling within the original jurisdiction of the High Court.) For much of the time since federation and with only a few small exceptions, the Commonwealth parliament has made very ample use of the 'autochthonous expedient', namely, its power to vest state courts with federal jurisdiction under section 77 (iii) of the Constitution (Cowen and Zines, 1978: 174; see also Commonwealth *Judiciary Act 1903*, s. 39). The main advantage of following such a course is that it avoids the creation of new courts and the risk of litigants having to commence actions in different courts in order to resolve their legal disputes.

The period under study was to witness the creation of two new federal courts, the Family Court of Australia in 1975 and the Federal Court of Australia in 1977. Those courts were vested with jurisdiction to deal with 'matters' arising under laws made by parliament pursuant to the power of the parliament to define the jurisdiction of any federal court other than the High Court under sections 76(ii) and 77(i) of the Constitution. In both cases the jurisdiction vested in those courts was made exclusive of other courts pursuant to section 77(ii). The power to create a federal court is taken to be implied from section 71.

The relevant provisions of sections 71, 76(ii), 77(i) and 77(ii) of the Constitution state:

> **71** The judicial power of the Commonwealth shall be vested in a Federal Supreme Court, to be called the High Court of Australia, and in such other

federal courts as the Parliament creates, and in such other courts as it invests with federal jurisdiction . . .

76 The Parliament may make laws conferring original jurisdiction on the High Court in any matter . . .

(**ii**) Arising under any laws made by the Parliament . . .

77 With respect to any of the matters mentioned in the last two sections the Parliament may make laws—

(**i**) Defining the jurisdiction of any federal court other than the High Court:

(**ii**) Defining the extent to which the jurisdiction of any federal court shall be exclusive of that which belongs to or is invested in the courts of the states . . .

The advantages usually cited in favour of creating federal courts with exclusive jurisdiction are the hope of achieving uniformity of interpretation more particularly in a specialised area of law and also the desire to adopt specialised procedures, for example, the degree of informality which should regulate proceedings in the family law area.

Reference has already been made to developments which have had the effect of expanding the perceived scope of the federal legislative power with respect to corporations and family law. In the case of section 51(xx), it has led not only to the valid enactment of monopolies and restrictive trade practices law, but also a whole range of provisions designed to deal with other unfair trade practices, especially as they affect the field of consumer protection. Thus section 52(1) of the Commonwealth *Trade Practices Act 1974* provides: 'A corporation shall not, in trade or commerce, engage in conduct that is misleading or deceptive or is likely to mislead or deceive.' (See also generally Part V, Divisions 1, 1A.)

The establishment of the two courts with exclusive jurisdication marks an expansion of federal judicial powers to complement the expansion of federal legislative powers.

It is widely acknowledged that within a comparatively short space of time the Federal Court has acquired a high reputation which in turn has helped to attract a highly significant and lucrative share of commercial litigation. (See, for example, Australian Constitutional Convention, Judicature Sub-Committee *Report on an Integrated System of Courts* Oct. 1984, para. 2.14: *Hansard (House of Representatives)*, 17 March 1987: 915.) Three members of the present High Court were elevated from the Federal Court (Brennan, Deane and Toohey JJ.). Perhaps one of the reasons why the Federal Court has had a great attraction for litigants (especially in the commercial law area) has been the shorter time required to bring a matter to trial than is the case with state supreme courts. Ultimately, however, such an advantage may diminish once the work of the Federal Court increases (Australian Constitutional Convention, *Proceedings*, Brisbane 1985, vol. 1, 155). On the other hand, it cannot be said that the working of the Family Court has enjoyed the same degree of public or professional acceptance or acclaim.

The creation of the new courts has brought to the fore difficulties that were not entirely unforeseen, namely, uncertainties about jurisdictional limits of the various courts particularly in the areas of trade practices and family law; the possibility of proceedings being instituted in different courts when they should be tried in the one court; the institution of proceedings in a wrong court; and the resulting expense and inconvenience experienced by litigants because of those difficulties. To a legal historian there is some similarity with the confusing position which existed in England before the fusion of the courts of Law and Equity as described by Charles Dickens in *Bleak House* in the fictional case of *Jarndyce v Jarndyce* :

> Equity sends questions to Law, Law sends questions back to Equity; Law finds it can't do this, Equity finds it can't do that; neither can so much as say it can't do anything, without this solicitor instructing and this counsel appearing . . .

All this has led to a succession of cases going to the High Court essentially for the purpose of resolving arid jurisdictional disputes. It will not be seen as the happiest chapter in Australia's legal history.

The judicial response

The High Court's response to these problems has been first to recognise that when an action is commenced in the exclusive jurisdiction of the Federal Court for a contravention of the Trade Practices Act, section 76(ii) of the Constitution is wide enough to enable the parliament to confer jurisdiction on the Federal Court to determine the non-federal aspects of a single justiciable controversy in which the issues raised under the federal law form a substantial part. 'Matter' in section 76(ii) is thought to be wide enough to encompass the claims based on state law when they arise from what is essentially the same set of facts as those which give rise to the federal claim (often referred to as 'accrued jurisdiction'). (*Philip Morris Inc. v Adam P. Brown Male Fashions*; *Fencott v Muller*; *Stack v Coast Securities (No. 9) Pty Ltd*; *Bargal Pty Ltd v Force*. As regards the accrued jurisdiction, if any, of the Family Court, see *Smith v Smith*.) In a case involving loss suffered by the purchasers of a wine bar as a result of misrepresentations made by the vendor at the time of sale, it enables the purchaser to sue for contravention of section 52 of the Trade Practices Act as well as any associated claims based on state law for fraudulent or negligent misrepresentation. Likewise, in cases involving section 52 and the claims of passing off at common law and also, until recently, defamation. (*Fencott v Muller*; *Philip Morris Inc. v Adam P. Brown Male Fashions* and as regards defamation, see *Australian Ocean Line v West Australian Newspapers*. The availability of section 52 of the Trade Practices Act to cover defamation was, however, curtailed by the enactment of the *Statute Law (Miscellaneous Provisions) Act (No.2) 1984*; s. 3 Sch. 1 insertion of s. 65A into *Trade Practices Act 1974*.)

To the litigant claiming a breach of section 52 it enables the whole action to be determined in the Federal Court whereas the section 52 claim could not be dealt with in a state court if the action was commenced in that court.

The majority of the High Court who accepted this interpretation of the concept 'matter' were not unaware of the impact of their view on the possible loss of jurisdiction to be suffered by the state courts.

> Lurking beneath the surface of the arguments presented in this case are competing policy considerations affecting the role and status of the Federal Court and the supreme courts of the states. There is on the one hand the desirability of enabling the Federal Court to deal with attached claims so as to resolve the entirety of the parties' controversy. There is on the other hand an apprehension that if it be held that the Federal Court has jurisdiction to deal with attached claims, state courts will lose to the Federal Court a proportion of the important work which they have hitherto discharged, work which the Federal Court has no jurisdiction to determine if it be not attached to a federal claim. Added force is given to this apprehension by the vesting of exclusive federal jurisdiction in the Federal Court, for example, by section 86 of the Trade Practices Act.
>
> There are those who consider that, in order to avoid jurisdictional conflicts, duplication of proceedings and diminution in status of the supreme courts, the Commonwealth parliament should not create federal courts or, if it does, should not give them an exclusive jurisdiction. On the other hand, others believe that federal courts should interpret federal laws and determine federal rights; and some go further and consider that parliament should vest an exclusive jurisdiction in a federal court in specialist fields in the hope that this will promote a more informed and uniform application of relevant federal laws (*Philip Morris Inc. v Adam P. Brown Male Fashions*, 513–14 per Mason J.).

The choice for these judges was made in favour of the interests of the litigants.

> With the force of these respective views we are not concerned. We must approach the question on the footing that parliament has decided for good reason to establish the Federal Court and to vest in it an exclusive jurisdiction under the Trade Practices Act. And we cannot assume that, in the event of a decision in this case adverse to the plaintiffs, parliament would be prepared to vest a concurrent jurisdiction under the Trade Practices Act in state courts. In deciding whether to attribute either a broad or a narrow content to 'matter', we should take into account that the adoption of the broad meaning will lead to the speedier determination of entire controversies between parties without undue duplication of proceedings. Perhaps the adoption of this view will have some adverse consequences for state courts, though this is by no means self-evident, but even if this be so, it is a consideration which is secondary to the interests of litigants. This circumstance is an additional reason for giving the word a broad rather than a narrow meaning (*Philip Morris Inc. v Adam P. Brown Male Fashions*, 514 quoted with approval by Mason, Murphy, Brennan and Deane JJ. in *Fencott v Muller, 609)*.

The cases involving these issues often gave rise to the kind of disagreements between the members of the Court which arose in relation to the scope of federal legislative powers. Some members of the Court either refused to accept the expanded notion of 'matter' referred to, or gave it a restricted meaning. For them the solution to the problems created in this area was to amend the *Trade Practices Act* so as to:

> provide that the jurisdiction of the Federal Court, at least in actions and other proceedings under Pt VI which relate to an alleged contravention of a provision of Pt V, should no longer be exclusive. The question whether conduct is misleading or deceptive does not require a specialist court to decide it—the supreme courts decide such questions every day—and the provisions of Div.2A of Pt V already recognise that no specialist court is needed to deal with matters of consumer protection. Now that the present cases have exposed the serious inconvenience of the present situation, I hope that the parliament will provide the remedy (*Stack v Coast Securities (No. 9) Pty Ltd*, 284–5 per Gibbs CJ.).

A second major problem which the High Court has had to face arose out of cases involving the sale of home units on the Gold Coast. The vendors sought specific performance to enforce the contracts against a falling market and proceedings were commenced for that purpose in the state Supreme Court. They could not have been commenced in the Federal Court. The purchasers, in an attempt to resist the claim, sought an injunction in the Federal Court to prevent the enforcement of the contracts, based on alleged contraventions of the Trade Practices Act because of alleged misrepresentations made to them by the vendors. The High Court unanimously decided that the accrued jurisdiction of the Federal Court to decide the state claims was not exclusively vested in the Federal Court. Furthermore, it was discretionary in nature with the consequence that both courts had jurisdiction. The Federal Court, however, had jurisdiction to deal with the *whole* controversy while the Supreme Court only had jurisdiction to deal with *part* of the controversy. In those circumstances only one court should exercise jurisdiction in these proceedings and *normally* the court to exercise that jurisdiction should be the court with authority to deal with all the issues, i.e. the Federal Court (*Stack v Coast Securities (No. 9) Pty Ltd*, 2995 and 298 per Mason, Brennan and Deane JJ., 299–300 per Murphy J). This would *not* apply as regards the disposition of non-federal issues where the state Supreme Court had already given summary judgement in favour of the vendor in regard to those issues (*Stack v Coast Securities (No. 9) Pty Ltd*, 295 per Mason, Brennan and Deane JJ, 300 per Murphy J).

It can be seen that the High Court had gone a long way towards unravelling the confusion involved in these jurisdictional tangles. The solutions adopted have generally favoured the authority of the federal courts in a way that tends to reflect the wider differences which exist between the members of the Court on federal issues. The attempts made by the Court to resolve these matters have been paralleled by attempts to resolve them at the political level. Had these attempts succeeded sooner, they would, of course, have obviated the need for a judicial solution.

The political response

A radical solution to the problem of state and federal courts was suggested by Sir Owen Dixon when he observed:

> [I]t would appear natural to endeavour to establish the courts of justice as independent organs which were neither Commonwealth nor state. The basis of the system is the supremacy of the law. The courts administering the law should all derive an independent existence and authority from the Constitution. Some practical difficulties would occur in carrying such a principle beyond the superior courts, but it is not easy to see why the entire system of superior courts should not have been organised and directed under the Constitution to administer the total content of the law. No doubt, some financial provisions would be required for levying upon the various governments contributions to the cost of administering justice. To make judicial appointments and deal with some other matters, it would have been necessary to create a joint committee. But it would not have been beyond the wit of man to devise machinery which would have placed the courts, so to speak, upon neutral territory where they administered the whole law irrespective of its source. (Dixon, 1935: 607; see also Cowen and Zines, 1978: 138–9 for a discussion of this solution.)

For a time, and somewhat surprisingly, it seemed that such a scheme might emerge from the recommendations of the Australian Constitutional Convention in 1978 and one of its committees in 1982. (Australian Constitutional Convention, *Proceedings*, Perth 1978, 150–65, 205 (Resolution 6). *Judicature Committee Report to Standing Committee D*, dated 26 September 1977, 29–31, 62–73 (Annexure D); *Fourth Report of Standing Committee D*, dated 27 August 1982, vol. 1, 12–18 especially 18.) By the time the Convention met again in 1983, however, support for such a course began to founder so that by 1985 it seemed to be accepted that the necessary support for such a scheme would not be forthcoming. (Australian Constitutional Convention *Proceedings*, Adelaide 1983, vol. 1, 9–37, 317 (Resolution 1); Brisbane 1985, vol. 1, 137–70, 422 (Resolution Item No. B4); *Judicature Sub-Committee Report on an Integrated System of Courts* dated Oct. 1984.) The practical details adverted to by Sir Owen have proved to be greater than he envisaged. Opposition to the proposals developed by the Convention committee included the use of an intergovernmental agreement (along the lines of the Financial Agreement in section 105A of the Constitution) to deal with the details of the scheme and the capacity of governments in such an agreement to override the Constitution; problems of accountability of the judiciary; and the opposition of the judges. Underlying these grounds was a more fundamental fear, namely, the loss of Commonwealth and state control over their own respective judiciary. The matter was graphically symbolised at one of the meetings of the

Convention when it was said by one speaker after pointing out that he was far from convinced that a persuasive case had been made out for an integrated court system:

> On the contrary, as I see it, it has within it the potential eventually to destroy the federal system by which we now live. The closest analogy I can draw to it would be to abolish state parliaments in favour of creating an integrated national legislature. Naturally, no member of parliament would have a bar of this; yet the inevitable effect of this proposal now before us seems to me to be in danger of passing us by (Australian Constitutional Convention; Proceedings, Brisbane 1985, 157).

In the event, the Convention finally settled on expressing support for a less ambitious and far more modest proposal, namely, what was referred to as the 'cross-vesting' of jurisdiction as between the Federal and Family Courts and the state supreme courts at the trial level. (See above references to the *Judicature Sub-Committee Report on an Integrated System of Courts* and *Proceedings* of the Convention, Brisbane 1985). Far from integrating such courts the proposal accepts their continued separate operation and existence. This probably constitutes a concession to the realities of a federal system of government. In that regard courts are in no different position to that occupied by other institutions or levels of government.

The Commonwealth has now agreed to two measures which show how the political processes can operate to ensure the continued operation of state governmental institutions, in this case their supreme courts, even though such assurances are not legally or constitutionally mandated. The Commonwealth has enacted legislation vesting state (and territory) courts with original and appellate federal jurisdiction concurrent with the Federal Court in civil matters arising under Part V, Divisions 1 and 1A of the Trade Practices Act, i.e. including, for example, section 52—a major modern source of commercial litigation. (Commonwealth *Jurisdiction of Courts (Miscellaneous Amendments) Act 1987*, s. 3, Schedule amendments to *Trade Practices Act 1974*. See also *Jurisdiction of Courts (Cross-Vesting) Act 1987*, s. 10). In this view of the writer this represents a major reversal of Commonwealth policy which should enable the state supreme courts to recover some of their lost importance and prestige. Secondly, and after quite lengthy and detailed discussions between Commonwealth and state law officers, the Commonwealth and the states have agreed to the enactment of complementary legislation to give effect to the cross-vesting proposal recommended by the Australian Constitutional Convention. Commonwealth legislation to that end has already been enacted. (*Jurisdiction of Courts (Cross-Vesting) Act 1987*. The Act is to come into operation on a date to be fixed by proclamation.)

Once the cross-vesting legislation is in operation federal legislation will vest the supreme courts of the states (and territories) with jurisdiction vested in the Federal and Family Courts, which the supreme courts do not otherwise possess. State complementary legislation will have a similar effect as regards vesting the Federal and Family Courts with jurisdiction vested in the state supreme courts. (*Jurisdiction of Courts (Cross-Vesting) Act 1987*, s. 4. It is recognised that there are doubts concerning whether Chapter III of the Constitution precludes federal courts being vested with jurisdiction derived from state legislation but see the opinion of Professor Zines in the Appendix to the *Judicature Sub-Committee Report on an Integrated System of Courts*, the answer to Question 1, 27–32.) Detailed and comprehensive provision is also made for the transfer of proceedings between these courts so that proceedings begun in an inappropriate court will be transferred to an appropriate court. (*Jurisdiction of Courts (Cross-vesting) Act 1987*, s. 5. The scheme extends to cross-vesting involving the supreme courts of different states as among themselves and also the territories.) It is envisaged that the cross-vesting provisions would need to be applied only in exceptional cases where there are jurisdictional uncertainties and where there is a real need to have matters tried together in the one court. The scheme seeks to ensure that no action will fail in a court through lack of jurisdiction and that as far as possible no court will have to determine the boundaries between federal and state jurisdictions.

There can be little doubt that one of the reasons why the states may have sought cross-vesting of jurisdiction is to arrest or reverse the loss of jurisdiction suffered by their courts (Australian Constitutional Convention, *Proceedings*, Brisbane 1985, vol. 1, 139). This was certainly the perception of the Federal Attorney-General (*Hansard* (*House of Representatives*), 17 March 1987, 915). It is recognised that the successful operation of the cross-vesting scheme will depend very much upon the way courts approach the legislation, particularly as regards the circumstances in which proceedings would be transferred between the courts concerned. In determining whether proceedings are to be transferred it needs to be borne in mind that it will no longer be the case that the relevant state courts will not enjoy the ability to deal with the whole proceedings—a factor which as seen tended to ensure that the balance of convenience would in many cases result in the Federal Court enjoying authority to determine the whole dispute between the parties. The machinery is therefore in place to enable the two kinds of courts to co-exist in a way that is designed to avoid arid and costly jurisdictional conflicts at the expense of the litigants.

This scheme envisages the establishment of a Committee of Chief Justices of State (and Territory) Supreme Courts and the Chief Judges of the Federal Court and the Family Court. Its purpose will be to monitor the operation of the scheme and to report regularly to the Standing Committee of Attorneys-General. The duration of the scheme will be subject to a trial period of three years after which each party to the scheme (Commonwealth and the states) will have the right to withdraw from it upon giving notice to the other parties. To this end provisions have been included in the federal legislation to enable the operation of the relevant provisions to be suspended after the expiration of the trial period. (*Jurisdiction of Courts (Cross-Vesting) Act 1987*, s. 16. See also *Hansard (Senate)*, 1 April 1987, 1567.)

Only a cursory glance at legal history is needed to remind us that conflict and competing jurisdictions between courts have been a feature of our English curial heritage. It is true that the main reason for this was that for a long time judges and court officials were very largely paid by fees from litigants, thus accounting for a search for business (Windeyer, 1957: 118). It would seem to be unlikely, though, that this was the only factor at work. In modern times and in Australia it may well be that federalism could prove to be another factor contributing to a competition over jurisdiction.

Irrespective of whether this is correct it would be welcomed if the comments that were made exactly a century ago about the perceived effect of the English Judicature Acts could be made in relation to our court system:

> It may be asserted without fear of contradiction that it is not possible in the year 1887 for an honest litigant in her Majesty's Supreme Court to be defeated by any mere technicality, any slip, any mistaken step in his litigation. The expenses of the law are still too heavy, and have not diminished *pari passu* with other abuses. But law has ceased to be a scientific game that may be won or lost by playing some particular move (Windeyer, 1957: 288–9 quoting the remarks of Lord Bowen).

Some concluding observations

A theme of this chapter has been to show how the High Court's interpretation of the Constitution has operated to produce change or at least the potential for change by expanding the perceived scope of national legislative powers. Such a result obviously widens the political choices and responsibilities of the federal government and parliament. Stress was placed in the chapter on the significant part played by literalism in the performance of the Court's role in constitutional interpretation.

To some it may perhaps seem surprising, at least at first sight, that federalism has not been used more extensively than it has as a reason for limiting the reach of Commonwealth legislative authority A similar complaint was raised recently in the USA when it was stated that: '[I]t is not an overstatement to say that, given the Supreme Court's Commerce Clause jurisprudence, the states exercise their reserved powers only at the sufferance of the national government (*Working Group on Federalism of the Domestic Policy Council, Report on 'The Status of Federalism in America*' (Nov. 1986), Executive Summary, 3).

However, federalism, at least as hitherto analysed, fails to yield a workable judicial standard or test for limiting the scope of Commonwealth powers. In particular, political scientists and others have yet to advance a definition of federalism which defines that concept in terms of which powers are inherently capable or appropriate for being exercised by the national or state levels of government, except perhaps as regards powers over defence and external affairs (Sawer, 1976: 107. The difficulty of devising objective and workable criteria for determining how power should be distributed between the Commonwealth and the states was recognised in Constitutional Commission: Advisory Committee on the Distribution of Powers, *Report*, June 1987, 1–4, paras 1.2–1.11.) Moreover some will point to the existence of alternative, non-legal and non-judicial mechanisms or pressures which will ensure the continued existence of federalism in Australia (Zines, 1987: 385–6).

The chapter also suggests that while change has occurred by virtue of judicial interpretation it has not been won or achieved without some costs and disadvantages. In the first place judicial change occurs gradually and over the course of time as witnessed by the failure of the Court to overrule *Huddart Parker & Co Pty Ltd v Moorehead* (1908) until the decision in the *Concrete Pipes* case (1971). Secondly, the results which can sometimes flow from the wording used to define Commonwealth legislative power may force the court to draw distinctions which would have little appeal to rational policy-makers charged with the task of drafting an ideal or new Constitution. This was illustrated in the chapter by the discussion of the plenary authority now exercised by the Commonwealth in regard to the *control of intrastate trade* when conducted by certain types of *corporations*, but not other types of corporations and more importantly, *ordinary individuals*. It was also illustrated by the developments involving the marriage and divorce powers given that those powers were based on marriage and not the broader concept of family or family relationships.

The court's declining, but not non-existent. role in supervising federal limitations on national legislative powers contrasts with the increasing role exercised by it in relation to the constitutional provisions which govern the composition and functioning of the federal parliament. Even there, however, it was suggested that the reliance placed on a literal approach to the interpretation of section 57 is likely to result in the scope of judicial review being narrowed as regards compliance with the provisions of that section.

Finally, the chapter discussed the tendency of federal institutions to grow and compete with those of the states. The courts have shown themselves to be much the same as other institutions or levels of government in that regard. The way in which political forces have responded to meet the threat posed by the Federal Court to the prestige and importance of the state supreme courts was said to illustrate how the political processes can operate to safeguard the continued operation of state governmental institutions by non-legal and non-judicial means. In this case the vehicle used for achieving this objective provides a further example of co-operative federalism in Australia.

Endnotes

1 It is generally accepted that the power does not provide the parliament with a direct power to fix the terms and conditions of employment but only the means of erecting the machinery of conciliation and arbitration to resolve industrial dispute extending beyond the limits of any one state: see *R v Commonwealth Conciliation and Arbitration Commission; ex parte Amalgamated Engineering Union (Australian Section)* (1967) at 242, 269; *1959 Report of Joint Committee on Constitutional Review*, para. 629, 87; Lane, 1986: 234–5.

2 According to the prevailing approach a mining company is likely to be treated as a trading corporation if it mines for the purpose of selling the same minerals, even if mining is not considered as 'trade'. It will suffice under the current approach if the sale of the mineral is a substantial activity or at least forms a significant proportion of the overall activities carried on by the corporation: see Lindell, 1984: 242.

3 *Attorney-General for NSW v Brewery Employees' Union of NSW* (1908), 501 per Griffin CJ. The same subject matter is generally taken to refer to the *connotation* rather than the *denotation* of a term—a distinction which is not without its difficulties: see *R v Federal Court of Australia; ex parte WA National League* (1979), 233–4 per Mason J.; Zines, 1987: 16–20.

4 *Farey v Burvett* (1916), 440 per Griffith CJ. and see Derham, 1961: 162–4. A similar approach was taken in *Bank of New South Wales v The Commonwealth* (*Bank Nationalisation* case) (1948) at 383 where Dixon J. treated the words 'whether by means of internal carriage or ocean navigation' as words of extension and not restriction in determining the forms of interstate trade which attracted the constitutional protection of section 92 of the Constitution. The Privy Council adopted the language and reasoning of Dixon J. as regards what formed part of interstate trade, commerce and intercourse: see (1949) 79 CLR 497, 632–3.

5 As regards the relationship between section 51(i) and 51(xxxv) see e.g. *R v Wright; ex parte Waterside Workers' Federation of Australia* (1955); *R v Foster; ex parte Eastern and Australian Steamship Co. Ltd (1959); Seamen's Union of Australia v Utah Development Co.* (1978) at 154. As regards the relationship between section 51(xxix) and section 51(xxx) see the *Seas and Submerged Lands* case (1975) 471 per Mason J. A notable exception to the general approach is to be found with the power of the Commonwealth to legislate with respect to the compulsory acquisition of property on 'just terms' in section 51(xxxv). This power is treated in the nature of a constitutional guarantee. See generally Zines, 1987: 20–3.

6 The powers in question are those contained in section 51(xxi) with respect to 'marriage' and section 51(xxii) with respect to 'divorce and

matrimonial causes; and in relation thereto, parental rights and the custody and guardianship of infants'. A substantial part of the discussion which follows in the text is drawn from material prepared by the writer as a member of the Advisory Committee on the Distribution of Powers for the report provided by that Committee to the Constitutional Commission: see generally Constitutional Commission, Advisory Committee on Distribution of Powers—*Report*, June 1987, ch. 4, 39–65, paras 4.1–4.98. The writer wishes to acknowledge the valuable assistance provided by Ms B. Guthrie, a legal officer with the Commission. However, the writer accepts sole responsibility for any errors and the correctness of the views expressed in the discussion.

7 For the validity of laws enacted at a joint sitting see *Cormack v Cope*; the *Petroleum and Minerals Authority* case and the *First Territory Representation* case As Professor Zines has observed from the *Cormack v Cope* to the *First Territory Representation* case the majority of the bench in favour of treating the issue as justiciable was reduced from 5:1 to 4:3 suggesting that the question may not be settled for all time: Zines, 1977b: 229 and see generally 227–33. For the validity of double dissolutions, see the *Petroleum and Minerals Authority* case at 120, 155–7, 178, 183. Possibly a challenge may be entertained if it is made before writs are issued for the election: see *ibid*. 157 per Gibbs J. See also Lindell, 1977: 158–160.

8 This may be implicit from the dismissal of the challenges raised against five of the six laws enacted at the joint sitting in 1974 i.e. other than the *Petroleum Minerals and Authority Act 1973*. In the *Petroleum Minerals and Authority* case, Gibbs J. said at page 144:

> The term 'deadlock' although commonly used in this context is perhaps misleading; to invoke s. 57 it is not necessary that the business of parliament should have come to a complete standstill or that the proposed law as to which a disagreement exists should be one of vital importance.

See also Pearce, 1977: 140–1.

9 See Sexton, 1978; Zines and Lindell, 1982: 721 n. (b). See now Commonwealth *Electoral Act 1918* ss. 46–50 as amended by the Commonwealth *Electoral Legislation Amendment Act 1983* and the Commonwealth *Electoral Legislation Amendment Act 1984*; and also the Commonwealth *Representation Act 1983*.

10 See *Fourth Report of Standing Committee 'D'* of the Australian Constitutional Convention dated 27 August 1982, vol. 1. paras 5.8–5.9, 56–7, published in *Proceedings of the Australian Constitutional Convention Adelaide 26–29 April 1983*, vol. 2.; Joint Select Committee on Electoral Reform (Commonwealth Parliament), *Report No. 1*, 'Determining the Entitlement of Federal Territories and new States to Representation in the Commonwealth Parliament' (Nov. 1985), paras. 4.7–4.13, 49–52.

11 For a legal analysis of a number of outstanding questions concerning the construction and application of section 57 of the Constitution, see Comans, 1985. Reference is there made to the application of section 57 in respect of a particular proposed law at each stage depending

on the retention of the identity of the proposed law as the proposed law originally passed by the House of Representatives, or that proposed law with such amendments only as have been made, suggested or agreed to by the Senate: *ibid*. 246. However, as is also shown by the article in question, the question of amendments that may be considered at a joint sitting gives rise to issues which have yet to be determined by the High Court : *ibid*. 249–50.

12 According to a former State Attorney-General, although no consistent method of consultation has been developed, it has been the case that the Commonwealth Attorney-General has written to the State Attorneys-General asking them to suggest appointees. The names put forward have been considered by the Commonwealth Attorney in making his proposals to the Cabinet and, in some cases, there has been additional consultation by telephone: *Proceedings of the Australian Constitutional Convention*, Brisbane 1985, vol. 1, 184.

Judicial decisions

Actors and Announcers' Equity Association v Fontana Films Pty Ltd (1982) 150 CLR 169.

Airlines of NSW Pty Ltd v New South Wales [*No. 2*] (1965) 113 CLR 1.

Attorney-General for NSW v Brewery Employees' Union of NSW (1908) 6 CLR 469.

Attorney-General (New South Wales) (ex. rel. McKellar) v The Commonwealth (1977) 139 CLR 527.

Australian National Airways Pty Ltd v The Commonwealth (1945) 71 CLR 29.

Australian Ocean Line v West Australian Newspapers (1983) 47 ALR 497.

Bank Nationalisation case: Bank of New South Wales v The Commonwealth (1948) 76 CLR 1.

Bargal Pty Ltd v Force (1983) 154 CLR 261.

Concrete Pipes case: *Strickland v Rocla Concrete Pipes Ltd* (1971) 124 CLR 468.

Cormack v Cope (1974) 131 CLR 432.

Cormick case: *In the Marriage of Cormick* (1984) 156 CLR 170.

CCSU v Minister for Civil Service [1985] AC.374.

CYSS case: *R v Coldham; ex parte Australian Social Welfare Union* (1983) 153 CLR 297.

Dowal v Murray (1978) 143 CLR 410.

Engineers' case: Amalgamated Society of Engineers v The Adelaide Steamship Co. Ltd (1920) 28 CLR 129.

FAI Insurance Ltd v Winneke (1982) 151 CLR 342.

Farey v Burvett (1916) 21 CLR 433.

Federated State School Teachers' Association of Australia v Victoria (1929) 41 CLR 569.

Fencott v Muller (1983) 152 CLR 570.

First Territory Representation case: *Western Australia v The Commonwealth* (1975) 134 CLR 201.

Franklin Dam case: *The Commonwealth v Tasmania* (1983) 158 CLR 1.
Gazzo v Comptroller of Stamps (Vic.) (1981) 149 CLR 227.
Herald and Weekly Times Ltd v The Commonwealth (1966) 115 CLR 418.
Huddart Parker & Co. Pty Ltd v Moorehead (1908) 8 CLR 330.
Jones v The Commonwealth [No. 2] (1965) 112 CLR 206.
Jumbunna Coal Mine N L v Victorian Coal Miners' Association (1908) 6 CLR 309.
Koowarta v Bjelke-Petersen (1982) 153 CLR 168.
Marriage Act case: *Attorney-General for Victoria v The Commonwealth* (1962) 107 CLR 529.
McKinlay's case: *Attorney-General for the Commonwealth (Ex. rel. McKinlay) v The Commonwealth* (1975) 135 CLR 1.
Melbourne Corporation v The Commonwealth (1947) 74 CLR 31.
Minister for Arts, Heritage and Environmental v Peko Wallsend Ltd (1987) 75 ALR 218.
Murphyores Incorporated Pty Ltd v The Commonwealth (1976) 136 CLR 1.
New South Wales v The Commonwealth (Seas and Submerged Lands case) (1975) 135 CLR 337.
Petroleum and Minerals Authority case: *Victoria v Commonwealth* (1975) 134 CLR 81.
Philip Morris lnc. v Adam P Brown Male Fashions (1981) 148 CLR 457.
Queensland Electricity Commission v The Commonwealth (1985) 59 ALJR 699.
Re F; ex parte F (1986) 60 ALJR 594.
Re Lee; ex parte Harper (1986) 60 ALJR 441.
R v Brislan; ex parte Williams (1935) 54 CLR 262.
R v Burgess; ex parte Henry (1936) 55 CLR 608.
R v Commonwealth Conciliation and Arbitration Commission; ex parte Amalgamated Engineering Union (Australian Section) (1967) 118 CLR 219.
R v Cook; ex parte C (1985) 156 CLR 249.
R v Federal Court of Australia; ex parte WA National League (1979) 143 CLR 190.
R v Foster; ex parte Eastern and Australian Steamship Co. Ltd (1959) 103 CLR 256.
R v Kirby; ex parte Boilermakers' Society of Australia (1956) 94 CLR 254.
R v Lambert; ex parte Plummer (1980) 146 CLR 447.
R v Toohey; ex parte Northern Land Council (1981) 151 CLR 170.
R v Wright; ex parte Waterside Workers' Federation of Australia (1955) 93 CLR 528.
Russell v Russell (1976) 134 CLR 495.
Seamen's Union of Australian v Utah Development Co. (1978) 144 CLR 120.
Second Territories Representation case: *Queensland v The Commonwealth* (1977), 139 CLR 585.
Smith v Smith (1986) 60 ALJR 508.
South Australia v O'Shea (1987) 73 ALR 1.
Stack v Coast Securities (No. 9) Pty Ltd (1983) 154 CLR 261.
Vitzdamm-Jones v Vitzdamm-Jones (1981) 148 CLR 383.
V v V (1985) 156 CLR 228.

References

Australian Constitutional Convention (1984), *Judicature Sub-Committee Report on an Integrated System of Courts*, Oct.

—— (1985) *Judicature Sub-Committee: Second Report to Standing Committee*, May.

Blackshield, A.R. et al. (1986), *The Judgments of Justice Lionel Murphy*, Primavera Press, Drummoyne, NSW.

Comans, C.K. (1985), 'Constitution, Section 57—Further Questions', *Federal Law Review* 15: 243.

Constitutional Commission (1986), Advisory Committee on the Distribution of Powers—Issues Paper.

—— (1987), —*Report*, June.

Cowen, Z. and Zines, L.R. (1978), *Federal Jurisdiction in Australia*, 2nd edn, Oxford University Press, Melbourne.

Derham, D.P. (1961), 'The Defence Power', in R. Else-Mitchell (ed.), *Essays on the Australian Constitution*, 2nd edn, Law Book Co., Sydney: 160.

Dixon, Sir O. (1935), 'The Law and the Constitution', *Law Quarterly Review* 51: 590.

Fourth Report of Standing Committee 'D' of the Australian Constitutional Convention dated 27 August 1982, vol. 1, published in *Proceedings of the Australian Constitutional Convention Adelaide 26–29 April 1983*, vol. 2.

Hanks, P. (1977), 'Parliamentarians and the Electorate', in G. Evans (ed.), *Labor and the Constitution, 1972–1975*, Heinemann, Sydney: 166.

Hansard (House of Representatives).

Hansard (Senate).

Jessep, O. and Chisholm, R.L. (1985), 'Children, the Constitution and the Family Court', *University of New South Wales Law Journal* 8: 152.

Joint Select Committee on Electoral Reform (1985), *(Commonwealth Parliament) Report No. 1*, 'Determining the Entitlement of Federal Territories and new States to Representation in the Commonwealth Parliament', Nov.

Judicature Committee Report to Standing Committee D, Australian Constitutional Convention, dated 26 September 1977.

Judiciary Act 1903.

Jurisdiction of Courts (Cross-Vesting) Act 1987.

Lane, P.H. (1986), *Lane's Commentary on the Australian Constitution*, Law Book Co., Sydney.

Lindell, G.J. (1974), 'Judicial Review and the Composition of the House of Representatives', *Federal Law Review* 6: 84.

—— (1977), 'Duty to Exercise Judicial Review', in L.R. Zines (ed.), *Commentaries on the Australian Constitution*, Butterworths, Sydney: 150.

—— (1984), 'The Corporations and Races Powers', *Federal Law Review* 14: 219.

Pearce, D. (1977), 'The Legislative Power of the Senate', in L.R. Zines (ed.), *Commentaries on the Australian Constitution*, Butterworths, Sydney.

Proceedings of the Australian Constitutional Convention, Melbourne, 24–26 September 1975.

Proceedings of the Australian Constitutional Convention, Hobart, 27–29 October 1976.

Proceedings of the Australian Constitutional Convention, Perth, 26–28 July 1978.

Proceedings of the Australian Constitutional Convention, Adelaide, 26–29 April 1983, vol. 1.

Proceedings of the Australian Constitutional Convention, Brisbane, 29 July–1 August 1985, vol. 1.

Report of Joint Committee on Constitutional Review (1959).

Report of Royal Commission on the Constitution (1929).

Report of the Parliamentary Joint Select Committee on the Family Law Act, 'Family Law in Australia', vol. 1.

Sawer, G. (1956), *Australian Federal Politics and Law 1901–1929*, Melbourne University Press, Melbourne.

—— (1976), *Modern Federalism*, Pitman, Carlton, Vic.

Sexton, M. (1978), 'The Role of Judicial Review in Federal Electoral Law', 52 *Australian Law Journal* 28.

Windeyer, Sir W. (1957), *Lectures on Legal History*, 2nd edn, Law Book Co., Sydney.

Working Group on Federalism of the Domestic Policy Council (1986), Report on 'The Status of Federalism in America', Nov., Executive Summary.

Zines, L.R. (1977a), *Commentaries on the Australian Constitution*, Butterworths, Sydney.

—— (1977b), 'The Double Dissolutions and Joint Sitting', in G. Evans (ed.), *Labor and the Constitution 1972–1975*, Heinemann, Sydney: 217.

—— (1983), 'The State of Constitutional Interpretation', *Federal Law Review* 14: 277.

—— (1987), *The High Court and the Constitution*, 2nd edn, Butterworths.

Zines, L.R. and Lindell, G.J. (1982), *Sawer's Australian Constitutional Cases*, 4th edn, Law Book Co., Sydney.

FEDERALISM, THE STATES AND INTERNATIONAL AFFAIRS

8

A POLITICAL SCIENCE PERSPECTIVE

Hugh Collins

By contrast with those older studies of Australian federalism from which this seminar has been taking its cues, the topic assigned to this session is novel. Neither the 1949 Australian Institute of Political Scientists' essays (Sawer et al., 1949) nor the 1951 ANU collection (Sawer, 1952) includes anything akin to this title among its chapter headings. The external order was not forgotten in those discussions, but it did not press urgently upon their consideration of the framework of domestic politics. Partly, the relationship between domestic structure and foreign policy was not discussed because it was not considered problematic. Thus, when examining the impact of federalism on public administration, Copland (1952: 135) explicitly contrasts the comprehensive jurisdiction of the Commonwealth in foreign affairs with the limited powers granted to it in social and economic affairs. Even Gordon Greenwood (1949: 43), that critic of federalism for whom national capacity for international action was vital, treats foreign affairs as a subordinate element in his case for extended Commonwealth powers. In 1987 the position is very different. What accounts for this difference? What significance is to be attached to it?

First, discussion of this topic arises simply as a reflection of political and governmental practice. Any description of Australia's interaction with the world necessarily includes the activities of the states and their agents as well as of the Commonwealth and its officers. We may rank overseas visits by state premiers alongside tours of duty by federal ministers. As well as the national diplomatic operations recently reviewed by Stuart Harris, a full account of Australia's overseas representation should arguably extend to the offices and officers of state governments stationed abroad (Department of Foreign Affairs, 1986). In Tokyo and Los Angeles, for example, five states have representation in some form alongside the diplomatic, trade and consular representatives of the Commonwealth (Ravenhill, forthcoming). There are also the transnational links created at provincial and municipal levels through sister-state relationships.

It may be objected that little of this is the stuff of high policy. There is not much in the preceding list of state activities to dent the Commonwealth's conventional pre-eminence in this sphere. Be that granted, it nevertheless remains the case that these activities raise questions of interest in the management of Australia's external relations. There is much here for the analyst of public administration in the federation to examine: we have moved a long way from the bureaucratic and political realities which Copland was observing.

To be sure, bringing Copland's assessment up-to-date might warrant only a paragraph or two in a more general survey. The second reason for paying specific attention to this topic is its recent significance as an area of constitutional conflict. *Seas and Submerged Lands; Koowarta; Franklin Dam*: these are the titles of successive acts in the judicial drama of the external affairs power. So far from putting a dent in the Commonwealth's capacities by their overseas activities, some states have considered their internal integrity to have been crushed beneath the weight of Canberra's plenary powers in foreign affairs. The 'great constitutional battle-ground' which Quick and Garran (1976: 631) discerned in section 51(xxix) has come to pass. So the claims for attention to this topic from a legal perspective at least will be apparent.

A political analysis of the topic may adduce a third reason for including it in our bicentennial reflections: it is upon this ground that the most intense battles of Australian federalism are likely to be fought in the last quarter of the Commonwealth's first century. A double dynamic will keep the states and the Commonwealth locked upon this ground. Internally, differences of interest, perception and party attachment will create opportunities and incentives for challenges to the limits of authority in this area. Externally, changes in the agenda, norms and institutions of international relations will provide occasion for testing the reach and responsibilities attached to the external affairs power.

We already understand the overseas engagements of the states as responses to emerging conditions of international interdependence (see Collins, 1983: 213–19). The states' quest for exports, investment and tourism reflects both the politicisation of many world markets and local demands for government activity in support of economic growth. The issue to be underlined here is that the changes which have bred these responses have reinforced a structural tension in the Australian political system. For the same pressures which have led to new patterns and levels of external activity by the states have simultaneously placed a premium upon the Commonwealth's search for coherent national management of Australia's external relations.

What particular Commonwealth governments regard as coherence for national policy is likely at any time to be viewed by particular state governments as intrusion or prejudice. As we enter this forest of political possibilities, the fire danger sign of constitutional conflict would seem to be set on 'high' for the foreseeable future.

For these reasons, the literature which describes state involvement in international affairs and which analyses the complications introduced by federalism into Australia's external relations has concentrated upon two aspects especially: the constitutional battle-ground, and the economic interactions, particularly in minerals and energy matters (see Ravenhill, forthcoming; Drysdale and Shibata, 1985). With such excellent recent reviews of these aspects of the problem available, and with the ground they cover now relatively familiar to us, I propose to make only a few observations on the constitutional politics of the external affairs power before taking up some other aspects of the topic that have been neglected in the literature.

Having just asserted that it is upon the battle-ground of section 51(xxix) that much future constitutional conflict will occur, it is important to emphasise that the extent and the stakes of conflict in this arena can be, indeed characteristically have been, exaggerated. One of the features of constitutional conflict in Australia requiring political analysis is the rhetoric of the adversaries. It seems well established in Australia's political style that in High Court battles the political victors and vanquished alike exaggerate the extremity of their position. This hyperbole may be deliberately intended to highlight the role of judicial review in changes in the federal balance, thereby removing the spotlight from the governmental actors and elements in the system which also contribute to change.

In assessing the political significance of a particular judgment by the Court, we should analyse the aftermath of the decision as carefully as the calculations which led to the case and the reasoning supporting the judgment. The *Franklin Dam* case, which provided so much grist to the mills of the doom-sayers of the federal compact, is illustrative here. To be sure, the Commonwealth's legislation was upheld. The dam was not built. But the Commonwealth and state governments have subsequently been entrammelled in extraordinarily complicated administrative negotiations. Nor has the Australian Labor Party, at state and federal levels, emerged electorally unscathed from its 'constitutional' victory (see Galligan, 1984: 102–23).

Constitutional battles in Australian federalism are rarely the zero-sum games that it suits the antagonists often to pretend. There are limits in practice and in politics to almost anything the Commonwealth or the states might wish to do with, for, or against each other. It is precisely the complexity of this political and administrative interdependence which creates the seeds of conflict at the same time as it constrains the outcomes of conflict.

Turning to aspects of federalism whose impact upon international affairs has received less attention in the literature, I have an agenda of four items for consideration.

First is defence. While the traditional symbols and apparatus of diplomacy—representation abroad, treaty powers, and so on—have received so much scrutiny, the relationship between defence and Australian federalism has been scarcely noticed. Such neglect is curious, because there are some highly significant issues involved, but instructive, because it reveals how far conceptions of defence are divorced from the issues which typically preoccupy the practitioners and analysts of intergovernmental relations. Very briefly, I propose to draw attention to three aspects which warrant more detailed study: defence procurement, defence posture, and defence policy.

Defence procurement involves a set of issues central to the strategies for industrialisation pursued by state and Commonwealth governments. A major defence contract is a prize zealously sought and jealously awarded. We need look no further than the decision in 1987 concerning the provision of submarines for the federal dynamics to be evident. In the long campaign associated with this decision, state governments were as much actors in the process as multinational weapons manufacturers. Nor, when reviewing the technical aspects of the contract, would the federal Cabinet's assessment have ignored the differential impact of its decision upon state and party fortunes. The final decision displayed that characteristically 'federal' formula: an attempt to find something in the barrel for each of the claimants.

Defence posture, particularly determining what forces are stationed where, can be a factor of immediate electoral significance to politicians in both levels of government. I do not attach special electoral significance to Mr Beazley's decision to shift a sizeable proportion of the Royal Australian Navy from constituencies in Sydney to divisions in Perth and Fremantle. But any change of this kind has implications for land use, housing, education, transport and business. Clearly decisions taken by one level of government have an important impact on the interests of the other level of government.

Defence policy is relevant because ideally it provides direction to the procurement and posture decisions. The Dibb Report and the subsequent Defence White Paper should be read as closely in state capitals as in the Russell Offices, for the realities with which these analyses deal have often been constructed by state governments. Thus, the development strategies of the Western Australian and Queensland governments, for example, have significant defence implications. Yet those pressing ahead with resource extraction and the provision of infrastructure in the north are rarely required to consider the national capacity to defend these developments. Indeed, these issues have only recently received scrutiny by our academic analysts of defence policy (see Langtry and Ball, 1986). The thrust of a defence policy aimed at self-reliance will require close interaction with agencies of state and local government.

Interdependence between levels of government in defence-related areas will have to be developed not least because the future defence tasks for Australia are likely to include some very messy low-level contingencies as well as the nastiness of terrorism. Our structures have not been shaped to deal with the darker side of politics. The inability of Australia's federal system to cope with thc narcotics trade suggests the obstacles to sustained defence protecting isolated oil rigs, quarantining against human and animal viruses, countering terrorism.

The second item on my agenda of neglected aspects of our general topic is the Senate. It may be surprising to include the federal element of the national legislature in this list; certainly the reasons for putting it here are far removed from the founders' intentions for that chamber. Yet what they designed has been used politically to great consequence in Australia's external policies. Two-and-a-half matters concern me here.

The first of these is the Senate's role in educating the parliament and the public in foreign affairs and defence matters. The Senate initiated the intensive committee work that has since been pursued by both Houses. The hearings and reports of parliamentary committees have been influential in many ways: in focussing attention upon issues; in providing detailed information through the submissions by government departments and voluntary agencies; in prompting reallocations of bureaucratic staff and administrative attention.

Secondly, if not a states' house, the electoral system and the nexus have made the Senate a house of minor parties and independents. In foreign affairs and defence issues the role of these parties has been demonstrably significant. Surely the defence and foreign policies of coalition governments in the 1960s and early 1970s were inseparable from the strategic position of the Democratic Labor Party in the Senate. More recently, the Democrats and the Nuclear Disarmament Party have provided a challenge to the bipartisan orthodoxies (or the margins of choice they offer) in issues such as arms control, uranium exports and foreign aid.

The pressures induced in government by this element of our federal legislature are the background to the remaining half of my two-and-a-half points. In any consideration of federalism, the states and international affairs we should not forget the Gair affair. Remember the elements: a government seeking to reduce its frustrations in the upper house and gain an additional seat; Mr Whitlam outwitted in this ruse by his arch foe, the Premier of Queensland; and the bait for Mr Gair, an Australian ambassadorship. It is to be hoped that the sordid spectacle of 1974 is not an exemplar for federalism, the states and international affairs overall.

The third item on my agenda is the influence upon Australia's external relations of the federal organisation of politics and society. As well as the formal federal framework and the federal character of the major political parties, many informal groups and associations are federal in character. It would be interesting to know the significance of this feature of Australian life for those groups with an interest in foreign policy and defence. This is really repeating in this context an observation by Professor R.S. Parker a decade ago: 'The politics of federalism cannot be adequately studied without reference to its impact upon the whole structure and operation of organised private interests' (Parker, 1977: 37).

Are there discernible differences in perception and attitude between state elements of private organisations? The Australian Institute of International Affairs is a body of this kind, whose history is perhaps better understood as a federation of branches than as a national organisation. Does its new national headquarters in Canberra, mirroring the pattern of many other organisations, represent a shift in the relationship between informal groups and federal politics?

Many organisations in the private sphere are closely associated with bilateral ties (for example, the Australian–American Association; the Australia–USSR Friendship Society); many of these groups are now built upon the interests of particular immigrant communities within Australia's multicultural society. When culture, sport, education, welfare and trade can become issues of directly political significance in relations between sovereign states, the impact of voluntary organisations upon the management of foreign policy can be profound. Thus, federal parliamentarians' dealings with the Department of Foreign Affairs may be primarily concerned with issues arising immediately out of the concerns of immigrant groups within their electorates. How such groups are organised, the pattern of their distribution nationally, and the consequences for state and national politics are questions still seeking answers. Research by Professor Warhurst and his colleagues may shortly improve our understanding of the local soil in which federalism is rooted.

Finally, no satisfactory account of international affairs can remain focussed upon a single national actor. Australia's engagement with the world prompts questions about the world's engagement with Australia. Two types of question arise here. The first is empirical. How have foreign states adapted their diplomatic and commercial interests here to Australia's federal structure? Behind the formal insistence upon approaching government only through Canberra, what daily lines of communication exist for foreign governments in Australian state capitals? Little is known on this. Nor is it a simple task to test how well foreign representatives understand the need to become acquainted with the federal character of Australian politics. It would be my guess that there is a livelier appreciation of this among the *corps diplomatique*, if only because the increased international activities of the states involve additional work for foreign embassies here. One clue to the interactions is the appointment to the staff of state governments, particularly in premiers' departments, of Australian diplomats to liaise with foreign governments and advise on international issues.

The other issue is normative. In international affairs Australia is precariously poised. As a nation we have a major stake in an international order conducive to peace, open to international trade, and supportive of humane values. Australia is one of the members of a small coalition able to promote broadly democratic values in world politics. It is desirable that Australia's domestic constitution assist rather than inhibit Australia's role in the world, not simply to maximise immediate self-interest but also to enable this nation and its citizens to participate effectively in matters of global concern.

Few discussions of the distribution of powers under the Australian Constitution take much account of the need to shape our form of government to meet our external circumstances as well as to suit our internal preferences. Such neglect is surprising when one considers the impact which the external order has had upon the shape of our polity and the conduct of our politics. A primary motive for federation, after all, was the perception of the vulnerability of the scattered colonies to foreign naval powers. The Financial Agreement is to be understood in the context of a world economic crisis, just as uniform taxation is inseparable from wartime emergency.

Australia's domestic order has had to respond in the past to the demands of our international circumstances. The needs today are, mercifully, different. But they are no less serious for being less dramatic. Any redesigning of Australian federalism requires an analysis of international affairs. Moreover, the politics of constitutional change in Australia is likely to respond to movements and events on the global scene no less than to currents of domestic opinion. Consider the impetus which such diverse interests as human rights organisations, on the one hand, and proponents of monetarism, on the other, have received from the example, the publications, and the organisation of such interests internationally. The sources for constitutional change lie beyond as well as within Australia.

The study of Australian foreign policy requires attention to the domestic sources of policy. It is a distortion to present Australia's external policies as if these were the decisions of a unitary state, yet that has been the dominant feature of this literature. One has only to attempt to deal with resources diplomacy, or with the international aspects of Aboriginal land rights claims, to confront the impact of Australia's domestic structure. Both in political action and in political analysis we have to grapple with the awkward and untidy realities of our situation rather than the rhetorical or reified simplicities that have served for some in the past.

References

Collins, H. (1983), 'Political Factors', in P. Dibb (ed.), *Australia's External Relations in the 1980s: The Interaction of Economic, Political and Strategic Factors*, Croom Helm, Canberra: 213–19.

Copland, D, (1952), 'The Impact of Federalism on Public Administration', in Sawer (ed.): 135–73.

Department of Foreign Affairs (1986), *Review of Australia's Overseas Representation*, AGPS, Canberra.

Dibb, P. (1986), *Review of Australia's Defence Capabilities: Report to the Minister of Defence*, AGPS, Canberra.

Drysdale, P. and Shibata, H. (eds) (1985), *Federalism and Resource Development: The Australian Case*, Allen & Unwin, Sydney.

Galligan, B. (1984), 'The Dams Case: A Political Analysis', in M. Sornarajah (ed.), *The South West Dam Dispute: The Legal and Political Issues*, University of Tasmania, Hobart: 102–23.

Greenwood, G. (1949), 'The Case for Extended Commonwealth Powers', in Sawer et al.: 37–63.

Langtry J.O. and Ball, D.J. (eds) (1986), *A Vulnerable Country? Civil Resources and the Defence of Australia*, ANU Press, Canberra.

Minister of Defence (1987), 'The Defence of Australia '87', Defence White Paper, AGPS, Canberra.

Parker, R.S. (1977), 'Political and Administrative Trends in Australian Federalism', *Publius* 7, 3: 37.

Quick, J. and Garran, R.R, (1976), *The Annotated Constitution of the Australian Commonwealth*, Legal Books, Sydney. First published 1908.

Ravenhill, J. (forthcoming), 'Australia', in H. Michelmann and P. Soldatos (eds), *Federalism and International Relations*, Oxford University Press.

Sawer, G. (ed.) (1952), *Federalism: An Australian Jubilee Study*, F.W. Cheshire, Melbourne.

Sawer, G. et al., (1949), *Federalism in Australia*, F.W. Cheshire, Melbourne.

9

A LEGAL PERSPECTIVE

Henry Burmester

International affairs since 1901 have been radically transformed so that there are few areas of government that do not have an international dimension. When considering the impact of international affairs on the legal position of the states in the Australian federation it is useful to keep this always in mind. Among the areas where international affairs now intrude into domestic legal arrangements, of particular interest to the Australian states are:

- **human rights**—international conventions lay down norms and standards on civil, economic and social rights as well as issues such as abduction of children, and racial and sexual discrimination. International bodies scrutinise Australia's discharge of its international legal obligations.
- **criminal law**—international conventions create international offences such as hijacking, interference with diplomatically protected persons, terrorism, torture. These offences are incorporated in the domestic criminal law. Extradition and mutual assistance arrangements are concluded to ensure criminals and international trafficking of money and drugs can be controlled.
- **environment**—international declarations on the environment and nature are adopted, and principles agreed dealing with international environmental law. Treaties are concluded on protection of migratory birds, the oceans and the atmosphere. Obligations are created for nations to take measures to protect their own environment as well as that of other countries and areas beyond national jurisdiction. Of great significance from the Australian legal perspective is protection of cultural and natural heritage under the World Heritage Convention.
- **private law**—uniformity in laws governing wills, service of process abroad, international contracts, carriage of goods by sea and other issues is sought to be achieved by adoption of treaties on these issues.

Whether this transformation in the significance of international affairs in the life of a federal state like Australia should alter the internal constitutional arrangements is central to the debate over the appropriate role of the Commonwealth and states in matters of international concern. There are those who say that unless rigid limits are set on the power of the central government to deal with such matters, then the whole constitutional structure in Australia will be subverted. Wilson J., for instance, in the *Franklin Dam* case (1983: 197), said: 'Of what significance is the continued formal existence of the States if a great many of their traditional functions are liable to become the responsibilities of the Commonwealth?'

This, he said, 'is not speculation'. The potential of the Commonwealth to legislate to implement any treaty:

> poses a serious threat to the basic federal polity of the Constitution. Such an interpretation, if adopted, would result in the Commonwealth parliament acquiring power over practically the whole range of domestic concerns within Australia (1983: 197).

Gibbs CJ. echoed similar views in the earlier case of *Koowarta v Bjelke-Petersen* (1982: 198) when he said:

> In other words, if (the external affairs power) empowers the parliament to legislate to give effect to every international agreement which the executive may choose to make, the Commonwealth would be able to acquire unlimited legislative power. The distribution of powers made by the Constitution could in time be completely obliterated; there would be no field of power which the Commonwealth could not invade, and the federal balance achieved by the Constitution could be entirely destroyed.

This view, however, has not received support from the majority of the High Court who have taken the view that a reduction in exclusive state power as a result of a great increase in matters which are the subject of international regulation or concern is merely an inevitable consequence of changes in the international environment. In constitutional terms, as Mason CJ. has put it, the difference between the original expectations and present day developments 'seems to have been a difference in the frequency and volume of external affairs rather than a difference in kind'. He rejected arguments based on a notion of federal balance (*Franklin Dam* case, 1983: 126).

On this view, there is no justification for special restraints or limitations on the external affairs aspects of Commonwealth power that are not imposed in relation to the interpretation and exercise of all other Commonwealth powers. The debate over the significance for Australian federalism of the increase in matters that involve international affairs is, however, a continuing one. It cannot be said that there is a political consensus in favour of the existing legal position, nor, however, is there any agreement on the need for, or shape of, changes to the legal framework to meet the changed situation.

An examination of discussion of this issue in recent years and a look back to discussion at the time of federation reveals, however, a similarity and continuity that has always ended in an affirmation of ultimate Commonwealth responsibility for the conduct of relations with other countries. While the constitutional status of Australia and its component entities has been transformed between 1901 and the passage in 1986 of the Australia Act, the basic approach to legal questions of responsibility for conduct and implementation of international affairs as between the Commonwealth and the states has not changed. Recent legal developments should not therefore be seen as radical legal departures. Rather, they primarily represent, it is suggested, changes in the political climate.

It is proposed to take a brief look at some of the earlier historical aspects of this question before outlining the constitutional position. This chapter will then examine the issues from today's perspective. In relation to this aspect, it will be convenient to divide the issue into:

1 the external dimension—the actual conduct of relations with foreign states and other international persons, including the conclusion of treaties and other international agreements;

2 the internal dimension—the allocation and implementation within Australia of legal responsibility for giving effect to domestic policies designed to further Australia's international relations. This embraces the regulation of relations between government and its citizens within Australia, such as the implementation in domestic law of treaty obligations.

Historical perspective

It is generally accepted (with the late Murphy J. as a notable dissentient) that the adoption of the Constitution in 1901 did not make Australia an independent nation in international law. Such independent status was achieved gradually through conventional growth and acceptance of Dominion status, marked by such events as the Balfour Declaration in 1926 and culminating in the Statute of Westminster in 1931 which was not formally adopted by Australia until 1942 (Zines, 1977). Nevertheless the Constitution has been seen as 'an "independence Constitution", that is as the constitutional basis for an Australian nation (although the "nation" was at the time, and for the time being, also a "colony")' (O'Connell and Crawford, 1984: 23–4).

While in 1901 Australia had substantial limits on its international competence, nevertheless as regards the internal allocation of responsibility for dealing with the international community, the imperial authorities, particularly as expressed through the voice of Chamberlain, had no doubt where responsibility lay. In the speech by Chamberlain on 14 May 1900 on the Constitution of Australia Constitution Bill in the House of Commons, he acknowledged that: 'everything which has to do with the exterior relations of the six colonies concerned will be a matter for the Commonwealth and not for the individual governments' (Greenwood and Grimshaw, 1977: 6).

While concerned to ensure appropriate imperial control in relation to matters involving dealings with foreign countries, Chamberlain anticipated in this speech the views he expressed so clearly in his 1902 despatch to the South Australian government in relation to the Vondel matter. He stated:

> Before the (Constitution) Act came into force each of the separate states, subject of course to the ultimate authority of the Imperial Parliament, enjoyed practically all the powers and all the responsibilities of separate nations. By the Act a new state or nation was created armed with paramount power . . . to deal with all political matters arising between them and any other part of the Empire or (through His Majesty's government) with any foreign power . . . Australia became one single entity . . . and the external responsibility of Australia except in regard to matters in respect of which a later date was fixed by the Constitution vested immediately in the Commonwealth which was armed with the paramount power necessary to discharge it (Greenwood and Grimshaw, 1977: 33).

In these sentiments Chamberlain echoed at least some of the founding fathers. Deane J. in the *Frankline Dam* case (1983: 255) reminded us of the 1891 statement of Sir Henry Parkes as to one of the objects of federation—the creation of 'one great union government which shall act for the whole'. Parkes said:

> That government must, of course, be sufficiently strong to act with effect, to act successfully, and must be sufficiently strong to carry the name and fame of Australia with unspotted beauty and with uncrippled power throughout the world. One great end, to my mind, of a federated Australia is that it must of necessity secure for Australia a place in the family of nations, which it can never attain while it is split up into separate colonies.

Despite these assertions of potential Commonwealth power, the reality was that foreign and defence policy of the new Australian polity was initially very much subject to and part of an overall imperial policy (Meaney, 1976). Nevertheless, as imperial relations evolved, as ideas of an imperial federation faded and instead considerable Dominion autonomy developed, so the Constitution showed its ability to reflect and adapt to the changing situation.

The Constitution

Executive power

The Constitution was largely silent about matters falling within the 'external' prerogatives of the Crown. Matters such as the appointment of ambassadors, the conclusion of treaties, and the declaration of war were regarded as matters that fell clearly within areas of imperial responsibility. Nevertheless, the Constitution contained a general executive power in section 61:

> The executive power of the Commonwealth is vested in the Queen and is exerciseable by the Governor-General as the Queen's representative, and extends to the execution and maintenance of this Constitution, and of the laws of the Commonwealth.

With the evolution of Australia into an independent nation, so the 'external' prerogatives devolved on the Commonwealth, to the exclusion of the states. (See Zines, 1977, for a detailed examination of this issue.) Section 61 is now generally accepted as the basis on which the Commonwealth exercises executive powers relevant to the conduct of foreign relations. This gives it in particular an unlimited power to *conclude* treaties.

Under section 2 of the Constitution there is power for the Queen to assign powers and functions to the Governor-General. In 1954 and 1973 the Queen assigned to the Governor-General the power to appoint certain diplomatic personnel but not other powers (for example, to execute Letters of Credence and Recall). These assignments were revoked in 1987, being regarded as anomalous and unnecessary. Section 61 alone suffices for the exercise of all the external prerogatives (O'Connell and Crawford, 1984: 27–8). Not only does the Commonwealth have executive power, but this executive power to conclude treaties, enter into diplomatic relations or declare war or peace is an exclusive Commonwealth power (Zines, 1977; Burmester, 1978: 261–2).

The Commonwealth is not, thus, hampered by the Constitution in the external aspects of the conduct of international relations. However, as will be discussed, this does not mean that problems do not arise between the Commonwealth and the states in this area. The implications of this devolution of power on the Commonwealth will be postponed till then.

Legislative power

Principal focus in considering the 'internal' aspect necessarily has to be given to the scope of the power to legislate with respect to external affairs in section 51(xxix) of the Constitution. Before doing that, however, it is useful to recall other legislative powers that the Commonwealth has and which enable it to control matters that are relevant to the conduct of international affairs. These powers include:

- s.51(i) — trade and commerce with other countries
- s.51(vi) — defence
- s.51(x) — fisheries in Australian waters beyond territorial limits
- s.51(xix) — naturalisation and aliens
- s.51(xx) — foreign corporations

s.51(xxx) — the relations of the Commonwealth with the islands of the Pacific

A number of other powers may at times be relevant, for example, section 51(xxviii)—the influx of criminals. The external affairs power has become significant as the issues that have become of international interest and concern have extended into areas such as human rights, environment, private law and matters not otherwise covered by Commonwealth legislative power. It is this development which has been of principal concern to the Australian states. The interpretation of the power has been a subject of controversy ever since 1900 when Chamberlain described external affairs as 'a phrase of great breadth and vagueness, which, unless interpreted and controlled by some other provision, might easily, it will be seen, give rise to serious difficulties' (Greenwood and Grimshaw, 1977: 7). During the Constitutional Conventions in the 1890s a specific reference to 'treaties' in this head of power was removed on the ground that it was a matter for the imperial authorities and not the Commonwealth (Thomson, 1977). This did not subsequently mean that the power did not extend to treaty implementation. The central issue since has, in fact, been the extent to which the power authorises legislative implementation of treaty provisions.

It is only with the *Franklin Dam* case in 1983 that there was a clear majority of the High Court indicating that the external affairs power would support Commonwealth legislation implementing in Australia *any* international treaty obligation, even if that obligation involved a matter of purely domestic significance and without any need to establish that the matter was one of international concern. Affirmation of this should not, however, be seen as a new turning. It was rather the logical outcome of earlier decisions and has been seen, at least by some, for example, Professor Sawer (1983–84), as merely a restatement of the effect of the earlier 1936 decision in the *Burgess* case (1936), which authorised air navigation regulations controlling all aircraft in conformity with the 1919 Convention on Aerial Navigation. Other decisions had upheld use of the power to implement certain treaty provisions, for example, *Airlines of NSW* case (1965), upholding certain air navigation regulations giving effect to the 1944 Chicago Convention.

The *Franklin Dam* decision removed suggestions that had arisen in 1982 in *Koowarta v Bjelke-Petersen* that some additional criteria had to be met, such as that the treaty dealt with a matter of international concern, before the external affairs power would support legislation. In that case three judges (Gibbs CJ., Wilson and Aickin JJ.) said the Racial Discrimination Convention could not be implemented by Commonwealth legislation. Three judges said it could (Mason, Murphy and Brennan JJ.), and Stephen J. said it could but only because racial discrimination was a matter of international concern. This same limitation had been suggested in the *Burgess* case in 1936 by Dixon J. who regarded as 'extreme' the view that merely because the Executive undertakes with some other country that the conduct of persons shall be regulated in a particular way, the legislature thereby obtains a power to enact that regulation (1936: 669). The suggested limitation was rejected by four judges in the *Franklin Dam* case (see Byrnes and Charlesworth, 1985 for a discussion of both the *Koowarta* and *Franklin Dam* decisions).

From the viewpoint of the states the decision in that case removed any hope they previously had that the High Court might impose some significant restraints on the powers of the Commonwealth parliament to legislate to implement treaty obligations. The restraints in future (as it should be added they had largely been in the past) would now need to be secured essentially by political and not legal means.

Without attempting any lengthy analysis of the case, the *Franklin Dam* case:

1 clarified that a requirement that a matter be one of international concern or significance was not an additional requirement where a treaty obligation was involved. It may however be relevant where a benefit under a treaty or some other international right is sought to support legislation;

2 reaffirmed the traditional limitations on the external affairs power, namely that:

  a a treaty cannot be used to support the exercise of legislative power if it has not been concluded in good faith—there is no example, however, of such an instance and it is difficult to envisage;

  b the general limitations and safeguards in the Constitution operate, for example, section 116 on establishment of religion; nor could one, by treaty, for instance seek to amend the Constitution to, for example, abolish upper houses;

3 recognised that the doctrine of implied state immunities—that a Commonwealth law cannot discriminate against a state or impair the existence or capacity of a state to function—could limit the legislative power. This does not necessarily prevent, however, a Commonwealth law controlling activity on state Crown land; and

4 reaffirmed that the law must be reasonably able to be considered an appropriate means of giving effect to a treaty obligation; in other words the law must 'conform' to the treaty. There continue to be differences in approach by the judges as to how strict this conformity must be.

There also now seems to be general acceptance by the High Court that the external affairs power authorises legislation to control areas, things or persons geographically external to Australia. This aspect of the power generally does not raise federal issues, except that it is significant in relation to control of activity in the three miles of territorial sea around Australia. The states were given title and concurrent legislative power over this area under the 1979 offshore constitutional settlement. The states have been particularly concerned to preserve their legislative powers over this area in relation to matters clearly of international concern such as pollution from ships.

There are still a number of areas where the scope of the power is unclear. For instance, does it extend to implementation of recommendations of international organisations or international declarations or resolutions? In 1936 in *Burgess* Evatt and McTiernan JJ. said that it did. In *Franklin Dam* Murphy and Deane JJ. contemplated that a law giving effect to international recommendations could be characterised as a law with respect to external affairs. Mason J. took the view that legislation could deal with 'benefits' under a treaty.

Nor is the power just confined to relations with other *states*. It extends to external affairs. Murphy J. recognised that relations with multinational corporations, international trade unions and other groups could be matters of external affairs. The extent of legislative power in this area remains, however, untested. Apart from by treaty, the judges have recognised that the Commonwealth has power to legislate in order to implement customary international law. It has also been recognised that the power extends generally to control of issues that directly affect relations with other governments such as exciting disaffection, preventing private mercenary armies entering another country, protecting the diplomats of a foreign State.

How far the power will enable a law to operate in relation to matters within Australia where there is no clear treaty obligation will, it seems, become largely a question of judgment on the part of judges. The external affairs power will, to this extent, become a purposive power, like the defence power, as the judges seek to determine whether a particular law is designed to give effect to or regulate some external affairs issue. This raises questions about the degree to which judges can and should question executive and legislative judgment about whether a matter raises an external affairs issue. It is partly the reluctance of judges to second guess the executive that leads the majority High Court judges to accept that a treaty obligation is sufficient by itself to give rise to an external affair (see Mason J. in *Franklin Dam*, 1983: 125). (See generally on the external affairs power, Zines, 1986.)

Having outlined the constitutional position it is appropriate to turn to consider the implications for the Australian states and their role in the conduct of Australia's international relations.

The external dimension

The power to speak for Australia and to deal and negotiate with other international actors is central to the external dimension of the conduct of a nation's international affairs. The Commonwealth, as indicated above, is in a strong legal position in this area. It has the external prerogatives to appoint ambassadors, to negotiate treaties. Its power in these areas is exclusive. As was said in a 1952 memorandum addressed to the Secretary-General of the United Nations: 'although the Australian Constitution is federal in character, the component states have no international status, and the making of treaties is a function of the federal executive alone' (UN Legislative Series, ST LEG/SER B/3, 1952). The international community has not sought to question this situation, which has generally been long accepted.

Latham CJ. in the *Burgess* case (1936: 645) said: 'other countries deal with Australia and not the states of the Commonwealth and this practice follows the evident intention of the Constitution'. Murphy J. has stated the position more broadly:

> [The states] have no international personality, no capacity to negotiate or enter into treaties, no power to exchange or send representatives to other international persons and no right to deal generally with other countries, through agents or otherwise (*Seas and Submerged Lands* case, 1975: 337).

This statement goes too far. The states do communicate with foreign states, conclude agreements in relation to trade and investment and maintain offices overseas. From a legal point of view these might, however, all be explained as no different from the activities of a large corporation with international connections. Nevertheless, the political reality is that a statement or dealing by a component political unit of a state is not the same as a statement or dealing by a business leader.

The states do compete with each other for foreign investment and for the development of export markets. This has led the states to open offices in a number of centres overseas such as Tokyo, Bonn and New York. Agents-General have been appointed to London, an office with colonial origins but now essentially an office with commercial functions like the other overseas state offices. As Campbell Sharman concluded after his 1973 survey: 'the dominant reason for the persistence and growth of state links with the international community is a commercial one' (Sharman, 1973). And while the states in their external dealings may not be able to act at the level of an international person, 'whatever the formal constitutional position, it is difficult in practice to exclude the constituent units of federal states from some forms of discussion and agreement at the international level' (O'Connell and Crawford, 1984: 34; for details of state overseas activity, see Ravenhill, forthcoming).

Nevertheless, the Commonwealth is concerned that these international dealings are kept limited. In this connection it is of interest that the passage of the Australia Act, which provided that the legislative powers of the states included power to make laws for the peace, order and good government of the state that have extra-territorial operation, also provided that this conferral of legislative power was subject to the proviso: 'nothing in this sub-section confers on a state any capacity that the state did not have immediately before the commencement of this Act to engage in relations with countries outside Australia'.

However, as Hocking in his study points out, the co-ordination and co-operation between Commonwealth and states that one might expect in this area does not appear to exist. Instead one can point to instances of states seeking to conduct their own foreign relations (see Hocking, 1984; Sharman, 1973).

Dr T.B. Millar instances the government of Queensland threatening to withhold coal mining leases from Japanese companies unless Japan bought Australian beef. This demonstrated, he said, 'how a state government could enter, perhaps critically, into national negotiations over trade or foreign investment' (Millar, 1978: 401). The Queensland Premier has often been outspoken in matters of foreign affairs, incurring the displeasure of foreign leaders. For instance, in 1984 he suggested Australian trade retaliation against New Zealand for its anti-nuclear stance. This provoked the Prime Minister of New Zealand to reply: 'The man has no mandate to run a defence, foreign relations or trade and industry policy' (*Canberra Times*, 9 October 1984).

It is difficult to see the Commonwealth legislating to prevent free speech by state politicians on matters of foreign policy. There will continue to be embarrassment, just as radio and television or newspaper articles can incur the wrath of foreign governments and can lead to diplomatic retaliation (for example, the expulsion of Australian trade officials from Teheran following a television programme poking fun at Iran's leaders).

Arising out of their international contacts, the states do conclude agreements, often with foreign states themselves or state instrumentalities. The extent to which such agreements are concluded is largely unknown. Many of these agreements would be similar to those concluded by a large mining corporation. They will derive their legal validity from a domestic system of law, often that of the state involved, and will be interpreted in the same way as private contracts. This is the case with the agreement between the South Australian Department of Agriculture and Libya on assistance in farming, which was subject to Libyan law (Ravenhill, forthcoming). There are, however, intergovernmental agreements the status of which is not so clear. Some agreements may not be intended to give rise to legal obligations but may be designed to be essentially political statements or 'best endeavours' type undertakings. These sorts of agreements are concluded between the Commonwealth and the states and there is no reason similar agreements cannot be concluded between the states and a foreign government. The Western Australian government apparently regards its agreement with Libya and certain commercial agreements as memoranda of understanding (Ravenhill, forthcoming). There are, however, other agreements the status of which is less clear (see Burmester, 1978: 262–6).

Unlike the Canadian provinces, particularly Quebec, the Australian states have not, however, purported to conclude agreements with international persons on the basis that the states themselves are international persons. In the 1970s there was some concern that the states might be seeking to assert such a capacity. In the 1976 Report of the Queensland Treaties Commission an argument was elaborated that the states had executive power to:

> make intergovernmental agreements which are legally binding even if they are non-justiciable in domestic courts . . . If such agreements are made with foreign governments and not with the Commonwealth or other Australian states, there is no reason to suppose that they may be any less a legal matter. The proper law may be municipal law or it may be international law. If it is the latter, the line between mere contract and a treaty becomes thin and the distinction a formality (Burmester, 1978: 263).

It is suggested that this attempt to blur the distinction is not an accurate portrayal of the legal position. An agreement that derives its validity from the international law plane can only be concluded between persons with international capacity. As indicated, the Australian states do not have this capacity. This is not just because of the provisions of the Australian Constitution, but also because no international capacity in the states has been recognised by any sovereign foreign states.

This is not the case in certain other federations, where a limited international competence in the component units appears to exist and certain agreements, mostly agreements dealing with common administrative border problems facing the component units, have been concluded between the component units and foreign states. These agreements may create legal difficulties in terms of accurate characterisation but in their own way they will help to solve some of the regional and border problems facing the component units (Di Marzo, 1980). In those federations, where a power for component units to conclude agreements at the international law level exists, it is usually exerciseable only with the approval of, or subject to some control by, the central government. (For a general discussion, see Burmester, 1978: 262–71.)

In the case of direct dealing and agreements, the Australian federal government is well placed to exercise control through its powers over overseas trade and investment. If it does not approve of a particular development it can prevent import or export approval. If a state were to conclude an agreement with a foreign state or entity that the Commonwealth considered undesirable or inappropriate it ultimately has sufficient legislative power, including use of the external affairs power, to override such an agreement or otherwise to control the external activities of the states (Sawer, 1984). The political implications of such action may, however, be another matter. Yet, if one imagines a radical state government sympathetic to the aspirations of a foreign government or liberation movement with which the federal government was not in sympathy, or to which it was deliberately opposed, then federal legislative intervention to restrict state dealings with that foreign state or entity is clearly possible. In most instances, however, one would expect political not legal solutions to be sought, although the ultimate ability of the federal government to prevent contact can clearly be a major factor in negotiating a satisfactory political compromise.

As mentioned, the Commonwealth can use its legislative power to override state executive action which it regards as prejudicial to the conduct of its foreign relations. Commonwealth legislation can also override any inconsistent state legislation pursuant to section 109 of the Constitution. Whether state legislative power extends to enable state laws to be enacted on matters of international relations is a more difficult question. Clearly state legislation can be passed to enact laws giving effect in the state, for instance, to particular treaty provisions. Whether a state could enact a law authorising the conclusion of a 'treaty' or dealing with some other aspect of relations with other countries is less clear. Barwick CJ. has said: 'whilst the power with respect to external affairs is not expressed to be a power exclusively vested in the Commonwealth, it must necessarily of its nature be so as to international relations and affairs' (*Seas and Submerged Lands* case, 1975). Professor Sawer concludes that while the Commonwealth's power to legislate in relation to foreign affairs may 'not in all respects [be] formally exclusive [it] is certainly paramount in a special sense' (Sawer, 1984: 47). In the USA, the Supreme Court has been willing more readily to exclude state law from areas of foreign relations concern (Burmester, 1978: 276–80). This is an area not yet explored by the High Court.

One area where the Commonwealth is involved in external dealings and where it has, in recent years, sought to accommodate state concerns and their wish to be involved in matters of international concern is treaty negotiation in relation to matters of state interest. The Commonwealth has included state representatives on delegations to certain international conferences and meetings. This had occurred on earlier occasions, but it has been formalised, and occurs more often, since the adoption in 1977 of Guidelines on Treaty Co-operation. Those Guidelines contained the following:

> In appropriate cases, a representative or representatives of the states are included in delegations to international conferences which deal with state subject matters; subject to any special arrangements, the purpose is not to share in the making of policy decisions or to speak for Australia, but to ensure that the states know what is going on and are always in a position to put a point of view to the Commonwealth. However, state representatives are involved as far as possible in the work of the delegation.

A similar statement appears in the 1983 revised guidelines adopted by the Labor government.

State representatives have been included on delegations to the Law of the Sea Conference, South Pacific Environment Protection Conferences, Human Rights Commission and Hague Conference on Private International Law meetings. These meetings deal with matters over which the states can point to a major interest in terms of traditional responsibilities for regulation of the subject matter. The states have also been represented in delegations to certain bilateral negotiations including those with Japan over fisheries and maritime delimitation talks with Indonesia. Queensland was not included, however, in delegations involved in negotiations with Papua New Guinea over the Torres Strait Treaty. There was, however, significant separate negotiation between the Commonwealth and Queensland as the negotiations between Australia and Papua New Guinea took place. The states have also been represented in delegations to meetings that do not have such a clear state interest such as the Preparatory Commission for the Law of the Sea Convention dealing with deep seabed mining; Tasmania is represented in the Antarctic minerals negotiations delegation. The normal practice at multilateral meetings of interest to all states is for representation to rotate among the states and for costs to be shared by all states.

The desire of the states to upgrade their status on delegations is reflected in the recommendation of the external affairs sub-committee of the Australian Constitutional Convention in 1984 that:

> The practice of state officers attending negotiating sessions as part of the Australian delegation should be encouraged. Where state officers do attend, they should attend as full members of the delegation being bound by the terms of the brief for the Australian delegation and responsible to the leader of the Delegation. This right as full delegate should include access to appropriate cables and communication facilities.

The same degree of co-operation and co-ordination that has been shown in the negotiation of treaties has not, however, been shown in other areas such as foreign trade and investment. In these areas the states compete among themselves and do not necessarily share the same perspective as the Commonwealth. The premiers of the states regularly travel overseas, for instance, seeking investment or markets, often at the expense of the other states. As T.B. Millar has summed it up:

> The Constitution and the facts of international living ensure that the Australian states will be fringe participants in Australia's external relations for as far ahead as one can see. And because they are constituents of the Australian Commonwealth and their electors are simultaneously federal electors, the federal government in foreign policy will always have to watch their interest, heed their fears and desires and try to restrain their excesses (Millar, 1978: 402).

This will be necessary notwithstanding the strong legal position of the Commonwealth.

The internal dimension

The area of greatest controversy relating to the Australian states and international affairs is the internal dimension—the implementation within Australia of international agreements or arrangements and domestic policies designed to further Australia's relations with other countries. The recent clarification of the extent of the external affairs power as a basis for Commonwealth legislation has been outlined earlier.

There are, however, a number of significant legal issues which arise that illustrate that, as a matter of practice, the states exercise considerable concurrent authority in this area. It is only in the exceptional case that the Commonwealth government legislates to exclude the states completely from a role in implementation of treaties of interest to the states or to override some strongly held state policy.

In many areas, for example treaties on defence or even trade in agricultural commodities, the states accept that it is appropriate for the Commonwealth to legislate. In other areas, the states jealously guard their role in legislative implementation, and often the Commonwealth has been happy to rely on state legislation and administration to implement particular treaties or policies. The current attitude of the Commonwealth to use of state legislation is reflected in the Guidelines on Treaty Consultation:

> The Commonwealth will consider relying on state legislation where the treaty affects an area of particular concern to the states and this course is consistent with the national interest and the effective and timely discharge of treaty obligations. However the government does not accept that it is appropriate for the Commonwealth to commit itself in a general way not to legislate in areas that are constitutionally subject to Commonwealth power.

The reliance on state legislation to implement treaties has a long history. Examples where the Commonwealth has relied on state legislation to implement treaties include treaties on migratory birds, oil pollution from ships and the International Covenant on Civil and Political Rights, although in this later case the Commonwealth has established its own investigatory body. International Labour Organisation (ILO) Conventions are another area where state legislation has been relied upon to implement treaty provisions. In part this reliance might, in the past, have been explained as a result of uncertainty about the scope of the external affairs power. But it also reflects a more fundamental political commitment to co-operation and hence a recognition that implementation of a treaty by state legislation is often appropriate. Reliance on state law thus continues, notwithstanding the clarification of the scope of the external affairs power.

Where the Commonwealth itself chooses not to legislate, the requirement to ensure that the laws of the states and the territories are all appropriate to give effect to a particular Convention, and the need to gain assurances from each state that they agree to ratification has, however, meant a large number of Conventions have not been ratified, or their ratification has been delayed even though the Commonwealth might be in favour of ratification. This has been particularly the case in relation to ILO Conventions (Byrnes, 1985). Reliance on state legislation does, of course, require, on the part of the Commonwealth, some assurance that the states will not turn around and change their law once Australia has accepted a treaty obligation (Burmester, 1978: 271). In international law it is Australia not the states that will have to answer for a breach of a treaty or other international law obligation. While appropriate assurances are sought from the states in this regard, and the agreement of the states to ratification obtained in cases where state law is being relied upon, this is essentially a political commitment. A state might decide for policy reasons some years later to alter its legislation. For instance, there are suggestions that recent Queensland industrial legislation may be in breach of ILO Conventions that Australia has accepted. Certain states passed legislation outlawing discrimination against women, including women working in mines, and this was inconsistent with an ILO Convention Australia had accepted outlawing women in mines. In such a situation Australia can either terminate its treaty acceptance (which is what was done in relation to the ILO Convention) or legislate to override the state law. Of course, it was the Commonwealth's decision to legislate to override state law that led to the *Franklin Dam* decision. In that case the Commonwealth government's assessment of what its international obligations entailed did not coincide with the view of the state government. Political solutions could not be found; the legal solution was resorted to and upheld. It seems important if a federal state is to be able to avoid breaches of its international obligations for which it will be held internationally responsible that it have the power to override state law in this way.

There are, however, instances where the federal government decides to legislate itself to implement a treaty and to exclude state legislation in areas that could be regarded as traditionally of state concern. If, for instance, the states delay or obstruct implementation of a treaty about which the Commonwealth feels strongly or which it wishes to move quickly to ratify it will sometimes enact Commonwealth legislation, possibly with 'roll-back clauses', i.e. clauses that enable the Commonwealth Act to be rolled back to enable state law consistent with the Convention to operate. An example is the *Protection of the Sea (Pollution from Ships) Act 1983*, which was amended in 1986 to cover the territorial sea after the states had not legislated quickly enough to cover that area. On the other hand, the Commonwealth regarded the dumping of radioactive wastes at sea as so important and a critical part of South Pacific Treaties on a Nuclear Free Zone and on the Environment that it legislated to control this activity completely, and did not provide for state law to operate in the area at all.

It is appropriate to mention at this point that reliance on the states to assist in the internal implementation of foreign relations policies can give rise to difficulties in areas other than that of treaties. While the Commonwealth is prepared to recognise a role for the states in relation to certain matters it is also concerned to protect its own ability to control within Australia sensitive issues involving its relations with foreign countries. As indicated above, it has significant constitutional powers quite apart from the external affairs power and many interests of its own. These need to be considered in determining the appropriate role for the states in relation to the internal aspect of Australia's international affairs. For instance, the Commonwealth sought to protect its primacy in this regard in the offshore area by explicit provision in the *Coastal Waters (State Powers) Act 1980*. In that Act the states were given legislative powers over the territorial sea. That area is, however, an area of international concern and an area where Australia has certain international obligations. In recognition of this, section 6 provides:

> Nothing in this Act affects the status of the territorial sea of Australia under international law or the rights and duties of the Commonwealth in relation to ensuring the observance, in relation to that sea or any other waters, of international law, including the provisions of international agreements binding on the Commonwealth and, in particular, the provisions of the Convention on the Territorial Sea and the Contiguous Zone relating to the right of innocent passage of ships.

Another example of potential conflict between state and Commonwealth internal policies was the threat by the Victorian Premier in 1976 to close Victorian ports to visiting United States warships. The Commonwealth government made it clear that it would, if necessary, pass legislation that would override any state attempt to interfere in what was seen as a matter of direct Commonwealth responsibility. The state Premier backed down and foreign warships continue to visit Victorian ports.

In order to protect their position in relation to matters of traditional state concern from the possibility of Commonwealth intrusion, the states have sought a number of protections. They have sought to address the problem identified by Wheare of 'how the power of the central government in foreign affairs, whatever its extent may be, is to be controlled so that in its exercise the divergent interests of the component regions in the federation shall be duly safeguarded' (Wheare, 1963: 183). A number of mechanisms have been suggested to control Commonwealth power. These have included:

- use of federal clauses
- formalising treaty consultation procedures, including possibly establishment of a Treaties Council
- greater parliamentary involvement
- constitutional amendment.

Federal clauses

During the period of the Fraser government, there was a sustained effort to give legal protection to the right of states to implement treaties by seeking the inclusion of federal clauses in treaties. These clauses would reduce the obligations of federal states in relation to matters falling within the competence of their component units. Federal clauses had been included in a number of treaties in the 1950s but by the 1970s and 1980s they were no longer generally acceptable to the international community. Non-federal states saw no reason why federal states should receive special treatment, particularly when the consequence was that the level of obligations accepted by federal states was reduced. Nevertheless, Australia did, between 1975 and 1983, expend considerable energy, with little return, seeking the inclusion of such clauses in certain treaties, particularly those dealing with private business law but also in human rights treaties, such as the proposed Convention on Torture (Burmester, 1985). The Hawke Labor government does not favour the inclusion of such clauses and has not supported their inclusion. This is made clear in the 1983 revised Treaty Consultation Procedures reproduced in the Appendix to this chapter.

The decision of the High Court in the *Franklin Dam* case (1983) has indicated, however, that federal clauses of the usual kind are of little legal significance under Australia's Constitution. Following the interpretation of the external affairs power to the effect that it enabled the Commonwealth parliament to legislate to implement treaty obligations, federal clauses which were premised on component units having legislative competence in relation to particular subject matters and the federal government competence in relation to certain other defined areas were held by the majority judges to be inapplicable to the Australian constitutional position.

A different kind of clause, a territorial units clause, has been favoured by Canada and it has gained acceptance in certain treaties dealing primarily with uniformity of private law rules. This clause enables Canada to adhere to treaties containing the clause only in relation to certain provinces and not others. Australia has not made use of such a clause, taking the view that treaties should apply uniformly across the country. The possibility exists, however, for the application of certain treaties only to certain states and this was recognised in the revised 1983 Treaty Consultation Procedures (see Appendix to this chapter). (For a discussion of Australian policy on federal clauses, see Burmester, 1985.)

Consultation

Another way in which the states have sought to protect their position is by formalising consultation procedures in relation to treaties. In an attempt to reassure the states that potential Commonwealth power would be exercised in a limited way the Fraser government agreed to adopt formalised procedures for consultations on treaties for the first time. The Premiers' Conference in 1977 adopted a set of principles and procedures that ensured the states were informed of treaty negotiations at an early stage and given an opportunity to make an impact in matters of interest. These were further developed and revised guidelines adopted in 1982. These procedures underwent some revision in 1983 under the Labor government but remain largely intact as a continuing restraint on unilateral Commonwealth assertion of power over matters of traditional concern to the states. As mentioned above, a copy of the present procedures is attached.

Another suggestion designed to ensure close consultation on treaty matters that emanated from the Australian Constitutional Convention is the idea of a Treaties Council, comprising Commonwealth and state officials who would report on treaties to which Australia contemplated becoming a party. This has not received any wide support. The Federal Republic of Germany has such a body. (See the paper prepared by this author for the external affairs sub-committee, Australian Constitutional Convention, 1984.)

Under these procedures, a regularly updated Treaties Schedule is provided to the states listing Commonwealth treaty action. The states are informed and consulted before the Commonwealth moves to implement certain treaties of interest to the states. An opportunity for the states to legislate to implement treaties continues to exist. For instance, the states have just passed legislation implementing the UNCITRAL Convention on International Sales. A number of other safeguards have been suggested by the states in an effort to limit Commonwealth powers to interfere with state domestic policies or laws.

Parliamentary involvement

Proposals have been made for changes at the federal level in the way in which treaties are handled. One suggestion is for greater parliamentary scrutiny and involvement which would at least expose any state concerns about a particular treaty and its method of implementation. In the USA it is argued that the requirement that two-thirds of the Senate approve ratification of treaties can act as some safeguard for the various state and regional interests of the nation. In Australia no such requirement for parliamentary approval exists before treaties can be concluded, other than the need for legislation to implement treaties affecting private rights.

Despite some suggestions from Senator Harradine that all treaties first be considered by a Committee of the Senate before ratification there has been surprisingly little support for greater parliamentary involvement (Notice of Motion, 21 February 1985). Such a proposal would ensure that the Senate, as the states house, and the community, including state governments, were aware of proposed treaty action and that appropriate consideration was given to the implications for federal relations including implications for legislative action. Greater parliamentary scrutiny could provide some safeguard against use of the treaty power to intrude into areas of state concern. It is of interest that the National Party 1987 election policy did contain a proposal that, except for treaties involving defence or national security, parliamentary approval should be necessary before ratification of a treaty.

The World Heritage Convention is given as an example of one treaty where greater parliamentary involvement at the time of ratification would have been desirable. No legislation was thought necessary to enable ratification of that Convention, which took place with no parliamentary involvement. However, legislation was subsequently thought appropriate some years later in order to enable the Commonwealth to discharge its obligations in a particular instance. If parliamentary scrutiny had occurred prior to ratification, the significance of the treaty for federal–state relations might have been appreciated and considered.

Constitutional amendment

Another way in which it has been suggested that limits on Commonwealth power in relation to the internal aspect of international affairs be reimposed is a constitutional amendment to limit the scope of the external affairs power. Agreement on an appropriate amendment that leaves the Commonwealth with essential power yet limits the treaty implementation aspect of the power is difficult to achieve. The Labor Party sees no need for a change. Senator Durack for the Liberal Party has proposed an amendment that would limit the external affairs power, so far as it operates with respect to persons, matters or things within the Commonwealth, to (1) persons, matters or things that have a substantial relationship to other countries, or to persons, matters or things outside the Commonwealth, and the enactment deals with, or with matters affecting or arising out of, that relationship; or (2) the operation of the enactment is related to the movement of persons, matters or things into or out of the Commonwealth. The amendment would not derogate from the executive power of the Commonwealth, including its treaty-making power (Constitution Alteration (External Affairs) Bill 1984).

The Australian Constitutional Convention external affairs subcommittee examined this whole issue extensively in 1983–84. There was no consensus however on any major reform. The Australian Constitutional Commission is also looking at this issue, but at the time of writing no proposals have been made for change in this area. It is of interest that all suggestions for change appear essentially negative, i.e. designed to confine Commonwealth power. There are no proposals to expand state capacity to participate in the conclusion of international agreements.

Conclusion

The Commonwealth, as a matter of constitutional law, now clearly has the power to conduct Australia's international relations and the power to implement domestically the policies and legislation necessary to enable that conduct to take place. What uncertainties remain about the scope of the external affairs power, such as the extent to which it extends to implementation of recommendations of an international body, are not considered significant legal impairments.

At the same time, the Australian federal system at the political level has been strong enough to ensure that in many instances the Commonwealth does not assert its undoubted power, but relies on state co-operation to enact legislation, or voluntarily to restrict their trade and investment policies or take other particular action. If, however, national interest is considered to require it, the Commonwealth has shown its willingness to intervene. The use of the World Heritage Convention both to stop the building of a dam in Tasmania and, most recently, to establish an inquiry into certain forestry issues in Tasmania indicates the extent to which a determined federal government can go in reliance on its external affairs power. These are, however, isolated examples. One can point to many more examples where the federal government has deferred to state concerns or sensitivities and only acted with the concurrence or agreement of the states. At the same time, there is no doubt that, on occasions, the federal system has served as a smoke-screen, particularly under the Fraser government, 'behind which a lack of commitment to a particular policy can conveniently be hidden' (see the detailed study on the implementation of treaties by Byrnes, 1985).

The political working of the federal system in the area of international affairs is where most attention will now need to be focussed, although the legal framework outlined in this chapter indicates a variety of ways in which political choices can be pursued.

APPENDIX

Principles and procedures for Commonwealth–State consultation on treaties—adopted at Premiers' Conference—June 1982, as subsequently endorsed by the Commonwealth in October 1983

The Commonwealth endorses the principles and procedures, subject to their operation not being allowed to result in unreasonable delays in the negotiating, joining or implementing of treaties by Australia.

A. Consultation

- **i)** The States are informed in all cases and at an early stage of any treaty discussions in which Australia is considering participation. Where available, information on the long term treaty work programs of international bodies is to be provided to the States.
- **ii)** Information about treaty discussions is forwarded to Premiers' Departments on a regular basis through the Department of the Prime Minister and Cabinet.
- **iii)** As a general practice, consultation is conducted by the functional Commonwealth/State Ministers or Departments concerned.
- **iv)** Existing Commonwealth/State Ministers' consultative bodies (such as the Standing Committee of Attorneys-General, the Australian Fisheries Council, etc.) may be used as the forums in which detailed discussions of particular treaties take place.
- **v)** Functional Departments keep Premiers' Department, State Crown Law Offices, the Commonwealth Attorney-General's Department and the Departments of Foreign Affairs and Prime Minister and Cabinet informed of the treaty matters under consideration.
- **vi)** When issues are to be discussed that are of particular significance to either State or Commonwealth authorities other than those directly represented on the Commonwealth/State consultative bodies, representatives of such authorities might be invited to attend the meetings in an observer role.

vii) The procedures outlined would not preclude direct communications between Premiers (and Premiers' Departments) and the Prime Minister (and the Department of the Prime Minister and Cabinet) on particular treaties. These channels may need to be invoked in cases where inter alia there is no established ministerial channel of communication, where ministerial councils are unable to reach final agreement or where significant changes in general policy are involved.

viii) Ministers and Departments, in considering treaty matters, may draw on legal advice and, through their Law Ministers, could refer any matter to the Standing Committee of Attorneys-General for advice. It is expected that, where a major legal issue arises in a consultative body, that body will avail itself of the legal expertise of the Standing Committee.

ix) The consultative process needs to be continued through to the stage of implementation where treaties bear on State interests. Where the preparation of reports to international bodies on implementation action takes place, States should be consulted and their views taken into account in the preparation of those reports.

B. Treaty negotiation process

i) Where State interest is apparent, the Commonwealth should, wherever practicable, seek and take into account the views of the States in formulating Australian policy and keep the States informed of the determined policy.

ii) In appropriate cases, a representative or representatives of the States are included in delegations to international conferences which deal with State subject matters; subject to any special arrangements, the purpose is not to share in the making of policy decisions or to speak for Australia, but to ensure that the States know what is going on and are always in a position to put a point of view to the Commonwealth. However, State representatives are involved as far as possible in the work of the delegation.

iii) It is normally for the States to initiate moves for inclusion in a delegation, but the Commonwealth should endeavour to keep State interests in mind.

iv) Unless otherwise agreed, the costs of the State representatives are a matter for State Governments.

C. Federal state aspects

i) The Government does not favour the inclusion of federal clauses in treaties and does not intend to instruct Australian delegations to seek such inclusion. The pursuit of federal clauses in treaties is generally seen by the international community as an attempt by the Federal State to avoid the full obligations of a party to the treaty. Experience at a number of International Conferences has shown that such clauses are regarded with disfavour by almost the entire international community. Experience has also shown that a Federal clause tailored to the needs of one federation will be unacceptable to other federations. Instructing an Australian Delegation to press for a federal clause only diverts its resources from more important tasks.

ii) The Government sees no objection to Australia making unilaterally a short 'Federal Statement' on signing or ratifying certain appropriate treaties, provided that such a statement clearly does not affect Australia's obligations as a party. An 'appropriate' treaty would be one where it is intended that the States will play a role in its implementation. An appropriate form for such a statement, acceptable to most States and the Commonwealth, is attached.

iii) The normal practice is that Australia does not become a party to a treaty containing a federal clause until the laws of all States are brought into line with the mandatory provisions of the treaty. However, where a suitable 'territorial units' federal clause is included in a treaty, the possibility of Australia acceding only in respect of those States which wish to adopt the treaty might be considered on a case by case basis where appropriate, perhaps in some private law treaties.

iv) The Commonwealth will consider relying on State legislation where the treaty affects an area of particular concern to the States and this course is consistent with the national interest and the effective and timely discharge of treaty obligations. However the Government does not accept that it is appropriate for the Commonwealth to commit itself in a general way not to legislate in areas that are constitutionally subject to Commonwealth power.

Federal statement

Australia has a federal constitutional system in which legislative, executive and judicial powers are shared or distributed between the Commonwealth and the constituent States.

The implementation of the treaty throughout Australia will be effected by the Commonwealth, State and Territory authorities having regard to their respective constitutional powers and arrangements concerning their exercise.

Judicial decisions

Airlines of New South Wales v New South Wales [*No. 2*] (1965) 113 CLR 54.
Franklin Dam case: *Commonwealth v Tasmania* (1983) 158 CLR 1.
Koowarta v Bjelke-Petersen (1982) 153 CLR 168.
R v Burgess; ex parte Henry (1936) 55 CLR 608.
Seas and Submerged Lands case: *New South Wales* v *Commonwealth* (1975) 135 CLR 337.

References

Australian Constitutional Convention (1984), External Affairs Sub-Committee, *Report to Standing Committee D*, Melbourne, September.
Burmester, H. (1978), 'The Australian States and Participation in the Foreign Policy Process', *Federal Law Review* 9: 257–83.
—— (1985), 'Federal Clauses', *International and Comparative Law Quarterly* 34: 522–37.
Byrnes, A. (1985), 'The Implementation of Treaties in Australia after the Tasmanian Dams Case: The External Affairs Power and the Influence of Federalism', *Boston College International and Comparative Law Review* 8: 275–339.
Byrnes, A. and Charlesworth, H. (1985), 'Federalism and the International Legal Order: Recent Developments in Australia', *American Journal of International Law* 79: 622–40.
Di Marzo, L. (1980), *Component Units of Federal States and International Agreements*, Sijthoff, Alphen.
Greenwood, G. and Grimshaw, C. (1977), *Documents on Australian International Affairs*, Nelson, Melbourne.
Hocking, B. (1984), 'Pluralism and Foreign Policy—the States and the Management of Australia's External Relations', *Yearbook of World Affairs* 38: 137–53.
Meaney, N. (1976), *The Search for Security in the Pacific 1901–1914*, Sydney University Press, Sydney.
Millar, T.B. (1978), *Australia in Peace and War*, ANU Press, Canberra.
O'Connell, D.P. and Crawford, J. (1984), 'The Evolution of Australia's International Personality', in K. Ryan (ed.), *International Law in Australia*, 2nd edn, Law Book Company, Sydney.
Ravenhill, J. (forthcoming), 'Australia', in H. Michelmann and P. Soldatos (eds), *Federalism and International Relations*, Oxford University Press.

Sawer, G. (1983–84), 'The External Affairs Power', *Federal Law Review* 14: 199–207.

—— (1984), 'Australian Constitutional Law in Relation to International Relations and International Law', in K. Ryan (ed.), *International Law in Australia*, 2nd edn, Law Book Company, Sydney.

Sharman, C. (1973), 'The Australian States and External Affairs: An Exploratory Note', *Australian Outlook* 27: 307–18.

Thomson, J.A. (1977), 'A United States Guide to Constitutional Limitations upon Treaties as a Source of Australian Municipal Law', *University of Western Australia Law Review* 13: 110–134.

Wheare, K.C. (1963), *Federal Government*, 4th edn, Oxford University Press, London.

Zines, L. (1977), 'The Growth of Australian Nationhood and its Effect on the Powers of the Commonwealth', in L. Zines (ed.), *Commentaries on the Australian Constitution*, Law Book Company, Sydney.

—— (1986), *The High Court and the Constitution*, 2nd edn, Butterworths, Sydney.

FEDERALISM, THE STATES AND ECONOMIC POLICY

10

AN ECONOMIC PERSPECTIVE

Cliff Walsh

INTRODUCTION

The perspective of 'Federalism, the states and economic policy' that I adopt in this chapter is essentially contemporary. Moreover it is principally concerned with the impact of fiscal relationships between 'levels' of government on the capacity of, and incentives to, the state local sector to pursue, according to their own priorities, the economic policies that they wish to pursue. That is, I am primarily concerned to raise questions about current fiscal federalism arrangements as they affect the states rather than to undertake an historical review of the development of state policies.

The purely fiscal perspective, of course, implies that I largely ignore some important features of Australia's federalism arrangements that unquestionably can have a significant impact on economic policy and the role of the states. For example, it means that I set aside consideration of the capacity of the Commonwealth to shape state economic and other policies through its use of its powers over trade (especially through the use of export controls), capital inflow (especially through rules governing foreign investment) and external affairs (through treaty 'obligations'). In recent years, in various ways, the use of these powers has had a significant effect on state development. Export controls and foreign investment rules have had a major influence on the development of Australia's mineral resources, especially in relation to sand mining and uranium. The external affairs power, on the other hand, was used to preclude Tasmania's proposed development of a hydro-electric scheme in the South-West (the Franklin Dam) as a result of its World Heritage Listing and to limit wood-chipping operations in Tasmania pending completion of an investigation of areas for World Heritage Listing, while its further use has been threatened in relation to the Daintree rainforests in Queensland.

Obviously, the use of such powers is a major issue in federalism and economic policy, broadly conceived. Indeed, in the case of the use of the external affairs power, some might argue that potentially it overshadows all other sources of constraint on the independence of the states. Nonetheless, I shall have little more to say about the direct use of such powers, for at least two reasons. First, to give them worthwhile consideration would require a full essay, and a greater knowledge of the relevant aspects of constitutional law than I can bring to bear. Second, but relatedly, in any event I am inclined to the view that developments in fiscal arrangements are of more fundamental and urgent concern. As significant as they may be, the use of the Commonwealth's trade or external affairs powers are inevitably selective, well publicised, subject ultimately to public opinion and open to legal challenge. By contrast, developments in fiscal arrangements are more pervasive, tend to have occurred by a process of slow attrition in less public view and, in my opinion, have reached an important watershed.

Some background observations

As I observed at the outset, my central concern is with the extent to which current fiscal federalism arrangements provide the states with the capacity independently to pursue the policies that they wish. This, of course, raises some important questions about the appropriate role of the states which cannot be answered satisfactorily merely by examining either the Constitution or the current effective role of the Commonwealth *vis-à-vis* the states. Let me state clearly then my own basic position, which will be amplified as consideration of the issues proceeds.[1]

In my view, whatever the historical circumstances of their establishment, one of the most important features of federal constitutions is their role in constraining the ability of governments to use in an exploitative way the coercive powers that are necessarily given to them. Even in countries without written constitutions, legislated or unlegislated 'conventions' and rules—for example, those governing the timing and conduct of elections—serve this purpose. Political federalism I take to be another such constraint adopted by some countries. On this view, the coercive powers of central governments are, and are intended to be, constrained both by the constitutionally defined limits on their roles and functions and by the fact that they are in effect put into competition with subnational governments that are given essentially equal rights in their own domains and given concurrent access to major revenue sources. The coercive powers of subnational governments are further constrained by their being put into political competition with one another, voters (and businesses) having the power to vote with their feet as well as through the ballot box.

From this perspective, of course, emphasis is placed rather more on *processes* than on outcomes *per se*. For example, whether federalism arrangements actually result in diversity in service levels among subnational governments is much less important than whether they give the subnational jurisdictions the capacity to choose independently the policies to pursue. In similar vein, how one judges the development of co-operative arrangements between national and subnational governments would be as much influenced by the extent to which they emerge from (and sustain) initial positions of equal power as by the ostensible worthiness of their purposes.

For another thing, other than where constitutions give national governments exclusive powers, or legislative precedence over shared powers, there should be no simple presumption that objectives defined by national governments should have unchallenged 'primacy' over subnational objectives.

Against this background, it will come as no surprise to learn that I regard the post-war development of fiscal federalism in Australia, and of the intellectual orthodoxy that has supported and sustained that developments with substantial concern. The financial dominance acquired by the Commonwealth and the related dependence of the state/local sector on Commonwealth grants seems to me to be fundamentally destructive of federalism, appropriately interpreted.

Let me say at the outset that my concern in this regard is quite unrelated to the current debate about whether the public sector is ' too big'. For reasons fully articulated elsewhere[2], I am of the view that major spending reform and reduction is desirable. I also strongly suspect that Australia's federalism arrangements have contributed to an over-expansion of public sector spending in the post-war period for reasons that go beyond the undoubted waste and duplication associated with many of the current programmes and administrative arrangements. But my principal concern here is with the quality and characteristics of the decision-making processes associated with the present structure of federalism arrangements more than with the specific details of the outcomes that have been produced by them or would be produced by alternatives.

Since the core of the concern revolves around the question of taxing powers, the bulk of my argument will focus on the role of Commonwealth assistance to the states. I will also, however, raise some issues relating particularly to the use of section 96 (specific purpose) grants and the role and influence of the Australian Loan Council.

Constitutional responsibilities and the division of taxing powers

The Australian Constitution, including amendments secured by referenda, gives a limited range of exclusive powers to the Commonwealth (especially the coining of money and the power to impose duties of customs and excise) but a much wider range of areas in which it has concurrent jurisdiction with the states but with Commonwealth laws taking precedence over state laws (including defence, external affairs, social welfare benefits, communications, foreign and interstate trade, taxation, corporations, immigration, patents, offshore fisheries and resources, some aspects of banking and insurance, arbitration involving interstate disputes and Aboriginal affairs). Though they have the power to refer matters to the Commonwealth, in all other things the states have a 'residual' exclusive jurisdiction, including over education; health; housing; urban development; environment; water supply and essential services; civil, criminal and commercial law; conditions relating to mining and agriculture; and the intrastate regulation of employment, working conditions, commerce and transportation.

As is now well known, despite the fact that in the post-war period this division of responsibilities has resulted in the states being responsible for (roughly speaking) a little more than 50 per cent of total public sector outlays, and despite their having concurrent powers over taxation save for customs and excise duties, the state–local sector raises only 20 per cent of taxation revenue—less than half of its revenue needs. Commonwealth grants represent over 50 per cent of state budget sector outlays, and more than 40 per cent of total state–local sector outlays.

Although the peculiar and economically dubious High Court interpretation of Commonwealth exclusive power over excise duties as precluding states imposing sales taxes on goods has contributed to this positon, the major factor has unquestionably been the Commonwealth's decision to retain exclusive power over income tax—a power initially acquired during the Second World War as a 'temporary' measure. This is particularly emphasised by observing that in 1938–39 the states collected over 70 per cent of total income tax revenue (individual and company), which represented over 45 per cent of state–local tax revenues. Overall, at that time state–local taxation revenue was about 47 per cent of total taxation revenue (compared to 20 per cent today) and Commonwealth assistance amounted to about 11 per cent of state–local receipts (compared to over 40 per cent today).

It is not only in comparison with its own earlier history that Australia's current division of own-source taxation revenues is peculiar. As Table 10.1 illustrates. Australia is considerably out of line with other major federal countries. As indicated in the final section of that table, for all the countries shown the ratio of the proportions of federal taxation to federal own-purpose outlays exceeds unity: that is, all federal governments collect more tax revenue than they need for their own purposes and make grants to other levels of government. But the Commonwealth government's 'excess tax ratio' of 56 per cent is almost double that of Canada and Switzerland (around 30 per cent), almost four times that of West Germany and more than four times that of the USA.

Particularly striking, moreover, is the fact that the Australian states' ratio of own-sourced revenue to own purpose outlays is only *half* of the next worst (Switzerland) and dramatically out of line with all others. Australian local governments (which admittedly generally have less important functions than those elsewhere) do comparatively well; it is the states that face the real 'own-sourced revenue squeeze'.

Like all international comparisons, these need to be treated with extreme caution because of problems in the comparability of data (including the complexities caused by social security levies and the exclusion of non-tax receipts) and because of institutional differences (including the respective roles of the different government levels). However, they certainly point to a remarkable difference in Australia relative to other countries, expecially for the state level which, the own-purpose outlays data confirm, have a more important role in Australia than elsewhere.

Faced with these imbalances, with recurring pressures to do something about the position of the states and with increasing pressures on their own budgets, Commonwealth governments have adopted a variety of responses. In the early 1970s, the pressure for a 'state growth tax' was eventually met by the Commonwealth transferring payroll taxation to the states. The Whitlam government, in pursuit of its regional and social policy objectives, on the other hand, substantially increased transfers to the states, including transfers for schools, and took over responsibility for higher education funding and for some state railway systems entirely, and adopted a cost-sharing arrangement for hospital funding.

The Fraser government initially offered a so-called 'new federalism' policy which, *inter alia*, gave the states the opportunity to introduce a marginal income tax surcharge or rebate, but no state has taken advantage of the opportunity—at least in part because the Commonwealth did not explicitly make room in an income tax structure already considered excessively burdensome. In relation to general revenue assistance, the Fraser government subsequently took a different tack with the introduction of various forms of tax sharing while, nonetheless, squeezing overall assistance to the states.

The Hawke government reverted to financial assistance grants initially with modest real growth 'guarantees' (guarantees that have now been cancelled as part of the strategy to substantially reduce prospective 1987–88 Commonwealth outlays) but squeezed other transfers and advances sufficiently so that total Commonwealth assistance actually fell in real terms in 1986–87.

In fact, the Commonwealth has been squeezing its assistance to the state–local sector over a substantial period, and more so recently. As a share of Commonwealth budget outlays, Commonwealth assistance has dropped from a peak of over 38 per cent in 1978–79 to less than 31 per cent in 1986–87, lower than its share prior to the 'Whitlam surge'. Indeed, prior to 1986–87, the Commonwealth had been increasing its own-purpose outlays as a share of GDP, while squeezing its assistance to the state–local sector. In 1986–87, more than half of the planned reduction in Commonwealth total outlays as a share of GDP was to be achieved by reduced assistance to the state–local sector: in fact, their assistance was reduced in real terms, while Commonwealth own-purpose outlays were constant in real terms. On the basis of the figures released in the May 1987 mini-budget, the squeeze clearly is to continue. Half of the proposed expenditure savings are cuts in state–local general purpose and specific purpose assistance. Even including the proposed assets sales, the Commonwealth's own-purpose outlays will be reduced by only 1 per cent in real terms compared to a 4 per cent real cut in assistance to the state–local sector. Excluding the assets sales, the Commonwealth's own-purpose outlays will actually increase in real terms.

The effects of intergovernmental grants

The Australian orthodoxy on fiscal federalism over the post-war period has, in general terms, favoured the dominance of the Commonwealth over financial resources. The essential ingredients in that support have been on the one hand the recognition that diversity among states in service provision may be a desirable thing, but at the same time a presumption that the 'national objectives' of macro-economic stability and income redistribution (including between the states) require substantial financial power on the Commonwealth's part in general, and control of the income tax in particular.

Nonetheless, particularly in recent years, even those who favour retaining Commonwealth dominance and broad uniformity in the tax system have expressed increasing concern about the implications of the extreme vertical imbalance that prevails. The states, it has been argued with increasing urgency, in large measure are able to avoid the opprobrium that otherwise would be attached to raising the revenue to fund their own expenditures and hence are more inclined to spend and less inclined to experiment. Commonwealth governments, moreover, have been able to give their policies and ideologies primacy even where they are constitutionally precluded from exercising decision-making power.

While obviously relevant and important, this line of argument greatly understates the nature of the problem. Just as important, the usual conclusion drawn from it—that greater revenue-sharing would overcome the potential problems—also misses a great deal that is important in sustaining what might be regarded as real federalism.

This orthodox approach pays only the slightest of lip service to the nature of the political processes through which decisions on the provision of public services are to be made; and it makes no allowance for the fact that federalism itself might be intended explicitly to be a political device in which giving genuine *independence* to sovereign subnational governments is as vital a matter as the outcomes that actually emerge.

Properly taking into account the nature of political processes suggests that the presence of large elements of grants in the funding of decentralised governments is likely to be a more serious problem than is typically conceded in federalism discussion. Such grants not only lower the apparent tax cost of decentralised service provision and encourage 'excess' demands for and supplies of services, they create the prospect of competitive bidding over the distribution of grants, with resources wasted in the bidding process and the prospect of politically rather than economically motivated outcomes.

Indeed, under federalism, a particularly potent special interest group is created. Local politicians can offer political support to federal level politicians in exchange for grants to their local jurisdictions: local citizens barely perceive that their federal taxes are raised (or benefits reduced) and in any event only bear part of the 'cost'. If federalism arrangements permit and encourage this 'trade' in grants, then what will emerge is a public sector within which the subnational sector is over-expanded at the expense of federal level services. The grants will, in general, be provided partly by increasing federal taxation and partly by reducing federal outlays compared to the no-grants situation. Whether the public sector as a whole will be overexpanded is an open question and one much less relevant than the observation that the presence of grants encourages behaviour that wastes resources in rent seeking, and distorts the pattern of real resource use (see Brennan and Buchanan, 1980; 1983; Grossman, 1987).

This line of reasoning does not deny the possible role of grants for 'horizontal balance' purposes, nor, necessarily, for correcting the consequences of benefit spillovers between jurisdictions (which otherwise would tend to result in undervaluation of public services *within* the jurisdiction). It does, however, suggest an important warning. The presence of significant grants in federal financial arrangements does more than just undermine the link between taxing and spending, damaging as that alone may be to responsible decision-making. It also creates the possibility of intergovernmental grants causing fundamentally more serious problems for the efficiency and the stability of political decision-making as they become the focus of increasing political pressure group activity, diverting attention and 'entrepreneurship' at all levels of government away from efficient, responsive and creative service provision.

As noted in my introductory comments, it is important to recognise that what also is missing from the orthodox 'economic' or 'fiscal' view of federalism arrangements is a perspective that focusses on its potential role as a constraint on the coercive power of government. From this perspective, another feature of the present fiscal federalism arrangements in Australia is that they severely restrict the potential benefits that would flow from tax competition between the states and/or local jurisdictions. If voters could clearly see that taxes were higher or lower in their state because of the spending policies and administrative practices of their state government, they would be better able to use the ballot box, or decisions to relocate, to secure tax or spending packages more in accord with their preferences—an observation consistent with the possibility that some would prefer higher levels of services which might be secured through governments running leaner, rather than spending (and taxing) more.

One thing that does seem clear is that independent access to taxation revenues sufficient to adequately carry out powers and responsibilities at all levels of government is an *essential* ingredient in sustaining the constraining role of federalism. Nothwithstanding the existence of an apparently open-ended (section 96) granting power in the hands of the Commonwealth under the Australian Constitution, the use of granting powers in a way that undermines the intention effectively to constrain coercive powers would be entirely contrary to the spirit of the interpretation of the purpose of political federalism suggested here.

It is important, however, to acknowledge that the use of grants to overcome constitutional constraints may not represent purely Commonwealth 'interference'. The centralisation of taxing powers in the hands of the Commonwealth, in exchange for grants, provides a mechanism by which *all* levels of government can minimise the impact of 'competition' on their ability to pursue their objectives without bumping into political restraints. The formation of a 'taxation revenue cartel' or 'fiscal club' can minimise the difficulties for them all of raising revenue beyond the levels that would be possible with independent behaviour and of avoiding the pressures towards 'leaner' government that might otherwise emerge. Of course, under these circumstances, we ought to expect other forms of ('non-price') competition to arise, particularly perhaps in terms of the expenditure policies offered by governments. Specifically, with grants intervening to reduce tax competition, spending policies might be expected to be over-expanded for reasons additional to those involved in responding to pressure groups discussed earlier.

It hardly needs to be pointed out, perhaps, that the Australian states have, indeed, vigorously pursued policies intended to secure development objectives through offering concessions/incentives to industries and activities to relocate. They have, too, vigorously lobbied the Commonwealth and its agencies to have national policies or the location of particular national projects designed to further their interests. There is considerable doubt, however, whether these policies and pressures have significantly altered the pattern of state development that would have occurred in their absence—though they may have acted to defend states against the similar policies pursued by others.[3] Making states more revenue independent by no means would eliminate potentially unproductive competitive behaviour, but it would increase the apparent cost to governments and taxpayers in terms of own-source revenue of such activities, and may induce such competition as occurs to take less wasteful forms. 'Competition-limiting' devices in federal systems, like barriers to competition in private markets, provide benefits to some, particularly public sector employees (including politicians) who obtain maintenance of employment, higher salaries and freedom from the more demanding environment of cost-minimising efficiency.

The general point, again, is that anything which interferes with the direct relationship between spending and taxing is likely to reduce the constraints built into the constitutional allocation of responsibilities and increase the likelihood of undesirable outcomes. The outcomes produced under 'pure' (competitive) federalism arrangements obviously may have 'costs' compared with some ideal (co-operative) alternative arrangements. But unless those ideal arrangements can be associated with a feasible political process that can secure and sustain their implementation—or which at least can be shown to do better—the practical significance of this observation is approximately zero. Nor is it the case that more 'competitive' federalism is inconsistent with co-operation emerging where desirable—but it would be co-operation based on more equal power between states and the Commonwealth.

It is true that the states have some capacity to expand their own taxation revenues even without access to sales taxes (on goods) and the income tax. They could increase their effort from existing taxes, not all of which are inherently inefficient or inequitable. But much of their current base contributes to the selective and inefficient nature of indirect taxation in Australia, and 'new' opportunities—such as a sales tax on services—are fraught with complexities that might best be avoided at state level. Some additional reduction in the reliance of the states on grants might also be secured, it is true, by more widespread application of user charges (for example, in the hospitals sector) or by cutting back on spending in areas where its effectiveness is questionable (schools, for example). Even so, if we seriously want to reduce the dependence of the states on Commonwealth grants, nothing short of a major shift of taxing capacity will do, and for this purpose only access to broad-based taxation of consumption expenditure and/or of income will generate sufficient revenues.

Returning taxing powers to the states

Much of the recent discussion about improving the quality of decision-making under federalism has conceded something of a case for increasing the states' access to revenue sources currently denied to them, but frequently has suggested that this should be achieved by formal revenue sharing with the Commonwealth. That is, the states, it is argued, should have some pre-specified share of one of the major revenue bases currently the sole preserve of the Commonwealth, in place of a substantial part of their grants.[4] Statistically, the dependence of the states would, indeed, be reduced; to the extent that the state tax share and the Commonwealth definitions of the base were less easily manipulated than grants, the states would have greater security; and somewhat clearer signals would flow to citizen-voters about who was really responsible for raising revenue. Nonetheless, while formal revenue sharing might be a step that would be better than nothing, it is hardly likely to herald a new era in federalism in which the power of the states *vis-à-vis* the Commonwealth is restored and creative competition and experimentation are encouraged. Indeed, to the extent that formula arrangements apply to state shares no additional competitive flexibility in tax rate setting is induced.

A somewhat bolder step has been supported by Russell Mathews (see Mathews 1986, for example) who has argued for the states being able to fix and vary their own income tax rates, provided they accept the Commonwealth Assessment Act and use the Commonwealth as the tax collection agent. Again, of course, the Commonwealth would withdraw some pre-specified part of its existing general purpose grants, and lower its own tax rates 'to make space' for the state taxes. With this I have much greater sympathy, since it would give the states a great deal more autonomy while retaining many of the advantages of uniform assessment and administration arrangements. However, the logic of my position on federalism compels me to say that I would support this arrangement only insofar as it were supported by the states themselves, and if any state wished to opt out of uniformity that would be a price that in the final analysis we should be prepared to consider paying to re-establish genuine federalism.

Moreover, the surely unintended preclusion of the states from sales taxation through the ridiculously broad High Court interpretation of the meaning of excises *also* should be overturned if the relevant constitutional amendment can be secured, as suggested in a partial analysis by the fiscal powers sub-committee of the recent Constitutional Convention. Again it would be advantageous—but not in my view an essential precondition—if the states and the Commonwealth could agree on an appropriately broadened common base, with a single collection agency. In the event that constitutional change proved impossible to secure, the formula-type proposal of the Commonwealth 'sharing' the sales tax with the states may be the only feasible option. It would be worth taking in that event, but would be distinctly inferior to genuine independence.

It will be objected by some that in expanding state taxing powers in these ways national stabilisation objectives would be put at risk. However, discretionary variations in tax rates are now an almost defunct stabilisation policy tool; and, even with much reduced tax revenues, the Commonwealth's ability to use tax changes for stabilisation purposes would not be directly affected. Depending on the nature of the state taxes there could perhaps be some loss of 'automatic stabilisation' from the income tax, but this would be neither very substantial nor unbearable.

What might be of more concern to those who give priority to the Commonwealth in stabilisation policy would be the threat that the states might use their new freedom to engage in 'balanced budget' pump-priming and would have more flexible tools for doing so than at present. This, of course, is an objection to any increased taxation power for the states. Indeed, taken to its logical limits, it is an objection to any independent subnational tax policy discretion. In any event, the states ultimately would be constrained by what their taxpayers would tolerate as a balanced budget tax increase, and unless all states co-ordinated their activities in appropriate ways the national impact need not be substantial.

Objections on national policy grounds also might be raised in relation to redistribution policy. Again, however, a number of counter-arguments exist. Most evidence suggests that, in practice, it is cash benefits rather than the structure of taxation that contribute most to redistribution through the tax/transfer mechanism. In any event, the presumption that states should not engage in redistribution is not universally accepted; their capacity to do so would be limited by the threat of migration of high income earners; and to totally preclude redistributional action by states would necessitate requiring them to eliminate all non-benefit taxation, a suggestion not seriously entertained by anyone, to my knowledge. Other federations live with state taxes, apparently without massive loss of effectiveness of national goals, redistributive or otherwise.

In a recent paper[5], I have provided some estimates of, and discussed the technical issues raised by, a states' income tax designed initially to replace all but the redistributional component of the present general revenue funds provided by the Commonwealth. My estimates suggest that something of the order of a 10 per cent states' income tax would be required with the Commonwealth cutting its rate scale to approximately 14 per cent, 19 per cent, 30 per cent and 39 per cent, to reduce its revenue and to cut grants by a little over $11 billion. I need not traverse this ground further, save to point out that this step alone would raise state taxation revenue from about 16 per cent of total taxation to almost 30 per cent; would lower Commonwealth taxation from 80 per cent of the total to about 68 per cent; would increase state–local own-sourced funding from about 46 per cent to about 65 per cent of their own-purpose outlays and would reduce Commonwealth assistance from 40 per cent of state–local receipts to about 22 per cent. There is no reason, of course, why the restoration of independence should stop at that point, whether or not the states also could be given access to broad-based sales tax. Indeed, as I shall argue in the next section, reducing the scope and role of specific purpose payments also would be desirable and they too could be part of the new deal on state taxes and Commonwealth withdrawal from grants and associated revenue raising. Nor does there seem any compelling reason why general purpose capital grants should be excluded from similar treatment.

None of this need reduce the capacity of the Commonwealth to maintain the provision of redistributional grants between the 'stronger' and the 'weaker' states. There are, nevertheless, some important questions to be raised about the nature and pattern of these grants suggested by recent analyses of these issues[6] and by concerns expressed by some of the states. However, while the impact of the Grants Commission procedures is clearly important to the ability of the states to independently pursue their economic policies, it is a subject that I do not have space to pursue beyond a brief comment.

Putting aside some nonetheless important issues about how sensitive the formulae are to some variables that in principle ought not to influence state *shares* (for example, the degree of concentration of revenue raising by the Commonwealth) and more generally putting aside questions about whether equalisation is appropriate at all, one doubt in my mind concerns the role of cost differences (or 'expenditure needs' as they are called). Australia is, I believe, the only federation to compensate for differences in the cost of providing a standard bundle of public services (arising from sparse population or whatever)—and such differential expenditure needs turn out to be the single most important variable.

Of course, remoteness and sparseness of population may both explain why the expenditure need variable is so dominant and to an extent underpin the politics of its inclusion. But to compensate for it on a routine formula basis is to underwrite what, from a national viewpoint, may be inefficient and unjustifiable location decisions. To this extent, at least, there is a significant difference, as I see it, between compensating for revenue needs and expenditure needs. Although a case could be made for eliminating expenditure needs entirely—leaving it to the states and/or the Commonwealth to make discretionary provision for subsidising remote public services—some less radical adjustments would be possible. For example, one could either reduce the weight attached to expenditure needs in general, or attempt to distinguish between cases in which cost differences are an inevitable by-product of economic activity from those that are the result of supporting the unsupportable.

In any event, there are a number of issues in need of reconsideration, and there is some hope, perhaps, that the inclusion in the Grants Commission's current reference to issues of economic efficiency might stimulate a wider debate about the desirable nature of 'horizontal equalisation'.

Specific purpose assistance

Specific purpose payments have been a major form of transfer from the Commonwealth to the states especially in relation to funding education, health, roads, public housing and local government, but extending over a very wide range of other state activities. In the mid-1970s, they reached almost a half of all Commonwealth assistance, and even today are about 37 per cent of total payments.

In some cases, they represent extremely high proportions of Commonwealth outlays on the relevant purpose, reflecting the fact that the Commonwealth is intruding where it has no direct constitutional power. For example, specific purpose grants represent 80 per cent of Commonwealth education outlays and contribute over one-third of state–local education outlays, for housing they represent 75 per cent of Commonwealth outlays and about 30 per cent of state–local outlays and so on. While I do not intend to pursue particular cases in any depth, some general observations are clearly highly relevant to the issue of the independence of the states to pursue their own objectives.

In a genuinely decentralised federalism, the scope of specific purpose payments should be severely limited. The need for a Commonwealth granting power is not denied: at the very least, it would be necessary to allow for inter-jurisdictional redistribution. There may also be cases where changes in technology or in tastes suggest that the original constitutional allocation of functions is no longer appropriate, and a transitional mechanism is needed until amendment of the Constitution is possible: but these arrangements should be merely temporary and transitional, and eventually should be tested through referenda.

To move towards genuine fiscal decentralisation on a revenue-neutral basis, most specific purpose grants should be absorbed into the general revenue financial assistance pool whether or not there was to be state income and/or sales taxation on the basis outlined earlier. Not only would such a move reduce the risk of unwanted paternalistic intervention by the Commonwealth, it should help also, within the context of a more competitive federalism, to create greater incentives at state level to rationalise the use of resources and possibly encourage the more widespread development of user-charging, where appropriate. Moreover, as the states themselves have begun to argue with greater vigour[7], there are very substantial savings in bureaucratic and other duplication to be made from rationalisation of current arrangements—a matter being looked into by a task force of Commonwealth and state officials.[8]

If specific purpose grants have any rationale, it is to change the *relative* cost to states of providing particular services. In theory, the purpose of these grants is to correct for the presence of inter-jurisdictional spillover benefits (or costs) that would tend to lead to under (over) evaluation of the benefits of particular forms of spending. Whether such spillovers are likely to be so significant in Australia (with large states) as to warrant, even in principle, the extensive array of grants we presently have is open to serious doubt. In any event, the wider the range of services to which they apply, the less the impact of the grants in changing the relative cost of different services.

In principle, moreover, there is no particular reason why the Commonwealth government should be the agency for arranging grants to correct inter-jurisdictional spillovers, where they are considered significant (for example, with education). Negotiation between the states—with, at most, the Commonwealth an observer–referee—would be the preferred means and it would be an interesting test of current arrangements to see what remained of inter-jurisdictional specific purpose grants under such an arrangement. Of course, much of the grant giving in practice reflects political imperatives from time to time and, too often for comfort, pure pork-barrel politics. The states usually have little incentive to refuse grants, whatever the intentions of the donor, particularly since they now typically do not have binding matching provisions.

It seems particularly clear that the (extreme) use of section 96 grants to transfer full effective spending power to the Commonwealth (as in higher education) is a means of completely circumventing constitutional processes. Without denying that changes in the distribution of spending powers (and concomitant tax powers) may be desirable over time, it might be argued that, for example, where Commonwealth outlays on functions not constitutionally within its province reach some specified proportion of total outlays on that function, it should be required to seek explicit approval for their continuation (or for a takeover) by referendum. More radically, Cheryl Saunders has argued that as part of a general reform of granting powers, section 96 ideally should be removed from the Constitution and replaced with new provisions that are constitutionally, politically and economically based on more secure foundations.[9]

The general point, of course, is that specific purpose grants are a potentially pernicious form of grant from the Commonwealth that can undermine the independence of the states, create perverse behavioural incentives and promote the wasteful grant-seeking competition discussed earlier. As significant as 'waste and duplication' may be where both the Commonwealth and the states are involved in the funding and supply of particular services, it is only the tip of the iceberg of costs associated with the Commonwealth's overuse of the section 96 granting power. The minimum requirement for change would be absorption of most of them into general revenue assistance as a step towards broader reform.

The role of the Loan Council

Finally, but inevitably, I turn to a brief consideration of the Australian Loan Council's part in securing greater independence for the states.

As a result of the Financial Agreement of 1927, the subsequent Gentlemen's Agreement of 1936 and increasing general financial dominance of the Commonwealth in subsequent years, the Australian Loan Council has become a major instrument for fiscal centralisation. Indeed, although substantial gains would flow from returning taxing powers to the states, it is difficult to see how *genuine* fiscal decentralisation could be secured without also substantially lessening Loan Council control.

Arguments for rescinding the provisions of both the Gentlemen's Agreement and the Financial Agreement have been presented by Ned Gramlich (1984) in his review of Australian federalism and will not be repeated here. What seems clear is that major arguments for retaining effective Commonwealth dominance of the Loan Council have centred on the need to control public sector borrowing requirements for macroeconomic purposes, and the fear of irresponsible borrowing by states and their instrumentalities. A number of points might be made in relation to this.

It is an interesting but open question how successful Loan Council controls have been in securing appropriately 'counter-cyclical' economic policy. As might have been expected *a priori*, there is substantial evidence that the states have at various times found ways to circumvent the controls when they otherwise would have been binding (i.e. constrained what the states actually wanted to do, as distinct from what they said they wanted to do). In 1981, for example, the use of domestic and overseas trade credits, roll-over of promissory notes and other short-term borrowing instruments, the use of simple leasing and leveraged-leasing deals, and a variety of other measures resulted in actual borrowings by relevant authorities of approaching *double* the approved programme. State officials have indicated that the controls have rarely altered plans significantly but have affected the cost of implementing them, though it is difficult to assess the extent to which the mere knowledge of the controls may have shaped the dimensions of ambitions.

Moreover, it has yet to be demonstrated that Loan Council decisions proved to be *effectively* counter-cyclical: for a variety of reasons, macroeconomic policy may be mistimed and misjudged, and the Loan Council has not been a very flexible instrument of macro-policy in any event. Equally important, there is the suggestion often made that, together with centralisation of taxation, Loan Council restrictions have imposed a substantial cost by distorting the balance between provision of public infrastructure capital and private capital formation, as well as between capital and recurrent outlays within the public sector.

Somewhat intriguingly, the present state–local sector *deficit*, currently a little below 3 per cent of GDP, is below that experienced throughout the 1960s and not significantly different from its average over the last twenty-five years or so. What has happened in the meantime, however, is that the Commonwealth has substantially reduced its advances to the states (i.e. borrowings it makes on their behalf), pushing the states into greater direct borrowing from the private sector—an outcome made even more inevitable by the fact that the Commonwealth has also reduced its current purpose assistance. And since the Commonwealth has not used its reduced borrowings on behalf of the states to reduce its total borrowing requirements, the pressure of total public sector borrowing requirements has expanded considerably.[10] To this extent, much of the criticism of state borrowings is misdirected, or at least based on a rather partial view of the underlying reasons.

Without denying the need in current circumstances to achieve reductions in the borrowing requirements of all levels of governments and their authorities, it is difficult to see present arrangements as *effective or desirable* mechanisms for achieving 'control' in the short run, or over the longer term.

The threat of 'excessive' borrowing would be somewhat reduced if the states had available to them more broad-based, flexible revenue-raising instruments as discussed earlier. Among other things, this would decrease the Commonwealth's general financial dominance, and hence partly offset the means by which it has sustained its complete dominance of the Loan Council. In any event, the present 'global limits' arrangements applied to authorities' borrowings contain a number of perverse features. For example, the knowledge that the limits might be reduced in future surely encourages states to borrow up to the limit at all times, and to 'store' unused funds for the tougher periods. Given this, moreover, reducing the overall limits may have a differential impact on states according to how extensive a cache of liquid assets their borrowing authorities previously had managed to establish.

Equally important, the limits process inevitably results in a creative but surely unproductive search for ways around them—for example, by entering into increasing 'arm's-length' joint venture arrangements with private sector organisations to, in effect, provide public sector capital (for example, in housing). Even when the global limits are not binding, the incentive to store up funds for future stormy days induces states to promote these deals.

As with the experience before the global limits, more recent experience confirms the ultimate futility of controls. Particularly (but not exclusively) in a context where the states are given, and must accept, greater revenue-raising independence, it is difficult in principle to see why considerably more 'freedom' could not be given over borrowing programmes, especially for semi-government borrowing. Save for a *possible* requirement that authorities which want such freedom must obtain a 'rating' in overseas public capital markets and take forward cover on overseas borrowings, there seems a good case for freeing the authorities entirely, especially those which have been 'commercialised'.

Highly developed international capital markets may not always work perfectly, but they should be capable of providing reasonable market discipline on borrowing capacities—much more so than was true in the 1920s and 1930s. Ultimately the cost of excessive borrowings would fall on the authorities and their state governments, and the perverse features of present arrangements—including the somewhat arbitrary distinction between types of borrowing—would be eliminated. One strategy available to the states in the absence of reform would be to privatise authorities, thus directly freeing them from control. This might be desirable on efficiency grounds, but to an extent is a measure of the contradiction in present arrangements where the private–public borrowing distinction is drawn so sharply.

As to the states' official borrowing programmes, the case for decontrol is considerably more contentious. The inability of state governments to borrow in their own names by the issue of securities is a severe restriction on fiscal freedom that appears inconsistent with genuine fiscal decentralisation. On the other hand, it might be argued that the states (and the Commonwealth) should not resort to borrowing other than in times of economic recession or to finance income-generating capital spending. This suggests a case for simultaneously returning to the states the power to borrow in their own right on public markets but imposing constitutional restrictions on the circumstances in which they (and the Commonwealth) should be allowed to do so. Granted, of course, that they have greater independence in revenue raising, it is interesting to observe in this connection that the state governments in the USA on  average run surpluses, offsetting part of the federal borrowing requirements.

I do not claim to have offered more than some thoughts about what might be considered so far as borrowing programmes are concerned. A great deal more analysis of the issues, of past experience, and of experience elsewhere where such controls are not applied, would be needed to fully resolve the issues. But they are unquestionably a vital ingredient of securing genuine independence in Australian federalism.

Conclusion

In current economic circumstances, faced with the need to reduce public sector spending and borrowing, the states have become something of a whipping boy at the hands of the Commonwealth. Without denying that the states have a role to play in redressing the public sector–private sector imbalances exposed by a balance of payments crisis, the ease with which the Commonwealth is able to *impose* its preferred outcomes is a reflection of what I see as an equally fundamental imbalance *within* the public sector itself.

In a sense, one is almost tempted to argue that it serves the states right for their acquiescence in the process by which the Commonwealth has acquired fiscal dominance over the post-war period. In early days, they were paid off in expanded grants—sometimes general revenue grants to enable their activities in general to share in the overall expansion of public sector resources, and sometimes in specific purpose grants as the Commonwealth sought to shift priorities in its direction. Now the states are facing the 'downside', with the Commonwealth equally setting the pace on reductions in resources. But the fundamental imbalance in fiscal powers laid bare in the process in my view is too significant to be shrugged off in this way.

Without totally contradicting those who would respond by saying that we are, after all, either one nation or we are not, I would argue that we are after all a federation or we are not—or at least that we have to make up our minds about whether we are. If we intend to be a federation, then the dominance of the Commonwealth should be neither a necessary nor a desirable feature of federal financial arrangements. The states should have in some sense 'equal financial power', a condition that would seem to require essentially *independent* financial power.

Table 10.1 International comparisons: percentage of total taxation and own-purpose expenditures by level of government—1983

	Federal					
	General taxation	Social security levies	Total federal	State	Local	Total
1 *% of total taxation*						
Australia	79.5	–	79.5	16.5	4.0	100
Canada	41.1	13.1	54.2	35.6	10.2	100
West Germany	32.6	35.7	69.4	22.3	8.4	100
Switzerland	28.5	31.2	59.7	22.9	17.4	100
USA	40.6	28.7	69.3	18.5	12.2	100
2 *% of own-purpose expenditure*						
Australia			50.9	42.1	7.0	100
Canada			41.6	38.9	19.5	100
West Germany			60.4	22.1	17.5	100
Switzerland			46.3	29.4	24.3	100
USA			61.7	16.2	22.1	100
3 *Ratio of taxation to expenditure proportions*[1]						
Australia			1.56	0.39	0.57	
Canada			1.30	0.92	0.52	
West Germany			1.15	1.01	0.48	
Switzerland			1.29	0.78	0.72	
USA			1.12	1.14	0.55	

[1] Calculated as crude ratio of percentages.

Source: OECD, Revenue Statistics of OECD Member Countries 1965–84.

Independence, however, does not necessarily imply that co-operation is not possible or desirable. To this extent—that is, understood as associated with greater financial autonomy—I am in sympathy with proposals such as that of Russell Mathews that we should be aiming towards a new financial contract with a federal fiscal council as part of it. Something of decision-making substance to replace the annual rituals of Premiers' Conferences and Loan Council meetings should be developed, but will only be achieved effectively if we rethink the role of the states.

The issue of financial arrangements seems to me of such importance that I have chosen to set aside many other issues that have a bearing on the states and economic policy. Included among these omissions are such issues as the role of the states in wages and industrial relations or in industry, trade and tariff policy, issues relating to minerals and energy, questions concerning state purchasing policies and wider issues concerning the role of local government. While they are undoubtedly important, in the main it seems to me that they are likely to be better understood and better tackled when the central features of the fiscal system are back in balance.

Endnotes

1 For a wider-ranging discussion, see Walsh (1986).
2 See, for example, Freebairn, Porter and Walsh (1987).
3 See, for example, Davis and McLean (1981) and Stutchbury (1981; 1984) and the chapters on individual states in Head (1986).
4 Peter Groenewegen appears to feel this to be appropriate within the context of a 'National Tax Council'. See, for example, Groenewegen (1981).
5 See Walsh (1987b). The estimates were made before the 1987 Premiers' Conference decisions, but provide a reasonable guide to the relevant orders of magnitude.
6 See Gramlich (1984) and Chessell (1986).
7 See SA Premier Bannon's Garran Oration (1987) and the Queensland government's submission to the 1987 Premiers' Conference.
8 A fact which Premier Bannon describes as implying that the matter is considered important, but not urgent!
9 See, for example, Saunders (1987).
10 The Business Council of Australia's analysis of state finances makes this point very effectively in an interesting general overview of the issues.

References

Bannon, J.C. (1987), 'Overcoming Unintended Consequences of Federation', *Australian Journal of Public Administration*, March 1987: 1–9.

Brennan, G. and Buchanan, J.M. (1980), *The Power to Tax*, Cambridge University Press, New York.

—— (1983), 'Normative Theory for a Federal Polity: Some Public Choice Preliminaries', in C.E. McLure (ed.), *Tax Assignment in Federal Countries*, ANU Press, Canberra.

Business Council of Australia (1987), 'Report on State Finances', *mimeo*, BCA, Melbourne: 36 pp.

Chessell, D. (1986), 'Horizontal Equity in the Australian Federal System', Paper presented to XVth Conference of Economists, Monash University.

Davis, K. and McLean, I.W. (1981), 'Economic Policy', in A. Parkin and A. Patience (eds), *The Dunstan Decade*, Longman Cheshire, Melbourne: 22–80.

Freebairn, J., Porter, M.G. and Walsh, C. (1987), *Spending and Taxing: Australian Reform Options*, Allen & Unwin, Sydney.

Gramlich, E.M. (1984), 'A Fair Go: Fiscal Federalism Arrangements', in R.E. Caves and L.B. Krause (eds), *The Australian Economy: A View from the North*, Allen & Unwin, Sydney: 231–74.

Groenewegen, P. (1981), 'Apportioning Taxation Powers in a Federation', in R.L. Mathews (ed.), *State Taxation in Theory and Practice*, Centre for Research on Federal Financial Relations, ANU, Canberra: 1–24.

Grossman, P. (1987), 'Federalism and the The Size of Government', University of Adelaide Working Paper no. 87–7.

Head, B. (ed.) (1986), *The Politics of Development in Australia*, Allen & Unwin, Sydney.

Mathews, R.L. (1983), 'The Commonwealth–State Financial Contract', in J. Aldred and J. Wilkes (eds), *A Fractured Federation? Australia in the 1980s*, Allen & Unwin, Sydney.

—— (1986), 'Changing the Tax Mix: Federalism Aspects', in J.G. Head, *Changing the Tax Mix*, Australian Tax Research Foundation, Sydney.

Queensland Government (1987), *Proposals by Queensland for Public Sector Restraint*, Queensland Government Printer, Brisbane.

Saunders, C. (1987), 'Commonwealth Power over Grants', in H.G. Brennan (ed.), *Constitutional Reform and Fiscal Federalism*, Centre for Research on Federal Financial Relations, ANU.

Stutchbury, M. (1981), 'The Dunstan Government and Industry Planning in South Australia', *Australian Quarterly* 53, 2: 198–213.

—— (1984), 'The Playford Legend and the Industrialisation of South Australia', *Australian Economic History Review* 14,1: 1–19.

Walsh, C. (1988), 'Federalism Australia-Style: Towards Some New Perspectives', in H.G. Brennan, B. Grewal and P. Groenewegen (eds), *Taxation and Fiscal Federalism: Essays in Honour of Russell Mathews*, Pergamon Press, Sydney.

—— (1987a), 'The Riddle of Financial Relations', in M. Birrell (ed.), *The Australian States: Towards a Renaissance*, Longman Cheshire, Melbourne.

—— (1987b), 'The Distribution of Taxing Powers Between Levels of Government: The Possibility of a State Income Tax Reconsidered', in G. Brennan (ed.), *Constitutional Reform and Fiscal Federalism*, Occasional Paper No. 42, Centre for Research on Federal Financial Relations, ANU.

11

A POLITICAL SCIENCE PERSPECTIVE

Brian Head

The argument of this chapter may be briefly stated as follows.

1 Despite the growth of Commonwealth influence over economic activity since the Second World War, the states remain very important regulators and promoters of economic activity in their respective regions.
2 Federal–state relations affect economic policy formation in complex ways, including tendencies towards conflict and rivalry as well as tendencies towards co-operation.
3 The underlying tendency in the use of state level economic powers is towards maximising growth within its own region (if necessary at the expense of other regions); the operative tendency in national economic powers is towards a greater measure of stabilisation, rational allocation, and equity.
4 While we might expect some *minor* changes in federal–state economic powers as a result of either constitutional amendment or restructuring of taxation arrangements, it seems likely that the key issues over the next decade must centre on federal–state administrative and legislative co-operation.
5 Some examples are drawn from the fields of industry policy and resource development, with incidental comments on environmental regulation and Aboriginal land issues.
6 The overall assumption of the chapter is that arguments for reforms based purely on economic principles of efficient resource allocation will continue to founder on the shoals of political bargaining; and that, contrary to the deregulatory thrust of economic rationalism, I claim that a continuing major role for the Commonwealth is highly desirable in ensuring that both economic and political 'markets' operate with a fair degree of concern for both equity and productivity.

Federal and state economic powers

Retention by the states of substantial powers of economic and social regulation, and of revenue raising, was a precondition for the success of the federation movement in the 1890s. At the same time, economic and political nationalism was an important element in the thinking of many of the federation founders. As Robert Garran wrote in 1895, the 'first step towards prosperity must be to strike off the provincial fetters which cramp the commercial and industrial growth of young Australia' (cited in Bannon, 1987: 8); and the first Prime Minister, Sir Edmund Barton, noted in 1902 his view that 'Provincialism dies a slow death, and all that is possible for a federal government, which must not nurse it, is to ease the pangs of its passing' (cited in Wright, 1970: xvii). Needless to say, provincialism has not withered; and the legal, political and rhetorical resources of state elites have placed some practical limits upon the steady, though intermittent, growth of central powers.

The states exercise considerable powers, within their own boundaries, over employment and working conditions, commerce and industry, commercial and civil law, water and energy supplies, urban development, environmental standards, health and educational services, rural land use, mineral development, fisheries, transport, policing, and welfare and recreational services. Commonwealth legislation, in areas specified in section 51 of the Constitution, is held to override any (inconsistent) state legislation, including such fields as taxation, interstate conciliation and arbitration, corporations, trade and commerce, immigration, copyright and patents, currency, banking, insurance, external affairs, defence, welfare benefits (since 1946), and Aboriginal affairs (since 1967). Moreover, in a number of fields the Commonwealth has exclusive jurisdiction, including control over Commonwealth employees and territories, and control over 'customs and excise' (later interpreted by the High Court as effective control over all consumption taxes). As will be seen in the following section, there are important policy areas where federal powers are inadequate, alone, to deal with key issues; other areas where federal policies are (sometimes) applied in ways which, intentionally or otherwise, conflict with the policy objectives of state governments; and further areas where state powers (for example, over land use) are much more substantial than federal powers. Federal–state co-operative arrangements have necessarily followed in the wake of such division of powers.

The Commonwealth's general responsibility for national economic management has been accepted broadly by all major political viewpoints in the post-war period, though debate over the scope and detail of interventionism in certain areas has remained heated. In particular, the system of fiscal centralisation which has prevailed since 1942 has been much discussed, and many plans for reassigning fiscal powers have been put forward. Many commentators in the 1970s, reacting against the centralising thrust of the Whitlam Labor government (mirroring earlier reactions against the centralisation phase of the 1940s), diagnosed the arrival of 'coercive' federalism and called for a reversion to a more 'balanced' and 'co-operative' model of federal–state relations.

According to the mainstream viewpoint, the states should be given a greater revenue-raising capacity, so that they can set their own spending and taxing priorities and thereby be held more accountable for their decisions. Towards this objective of greater financial independence, the search for a state-level 'growth' tax (Gates, 1974) has led to the ceding of land tax, entertainment tax and payroll tax to the states (Groenewegen 1983b: 180). Legislation in 1976 by the Fraser government clarified the option for states to request an income-tax surcharge (or reduction) on residents of their own states. A small reduction in the specific purpose component of Commonwealth payments to the states has been achieved since the mid-1970s. And much discussion continues concerning state access to a consumption tax and/or to a 'real' bite of income taxation (Walsh, 1985). In the absence of systematic reform, the Australian system of fiscal federalism is claimed to be highly inefficient. Yet it continues to resist changes, largely owing to the political expediency of state leaders who do not have to face the political responsibilities for raising the bulk of their revenue. According to one major critic:

> The Australian fiscal system . . . maximises the amount of political noise and minimises the degree of electoral accountability, financial responsibility, economic efficiency and effective policy choice. In acquiescing in the continued operation of such a system, the states have shown that they are more concerned with political opportunism than with financial independence, insisting on state rights in virtually every aspect of public policy except the crucial area of fiscal policy (Mathews, 1983: 48).

The states have little *political* incentive to demand open access to tax sources whose differential rates might raise the stakes in interstate competition, over and above the competition already implicit in their various programmes of industry subsidies and service provision.

Social scientists examining Australian federalism, faced with continuing evidence of increased Commonwealth fiscal and legislative powers, have generally assumed that the states now have less control over significant economic policy decisions than at any period since the concerted centralisation of the Second World War. The notion of Commonwealth aggrandisement at the expense of the states is based, however, on a dubious assumption that power relations have a zero-sum quality, i.e. the assumption that any gain in influence by one side must involve a loss in influence by the other side. This is much too simplistic an approach to studying power relations in a complex web of interactions. A preferable approach, in my view, is implicit in the following comments by Dr Cheryl Saunders on the common claim that Commonwealth environmental legislation erodes the rights of states:

> it is a claim that serves no other purpose than to perpetuate the anachronistic distinction between centralism and states rights, a distinction that bedevils debate on almost any aspect of Australian federalism. It is time the debate moved to another plane: to consider, for example, the role which it is appropriate for the different levels of government to play in relation to particular matters and how any necessary co-ordination between them should be achieved (Saunders, 1985: 30).

The viewpoint of this chapter is that the states remain very important regulators and promoters of economic activity in their own regions; and they have major legal, administrative and political resources available which enable them either to veto or to force compromises in federal policies (Sharman, 1980). But *a priori* arguments about an ideal-rational allocation of powers between the federal and state levels are less important than the specific forms of grassroots co-operation and co-ordination which have been developing in many policy areas with a view to improving efficiency, overcoming duplication, and raising the quality of services (Bannon, 1987).

One of the important elements of modern public policy is the politicisation of economic issues. It is therefore necessary to take account of the broader politico-economic context of intergovernmental relations, and to recognise that 'solutions' are likely to be untidy and 'second-best' options rather than optimally rational. Federalism is based not on a natural equilibrium, but on two sets of competing definitions of policy objectives: among the states (horizontal) and between the federal and state levels (vertical). Moreover, the relevant context of policy debates often involves wider considerations: international patterns of trade and investment, currency movements, international treaties, and bilateral or multilateral negotiations. Neither the federal nor state governments are able to escape the constraints of operating within the framework of a multi-layered system.

Federal–state conflict and co-operation

The first report of the Commonwealth Grants Commission (1934) noted that while rural industry development policies were largely controlled by the states, the major form of industry assistance for manufacturing—the tariff—was controlled by the Commonwealth, leading to

> a lack of co-ordination and consistency in the two policies. There is almost a competition between the two factors of development; each frustrates the effect of the other; the burdens created by the one make the protection required for the other the greater, so that the clash we noticed earlier becomes more intense as each protective effort grows (CGC, 1934: 62).

Differences in state economic structures are significant factors in generating conflict or co-operation in economic policy. Although the

Australian states are more homogeneous in economic and social characteristics than are the states in some other large federal systems (Mathews (ed.), 1981), it is nevertheless also true that differences in rural and urban industries, and in patterns of urbanisation and land settlement, and consequential priorities in state development policies, tend to crystallise into a distinction between the 'core' or 'inner' states (Victoria and New South Wales) and the other states (which can be ranked in various degrees as 'outer' or 'peripheral'). The economic interests espoused by the states most reliant on rural exports have been somewhat different from those of the states most reliant on import-substitution manufacturing.

The federal system of government is supposed to be particularly appropriate for dealing with problems arising from regional diversity in a nation with a large land area; federal institutions are designed partly to express and partly to reconcile these conflicting interests. The history of the Commonwealth Grants Commission and the differential per capita funding ('relativities') of the states in tax reimbursement grants have entrenched a principle of fiscal equalisation (i.e. a recognition that some states should be compensated if their costs of service delivery are higher than average, or if their revenue-base is inadequate). Some commentators have seen this as a disguised subsidisation of inefficient location of population (for example, Gramlich, 1984: 247, 273). This argument has suited the political leaders of the more populous states, who have forcefully argued to the Grants Commission in recent years that the level of fiscal cross-subsidisation is excessive. The political reality is that the premiers of less populous states have lobbied successfully to delay or modify Grants Commission recommendations which tended to reduce their per capita funding levels. But arguments over relativities are to be expected in a system of centralised revenue-collection and diverse expenditure authorities. This chapter will focus, however, not upon taxation issues but upon economic regulation and expenditure policies of the federal and state governments. Local government in Australia (ACIR, 1984a; Chapman and Wood, 1984) has historically been a very weak element in the field of public policy, and its role is not addressed in this discussion.

It is necessary to note some important policy areas in which federal and state objectives may diverge, or where federal policies require the assistance of the states, or where federal policies have differential impacts on the various state economies—policy areas which either have a high risk of conflict or where the need for co-operation is widely understood.

1 **Tariff protection** assists local industry by raising the price of imported goods, but thereby inflates the cost of inputs for other industries including the more internationally competitive export industries. The divisions among industry sectors on this issue are largely reflected in state policy differences—the 'manufacturing' states, having more to lose, have generally lobbied the Commonwealth to retain protective

measures, while the rural-exporting states have generally attacked the tariff system and urged restructuring of industries to achieve greater efficiency—the view adopted by most of the economics profession.

2 **Exchange rates** have, historically, been subject to federal government adjustment (until the 'managed float' of the Australian dollar in December 1983). Currency adjustments greatly affect the demand for imports, the capacity to service foreign loans, the inflow of foreign tourists, the competitiveness of export industries; and can provide indirect protection for local manufacturers. As different sectors of the economy are advantaged (or otherwise) by changes in the exchange rate, this is translated into regional effects depending on the location of certain industries.

3 **Foreign investment**, an area of federal regulation, has been a field of lively debate during the last twenty years owing to Commonwealth concerns to increase the level of Australian equity in major projects (Stevenson, 1976; Anderson, 1983). Federal controls have been perceived as discouraging investment in particular industries, and thus have been bitterly criticised by state political and business leaders whose main concern is to attract new capital. The 50 per cent local equity rule for major projects has contributed, in the mining industry, to a decline in the very high levels of foreign control typical of the first resources boom of the 1960s and 1970s.

4 **Export controls** have been exercised by the federal government with various objectives: to conserve resources (the iron ore export embargo 1938–60), to set minimum prices for mineral exports (to maximise government and corporate incomes), to restrict the size of the uranium industry (only three mines were granted export licences by the federal Labor government in 1983), and to prevent mining or logging in environmentally sensitive areas (even where the developers held state government licences for production). Clearly the states, in championing the interests of capital in their territory, have found such controls unacceptable forms of intervention.

5 **Control of offshore resources** is formally a federal power, and this was successfully asserted in the Labor government's 1973 legislation. However for practical purposes some form of federal–state administrative agreement and royalty-sharing formula had been seen as necessary—these had been embodied in federal and state statutes in 1967, and in revised form in 1980 after the political debates generated by Labor's 1973 legislation (Crommelin, 1985: 100). The federal government also gains substantial revenue from its excise on locally produced oil and LPG products (introduced in 1978 to raise the domestic price to import parity following the OPEC oil price rises). Recent plans for a federal resource-rent tax have been strongly opposed by the states.

6 **Public sector borrowing** has been regulated by the Loan Council since

1927, in the wake of undisciplined state borrowings in the 1920s. Loan money has traditionally been the major source for state capital works programmes, whether by departments or statutory authorities (ACIR, 1982). The Campbell Report on the financial system in 1981 recommended 'freeing up' the restrictions on statutory authorities' borrowing; this was agreed at the Loan Council meeting in 1982, but such borrowings were brought back under the 'global limits' allowed to the states in 1984. Generally speaking, federal government concerns to peg back deficits and the public sector borrowing requirement have been translated into cutting back on state public works.

7 **Wages and prices** regulation is an area of massive federal–state complexity. The Commonwealth's influence over wage levels is indirect: for example, by making submissions to the Commonwealth Conciliation and Arbitration Commission, by negotiations with trade unions for a form of voluntary incomes policy (the 1983 Accord between the ALP and the ACTU), and by influencing the inflation rate through macro-policies. The states have considerable potential powers for price control and for wages restraint but in recent decades have preferred to rely on arbitration tribunals for wages policy and left prices to the market. Federal referenda, to grant control of these areas to the Commonwealth, were unsuccessful in 1973. A voluntary 'wage freeze' lasted only a few weeks in 1977; another in 1982 was more successful, backed by the Arbitration Commission. Controversy in the area of wage and price controls has largely been on party lines, but this spills over into federal–state relations depending on the party complexion of the various governments.

8 **Federal government contracts** for procurement of equipment or for the location of defence or administrative personnel may have important regional effects. The decision in 1987 to award the submarine construction contract to a consortium based in South Australia; the recent decisions to upgrade a naval base in Western Australia, an airforce base in the Northern Territory and an international airport in Cairns—such decisions have major implications for a regional economy. More generally, federal government procurement policies and offsets clauses for foreign suppliers may act as a form of industry assistance for state-based industries.

9 **Aboriginal land issues** have come within the field of Commonwealth policy since the 1967 referendum, but Commonwealth administration of Aboriginal affairs in the Northern Territory has a much longer history. Social and moral issues have made this a sensitive policy area, exacerbated by entrenched state policy outlooks. The 1976 federal legislation granting an Aboriginal veto over exploration and mining in the Northern Territory has failed to become a model for state legislation. Federal Labor's quest for uniformity, through persuasion and threats of overriding legislation, was abandoned in 1986; and the 1976 Act was amended in 1987 to make it more 'flex-

ible'. States' rights rhetoric has been pushed to a high pitch on this issue by the Queensland government, which even regarded the purchase of a pastoral property by the federal Aboriginal Land Fund Commission as a breach of 'co-operative federalism' (*National Times*, 14 February 1977).

10 **Immigration policy** is a federal arena in respect to the selection and numbers of immigrants. The burden of post-arrival services falls upon the states, but Commonwealth funds provide for specific welfare and educational needs of many immigrants, broadening out into support for multiculturalism. Such areas as housing, training and employment are typically matters of federal–state consultation and joint funding programmes.

11 **Industrial relations** issues are clearly of great importance for both the national and regional economies of Australia. As with wage issues, noted earlier, the wider field of industrial relations is highly complex (Dabscheck and Niland, 1981) and has been a political minefield for several governments. The importance of industrial relations in export industries and in debates concerning a more 'flexible' labour market has given a sense of urgency to both federal and state governments' proposals for reducing disputations, increasing productivity, restructuring some industries and reducing demarcation disputes by facilitating industry-based unionism. Overlapping federal and state jurisdictions and the different political agendas of some governments have proved inimical to consensual reforms.

On the basis of these policy areas, together with evidence on the well-known aspects of the federal government's macro-economic stabilisation policies, I would like to suggest two kinds of comment. Firstly, at a high level of abstraction, the states and the federal government represent countervailing tendencies in economic policy directions. Secondly, the way forward in some crucial areas of policy involves intricate federal–state co-ordination and consultation, rather than one level vacating the field.

Two logics?

As noted above, it is possible to claim that the general thrust of state-level economic policy is centred on regional development and the promotion of locational incentives to attract capital and population inflows. The economic logic of state-building is territorial (focussed on activity built up within its borders) and expansionary (the ideology of growth and development). Of course, there are major limitations upon these tendencies—constraints stemming from the effects of recession, industry restructuring, specific problems confronting sub-regions dependent on one industry or one crop, federal policies, etc. But in principle the states are in competition with each other (though also, indirectly, with overseas sites) for scarce investment funds and labour skills. The states have, historically, created a panoply of industry assistance measures to attract mobile millions and footloose firms—cheap land, subsidised energy prices, cheap loans, public infrastructure, public housing, workforce training, government purchasing, reduced royalties, relocation subsidies, and so on. The states have been distrustful of both market forces and of the federal government. They have sought to create a policy environment sheltered as far as practicable from external economic and political forces. When the federal government wants austerity, the states usually want to continue the party; and all the more so when there are party differences between Canberra and the states.

On the other hand, the economic logic of national-level government in the post-war period has been to increase overall economic activity through policies aimed at improving efficiency and productivity, while ensuring that relevant standards of equity and service provision are maintained for all citizens. Again, this tendency is constrained to some extent by politically determined patterns of international trade, by the influence of significant interest groups seeking special deals, by state governments requesting special projects (roads, dams) to help their electoral survival, by unemployed workers requiring public works programmes in depressed industrial regions, etc. But behind such pork-barrelling, lobbying and concessions, the logic is towards general rules rather than *ad hoc* subsidies, a logic which should increasingly inform the taxation debate as well as the public expenditures debate. The same tendency that points towards lower tariffs also points towards lower priority for decentralisation or regional subsidies.

To the extent that somewhat different economic logics tend to govern the directions of federal and state policy-making, we might expect the federal government to bring a mediating and moderating influence to bear in federal–state consultations to achieve rational co-ordination in areas of overlapping jurisdiction. The extent of federal–state co-operative arrangements is already immense (ACIR, 1983; 1986). These include ministerial councils and associated standing committees of officials; statutory commissions (Snowy Mountains, River Murray, National Companies and Securities Commission); marketing boards for primary produce; and joint administrative arrangements such as the offshore resources agreement. The involvement of the states in traditional forums such as the Premiers' Conference and Loan Council has been slightly broadened to include participation in new forums, including the Constitutional Convention (1973–85), economic policy summits, and (minor) representation on the Economic Planning Advisory Council.

Intergovernmental co-operation is highly desirable but is not without costs—whether the (apparent) reduction of 'autonomy' for ministers or the problems of accountability created by a myriad of new intergovernmental structures. These problems might be 'expected to grow with the complexity and numbers of the intergovernmental arrangements themselves' (Saunders, 1986: 173). Some of these issues will now be addressed in two policy areas: industry policy and resource development.

Industry policy and federalism

Policy co-ordination and planning in Australia has generally been short term, *ad hoc* and advisory in nature (Wiltshire, 1986: 66); other federations such as Canada have had similar experience (Thorburn, 1984). The hostility towards more integrated planning and co-ordination stems partly from business fears of over-regulation, partly from economists' arguments about the superior efficiency of markets as resource allocators, and partly from lack of experience and resolve among senior politicians and officials in the various levels and agencies of government. Thus, the Vernon Committee's mild proposal for an Economic Council to provide advice on medium-term economic trends was rejected by the conservative Menzies government in 1965 as impractical and dangerous. Twenty years later, the federal Labor government's Minister for Industry was still anxious to assure the public that the Australian government's plans for revitalising and restructuring manufacturing were not 'prescriptive' or imposed, but a pragmatic product of tripartite consultation on an industry-by-industry basis.

The uneven concentration of manufacturing among the states at the time of federation continued more or less unchanged until the 1940s (Hughes, 1964), the distribution being reinforced by the operations of Commonwealth tariff policy. Governments in the less populous rural states responded somewhat differently to the experience of the Great Depression, when commodity prices slumped and exposed the vulnerability of those regional economies dependent on rural exports. The South Australian government initiated schemes of industry assistance and public housing which attracted manufacturing investment, and a decade later this model was taken up—especially in processing industries—by Western Australia and Tasmania. In Queensland, on the other hand, the sugar industry had been protected by domestic price schemes, and the state government drew no lessons about the necessity of diversification and industrialisation. The 'comparative advantage' of Queensland minerals and energy in the 1960s led to a boom in mining and mineral processing rather than in broad-based industrialisation. Patterns of urbanisation in each state also tended to reinforce patterns of industrial investment, with the bulk of the nation's manufacturing clustered in half a dozen large coastal cities from Adelaide around to Newcastle.

With virtually all state governments intent upon attracting new investment, encouraged by the Menzies government, a pattern of interstate competition emerged for the establishment of (often foreign-controlled) plants in chemicals, oil refining, vehicle assembly, metal processing and light industry. In this post-war period, the subsidies offered for large projects were very substantial, reflecting not only the technological and financial weakness of the states in the global economy, but also their intense rivalry as bidders for scarce funds. One result of this process was a net loss to state revenues (stemming from underpricing of energy, water, freight charges, land, and other public services or assets, not balanced by corporate payments of royalties and state charges). Another result was a proliferation of relatively small plants which soon became uncompetitive and which were not upgraded. In the iron and steel industry, perhaps the best-known example, the South Australian government heavily subsidised the establishment of BHP's Whyalla operation, but had no way of preventing its closure some decades later (Aungles and Szelenyi, 1979). The Western Australian government offered major concessions to obtain BHP's plant at Kwinana, which closed down as part of an industry rationalisation. The Industries Assistance Commission's inquiry into the iron and steel industry criticised these concessions and regional fragmentation as contrary to the national economic interest:

> While policies which foster industrial development in a particular region may be beneficial to that region, they distort industrial development and impose costs on the nation as a whole, where, in the absence of government intervention, the development would have taken place elsewhere (IAC, 1980: A7).

Similar comments have been commonly made in relation to cheap energy pricing policies, where federal authorities have argued for full cost-recovery instead of bargain-basement concessional pricing by state authorities. The same criticism has equally been voiced by editorial writers in the national press:

> But even if a project is profitable from one premier's viewpoint, this does not necessarily make the nation any better off, especially if generous concessions are offered to attract the project . . . We have witnessed only recently the destructive competition between states in attracting aluminium smelters (*The Australian*, 22 November 1982).

The use of state industry-assistance measures to attract investment has occurred in the wider framework of a Commonwealth tariff to assist some import-competing sections of manufacturing. The federal government also assists industry through government procurement policies (marginal advantages for domestic suppliers) and 'offsets' provisions in overseas contracts (a proportion of the work to be subcontracted to domestic firms). It is well known that the broad tendency in tariff policy since the late 1960s has been towards gradual reductions in the level of protection, signalled dramatically by the 1973 decision to cut tariffs by 25 per cent in all categories. The social and political costs of tariff reduction are very important, all the more so in a period of recession and de-industrialisation. The economic rationalists who favour radical restructuring of industry by exposing it to the wholesome winds of market forces have been opposed by those who have found evidence that under present conditions (politicised trade blocs, static world trade, dumping, etc.) this beneficent breeze would become a destructive gale. The debate on industry policy is also closely tied to the prospects of industrial enclaves: the effects of tariff reduction are regionally specific (IAC, 1977; 1981; BIE, 1985; EPAC, 1986). Therefore the state governments have been vitally concerned to influence federal decisions on tariff levels for particular industries. In the case of the iron and steel industry, the Commonwealth has also directed specific purpose payments to certain states for 'regional adjustment' schemes to cope with the effects of industrial decline.

The Steel Industry Plan (1983) was negotiated as a series of trade-offs: federal guarantees of the domestic producer's market share, in return for corporate investment, productivity and industrial relations agreements, etc. for a period of five years. The negotiations, mainly through the tripartite Australian Manufacturing Council (AMC), inevitably also involved leaders of the states most affected by losses of jobs and investment. Similarly, the industry plan for passenger motor vehicles (1984), and arrangements for other ailing industries (such as heavy engineering and textiles, clothing and footwear) involve complex negotiations on assistance measures by federal and state governments, employers and trade unions. The more competitive sectors of manufacturing are less likely to come under the ambit of an industry plan; they will be offered general incentives for technical excellence and export-orientation to achieve maximum efficiency, but otherwise will not be subject to industry-specific regulation, and thus not subject to intensive federal–state bargaining.

Three other comments may be appropriate on this theme. One is to note the abolition in 1986 of 'state preference schemes' (under which governments had granted a preferential margin, around 10 per cent, to local tenderers). This economic-rationalist decision emerged from years of negotiation in the Ministerial Council; it represents a major exception to the general pattern of state orientations toward locational incentives, but it also reflects the anticipated interests of the major manufacturing states. A second, and related, issue is the beginning of a new direction at state level in shifting the emphasis of industry assistance away from decentralisation objectives, towards rewarding firms with growth potential especially in exporting (Victorian Government, 1984; 1987). The new policy is intended to encourage high-technology firms with prospects of expansion; it is tied to moves towards better co-ordination of public sector and private sector and moves to streamline business regulation, a direction shared by other 'new-managerial' Labor state governments.

Finally, there is the issue of co-ordinating federal–state planning and administrative machinery. Can the Ministerial Council, in conjunction with the federal government's tripartite advisory body (the AMC), provide an appropriate climate for long-term policy formation *and* for the reconciliation of federal–state and interstate conflict? Leaving aside the economic-rationalist condemnation of industry policy (as less efficient than market forces), we can point to the establishment of a federal–state National Industry Extension Service to act as an information broker between corporate, public sector and research institutions; the Commonwealth tax incentives for R & D expenditure; and other evidence of integrated concern for technological development. On the other hand, the states continue to offer locational incentives to poach high-technology firms. The complex problems of industry policy in a federation are noted in the Canadian context by Richard Simeon:

> Thus, we have a clash at two levels. At the level of the *substance* of industrial strategy, the questions are: where development will take place; what sectors will be emphasised; and how the conflict between the desire for regional growth can be reconciled with the desire to promote redistribution and maximisation of aggregate growth across the whole country. At the level of *procedures*, there is the question of how such a reconciliation might be brought about, and who is to make industrial policy. Is it Ottawa [Canberra] alone, the provinces [states] acting independently, or some combination? (Simeon 1979: 22–3)

Any scenario in which only the Commonwealth, or only the various states, formed industry policy is not practicable, owing to the major stake which each level of government necessarily holds in this field and owing to the different policy instruments available to each level. The future lies with finding appropriate *procedures* for consultation and reconciliation of opposing interests, however difficult that may be, perhaps where each level has a voice in influencing the plans of the other level. The product would inevitably be incomplete and remain partially *ad hoc*, reflecting the politicised differences in regional needs, the lobbying of industry sectors, and the unpredictability of the external economic environment.

Federalism and resource development

The exploitation of natural resources is regulated in most essentials by the states—mining, forestry, agricultural and fisheries industries have long been central objects of state administration. These industries have typically been major users of public infrastructure—especially transport, energy and water supplies—in rural and coastal areas. The states have historically been the suppliers of roads, ports, railways, dams and irrigation, power generation and other technical infrastructure; together with urban social infrastructure in remote development areas—schools, health services, police, etc. The states notoriously overinvested in rural public works in the 1920s, in conjunction with inefficient rural settlement schemes. These problems were relevant to both the creation of the Loan

Council in 1927 and to the continuing financial disabilities of some states analysed by the Grants Commission in 1933–34. The costs and benefits of public funding for 'Northern Development' have been strongly debated for many decades. The Commonwealth's vulnerability to schemes for subsidising infrastructure in remote areas, arising from its defence policy posture and from its administrative responsibility in the Northern Territory, may be illustrated by the successful lobbying of Western Australia to establish the Ord River project in the early 1960s.

The resources boom of the 1960s raised the issue of public investment in infrastructure with a new urgency. The resource-rich 'peripheral' states in particular saw resource development as offering the prospect of a new fast-growth track for previously backward regions. The Loan Council rationing of public works borrowing was seen as an irksome restriction. The Premiers of Queensland and Western Australia sought the deregulation of loan funds for major resource infrastructure. As Sir Charles Court said in 1964, an expansion of loan monies was necessary

> so that a state such as Western Australia can, in the national interest, effectively and safely have an accelerated rate of growth greater than the national average. We certainly cannot achieve it alone or under the present Commonwealth–state financial agreement (cited in Head, 1982: 62).

In 1978, the Loan Council created a new category of borrowing for large-scale resource infrastructure, a decision which fitted in with the Fraser government's concern to expand resource-exporting industries. However, no new funds were made available after two years of this scheme owing to other policy objectives: the need to lower the public sector borrowing requirement and general policies of public sector restraint. Moreover, loan monies for other state purposes had been proportionately cut to allow 'room' for major projects. The states increasingly resorted to backdoor methods in the 1980s to overcome Loan Council restrictions: leveraged leasing, 'front-end' payments by private developers for railways, privatisation of new projects such as Sydney's Darling Harbour Tunnel. Commonwealth policies towards state capital works programmes have been marked by suspicion, arising from overcapitalising in state electricity generation during the resources boom and a blowout in overseas debt. In general, the states are portrayed by the Commonwealth as more profligate in spending. And in the current climate of federal politics, the rival party leaders have been trying to outbid one another in cutting grants to the states as a means of trimming the federal deficit. The two logics of federal restraint and state expansionism were nicely illustrated by the Janus-faced performance of the state-aggrandising Queensland Premier in May 1987 when, having announced his intention to move into federal politics on a platform of slashing expenditure and taxation, he was obliged to advocate major reductions in grants to his own state. The strategy was not electorally successful.

The planning and financing of infrastructure has raised many issues, such as acceptable levels of public subsidies to the private sector, appropriate forms of public royalties and revenues, environmental protection, Aboriginal land and heritage issues, and conflicts between state and federal views of the national interest (Head, 1982; 1986b; Perkins, 1985; O'Faircheallaigh, 1987: ch. 2; ACIR, 1984b; 1985). There is a range of views on each of these questions which cannot be summarised here. I will conclude by noting two policy areas which seem pre-eminently in need of a federal–state co-operative approach—the area of conservation and land use, and the area of Aboriginal rights. Both these areas have major importance for the political economy of development and for federal–state relations.

Since the 1960s there has been a growing awareness that unrestrained economic development has unacceptable side-effects—chemical pollution, soil erosion, water salinity, despoliation of forests, etc. Moreover, there have been a series of conflicts arising from competing land uses: in cities, between residential, industrial, commercial and 'green-belt' zones; in rural areas, between pastoralism, crops, mining and forestry. Most state governments established monitoring and planning procedures to give more attention to the environmental impact of proposed developments, and the federal government passed environmental-impact legislation in 1974 to ensure that export industries did not breach conservation principles. As the Lake Pedder and Franklin Dam issues demonstrated, state governments do not always give a high priority to environmental considerations when these conflict with perceived 'development' opportunities. The Queensland government was at one time willing to contemplate oil drilling on the Great Barrier Reef until reaching agreement with the Commonwealth on funding for a marine park. Co-ordination of state and federal policies on parks and wilderness areas has taken some small steps, and ministerial councils operate in a number of relevant fields. The Senate Standing Committee on Science, Technology and the Environment tabled a report on *Land Use Policy in Australia* (1984) which recommended improved co-ordination between levels of government, the negotiation of a national set of objectives, and procedures for resolving the competing priorities of conservation and development, neither of which deserves to be sacrificed.

Finally, the issue of Aboriginal claims to economically viable tracts of traditional land and protection of sacred sites overshadows many issues of land use especially in northern and central regions of Australia. As noted above, the right of veto granted to Aborigines by the federal government's Northern Territory legislation in 1976 was modified in 1987 to facilitate mineral exploration and production. The Australian Mining Industry Council (the main lobby group of mining firms) and the conservative state governments in Queensland and (until 1982) Western Australia had seen land rights as 'apartheid'. Some other state governments and the federal government have, by contrast, taken a more balanced view concerning the need for Aboriginal self-determination and economic viability. There is considerable evidence that recent federal governments have shied away from confronting the states on land rights issues (for example, Aurukun 1978, Noonkanbah 1980; abandonment of national legislation 1986). Decentralised and diverse policies are now in place and are unlikely to be dislodged by Canberra's strategies of persuasion and bluff. The federal opposition's 1987 election policy involved returning Aboriginal land issues to the states, putting aside the Commonwealth powers gained by referendum in 1967. In administrative terms, this is a policy field in which federal–state co-operation is highly desirable to ensure that equity can emerge and that some general rules can be recognised. But the federal Labor policy of uniform national land rights (1983–86) failed on the shoals of federalism, notably the political and administrative difficulties of reaching consensus in the face of diverse perceptions of the nature of the problems at the local and regional levels.

Conclusion

I am sceptical of any argument which assumes that the relative power either of the Commonwealth or of the states is likely to be eroded or enhanced substantially in the short-term to medium-term. Entrenched political realities and the growing webs of co-operation and interdependence will constrain any major shifts in the federal–state power 'balance'. In any case, the accretion of power to one or other level is not, in itself, a viable solution to the problems of the federal system in Australia. Rather, the future health of federalism depends primarily on improving the quality of federal–state administrative co-operation. This claim places less weight on highly politicised and ideologically charged avenues of reform such as reassignment of constitutional powers including revenue-collection powers (McMillan et al., 1983). These directions of reform have an understandable appeal in elegance and rationality and particular reforms are highly desirable—including the proposal, in the unsuccessful referendum of December 1984, to broaden the constitutional provision for voluntary interchange of powers between the federal and state levels. However important such solutions, and however much they might facilitate administrative rationality, the day-to-day realities of federalism will reflect mundane and complex negotiation.

Federalism will remain based on hard-nosed bargaining and bullying, intractability and political stand-offs; *as well as* reasoned attempts to induce co-operation in policy areas where uniform standards are seen to have wide benefits and where policy co-ordination can reduce the costs of service delivery. Contrary to some widely held views, I would argue that federalism does not necessarily prevent the achievement of national objectives in such areas as social welfare (Birch, 1955) or economic growth (Greenwood, 1946). But federalism does insert multiple points of politicised pressure into the fields of policy formation and implementation, and therefore the route to be followed in policy innovation can be extremely cumbersome and strewn with compromises. This is perhaps the answer to those analysts who worry lest intergovernmental relations should slip into the hands of small élites of senior bureaucrats—mandarin managerialism—and thereby displace the democratic primacy of parliaments, parties and ministerial accountability. Federalism is a political animal.

References

Aldred, J. and Wilkes, J. (eds) (1983), *A Fractured Federation? Australia in the 1980s*, Allen & Unwin, Sydney.

Anderson, D.L. (1983), *Foreign Investment Control in the Mining Sector: Comparisons of Australian and Canadian Experience*, Centre for Resource and Environmental Studies, ANU, Canberra.

Aungles, S. and Szelenyi, I. (1979), 'Structural Conflicts between the State, Local Government and Monopoly Capital—the Case of Whyalla in South Australia', *Australian and New Zealand Journal of Sociology* 15(1): 24–35.

ACIR (1982), Advisory Council for Intergovernmental Relations, *The Australian Loan Council and Intergovernmental Relations*, Report no. 5, ACIR, Hobart.

—— (1983), *Register of Commonwealth–State Cooperative Arrangements*, ACIR, Hobart.

—— (1984a), *Responsibilities and Resources of Australian Local Government*, Report no. 7, ACIR, Hobart.

—— (1984b), *Intergovernmental Aspects of Major Resource Projects and their Infrastructure*, Discussion paper no. 15, ACIR, Hobart.

—— (1985), *Resource Development and Intergovernmental Relations*, Report no. 10, ACIR, Hobart.

—— (1986), *Operational Procedures of Inter-Jurisdictional Ministerial Councils*, Information paper no. 13, ACIR, Hobart.

Bannon, J.C. (1987), 'Overcoming the Unintended Consequences of Federation', *Australian Journal of Public Administration* 46(1): 1–9.

Birch, A.H. (1955), *Federalism, Finance and Social Legislation*, Oxford University Press, Oxford.

Bjelke-Petersen, J. (1983), 'Federalism: A Queensland View', in Patience and Scott (eds): 63–74.

BIE (1985), Bureau of Industry Economics, *The Regional Impact of Structural Change*, Research report no. 18, BIE, Canberra.

Burke, B. (1984), 'Federalism after the Franklin', *Australian Quarterly* 56(1): 4–10.

Business Council of Australia (1987), 'State Finances: Lifting the Veil', *Business Council Bulletin* 34 (May): 20–34.

Canada: Science Council (1979), *The Politics of an Industrial Strategy: A Seminar*, Science Council of Canada, Ottawa.

Caves, R.E. and Krause, L.B. (eds) (1984), *The Australian Economy: A View from the North*, Allen & Unwin, Sydney.

Chapman, R. and Wood, M. (1984), *Federalism and Local Government*, Allen & Unwin, Sydney.

CGC (1934–), Commonwealth Grants Commission, *Reports on Financial Assistance to the States*, Government Printer, Canberra.

Cousins, D. and Nieuwenhuysen, J. (1984), *Aboriginals and the Mining Industry*, Allen & Unwin, Sydney.

Crommelin, M. (1985), 'The Mineral Exploration and Production Regime within the Federal System', in Drysdale and Shibata (eds): 90–104.

Dabscheck, B. and Niland, J. (1981), *Industrial Relations in Australia*, Allen & Unwin, Sydney.

Drysdale, P. and Shibata, H. (eds) (1985), *Federalism and Resource Development: the Australian Case*, Allen & Unwin, Sydney.

EPAC (1986), Economic Planning Advisory Council, *Regional Impact of Industry Assistance*, Council paper no. 20, EPAC, Canberra.

Galligan, B. (1982), 'Federalism and Resource Development in Australia and Canada', *Australian Quarterly* 54(3): 236–51.

—— (ed.) (1986a), *Australian State Politics*, Longman Cheshire, Melbourne.

—— (1986b), 'The Political Economy of the States', in Galligan (ed.): 244–65.

Gates, R.C. (1974), 'The Search for a State Growth Tax', in R.L. Mathews (ed.): 159–77.

Giblin, L.F. (1949), 'Financial Aspects of the Constitution', in G. Sawer et al., *Federalism in Australia*, Cheshire, Melbourne: 89–108.

Grabosky, P. and Braithwaite, J. (1986), *Of Manners Gentle: Enforcement Strategies of Australian Business Regulatory Agencies*, Oxford University Press, Melbourne.

Gramlich, E.M. (1984), '"A Fair Go": Fiscal Federalism Arrangements', in Caves and Krause (eds): 231–74.

Greenwood, G. (1946), *The Future of Australian Federalism*, Melbourne University Press, Melbourne.

Groenewegen, P.D. (1983a), 'The Fiscal Crisis of Australian Federalism', in Patience and Scott (eds): 123–58.

—— (1983b), 'The Political Economy of Federalism 1901–1981', in Head (ed.): 169–95.

Harman, E. and Head, B.W. (eds) (1982), *State, Capital and Resources in the North and West of Australia*, University of Western Australia Press, Nedlands.

Harris, S. (1985), 'State and Federal Objectives and Policies for the Use and Development of Resources', in Drysdale and Shibata (eds): 67–89.

Harris, S. and Perkins, F. (1985), 'Federalism and the Environment: Economic Aspects', in Mathews (ed.): 35–46.

Harris, S. and Taylor, G. (eds) (1982), *Resource Development and the Future of Australian Society*, Centre for Resource and Environmental Studies, ANU, Canberra.

Head, B.W. (1981), 'Some Economic Bases of Interstate and Federal–State Conflicts', *Journal of Australian Studies*, 9: 49–60.

—— (1982), 'The State as Entrepreneur: Myth and Reality', in Harman and Head (eds): 43–74.

—— (1983a), 'The Political Crisis of Australian Federalism', in Patience and Scott (eds): 75–93.

—— (ed.) (1983b), *State and Economy in Australia*, Oxford University Press, Melbourne.

—— (1984), 'Australian Resource Development and the National Fragmentation Thesis', *Australian and New Zealand Journal of Sociology* 20(3): 306–31.

—— (1986a), 'Economic Development in State and Federal Politics', in Head (ed.): 3–55.

—— (ed.) (1986b), *The Politics of Development in Australia*, Allen & Unwin, Sydney.

Hielscher, L. (1982), 'The Issues for State Governments', in Harris and Taylor (eds): 109–20.

Hughes, H. (1964), 'Federalism and Industrial Development in Australia', *Australian Journal of Politics and History* 10(3): 323–40.

IAC (1977), Industries Assistance Commission, *Structural Change and Economic Interdependence*, AGPS, Canberra.

—— (1980), *Iron and Steel Industry*, Report no. 249, AGPS, Canberra.

—— (1981), *The Regional Implications of Economic Change*, AGPS, Canberra.

Knight, K.W. (1974), 'Federalism and Administrative Efficiency', in Mathews (ed.): 43–56.

Loveday, P. (1982), *Promoting Industry*, University of Queensland Press, St Lucia.

McCarrey, L. (1987), 'The Last of the Big Spenders', *IPA Review* 41(1): 43–5.

McMillan, J., Evans, G. and Storey, H. (1983), *Australia's Constitution: Time for Change?*, Allen & Unwin, Sydney.

Maddox, G. (1973), 'Federalism: Or Government Frustrated', *Australian Quarterly*, 45(3): 92–100.

Mathews, R.L (ed.) (1974), *Intergovernmental Relations in Australia*, Angus & Robertson, Sydney.

—— (ed.) (1976), *Making Federalism Work*, Centre for Research on Federal Financial Relations, ANU, Canberra.

—— (ed.) (1981), *Regional Disparities and Economic Development*, Centre for Research on Federal Financial Relations, ANU, Canberra.

—— (1982), 'Resource Development and Fiscal Equalisation', in Harris and Taylor (eds): 121–45.

—— (1983), 'The Commonwealth–State Financial Contract', in Aldred and Wilkes (eds): 37–62.

—— (ed.) (1985), *Federalism and the Environment*, Centre for Research on Federal Financial Relations, ANU, Canberra.

Norrie, K.H. (1979), 'Regional Economic Conflicts in Canada: Their Significance for an Industrial Strategy', in Canada: Science Council: 55–83.

O'Faircheallaigh, C. (1987), *Mine Infrastructure and Economic Development in North Australia*, North Australia Research Unit, Canberra.

Painter, M. (1986), 'Administrative Change and Reform', in Galligan (ed.): 194–213.

Partridge, P.H. (1952), 'The Politics of Federalism', in G. Sawer (ed.), *Federalism: An Australian Jubilee Study*, Cheshire, Melbourne: 174–99.

Patience, A. and Scott, J. (eds) (1983), *Australian Federalism: Future Tense*, Oxford University Press, Melbourne.

Perkins, F. (1985), 'Financing and Charging for Infrastructure', in Drysdale and Shibata (eds): 151–76.

Pooley, F.G.H. (1985), 'State and Federal Attitudes to Foreign Investment and its Regulation', in Drysdale and Shibata (eds): 140–50.

Saunders, C. (1985), 'Political and Constitutional Aspects: Commentary', in Mathews (ed.): 30–4.

—— (1986), 'The Federal System', in Galligan (ed.): 158–76.

Saunders, C. and Wiltshire, K.W. (1980), 'Fraser's New Federalism 1975–1980: An Evaluation', *Australian Journal of Politics and History* 26(3): 355–71.

Senate, Standing Committee on Science, Technology and the Environment (1984), *Land Use Policy in Australia*, AGPS, Canberra.

Sharman, C. (1980), 'Fraser, the States and Federalism', *Australian Quarterly* 52(1): 9–19.

Simeon, R. (1979), 'Federalism and the Politics of a National Strategy', in Canada: Science Council: 5–43.

Smith, B. (1982), 'Environmental Issues and Policy', in Harris and Taylor (eds): 226–38.

Stevenson, G. (1976), 'The Control of Foreign Direct Investment in a Federation: Canadian and Australian Experience', in R.M. Burns et al., *Political and Administrative Federalism*, Centre for Research on Federal Financial Relations, ANU, Canberra: 39–70.

—— (1977), *Mineral Resources and Australian Federalism*, Centre for Research on Federal Financial Relations, ANU, Canberra.

Stilwell, F.J.B. (1983), 'Is There an Australian Economy?', in Aldred and Wilkes (eds): 19–36.

Thorburn, H.G. (1984), *Planning the Economy: Building Federal–Provincial Consensus*, Canadian Institute for Economic Policy, Ottawa.

Victorian Government (1984), *Victoria: The Next Step: Economic Initiatives and Opportunities for the 1980s*, Government Printer, Melbourne.

—— (1987), *Victoria: The Next Decade: Leading Australia into the Next Decade*, Government Printer, Melbourne.

Walsh, C. (1985), The Riddle of Financial Relations, Paper presented to AIPS conference on the Australian states, July.

Warhurst, J. (1983), *Central Agencies, Intergovernmental Managers, and Australian Federal–State Relations*, Occasional paper no. 29, Centre for Research on Federal Financial Relations, ANU, Canberra.

—— (1986), 'Industry Assistance Issues: State and Federal Governments', in Head (ed.): 56–71.

Warhurst, J., Stewart, J. and Head, B.W. (1988), 'The Promotion of Industry', in B. Galligan (ed.), *Comparative State Policies*, Longman Cheshire, Melbourne.

Weller, P. and Smith, R.F.I. (1976), 'Setting National Priorities: The Role of the Australian Government in Public Policy', in Mathews (ed.): 81–96.

West, K. (1983), 'Federalism and Resources Development: the Politics of State Inequality', in Patience and Scott (eds): 107–22.

Wettenhall, R.L. (1983), 'The Administrative Crisis of Australian Federalism', in Patience and Scott (eds): 159–87.

Whitlam, E.G. (1983), 'The Cost of Federalism', in Patience and Scott (eds): 28–48.

Wiltshire, K.W. (1976), 'Setting State Priorities: the Role of the States in Public Policy', in Mathews (ed.): 97–131.

—— (1985), 'The Significance of the States', in D. Woodward et al. (eds), *Government, Politics and Power in Australia*, 3rd edn, Longman Cheshire, Melbourne: 121–30.

—— (1986), *Planning and Federalism: Australian and Canadian Experience*, University of Queensland Press, St Lucia.

Wright, D.I. (1970), *Shadow of Dispute: Aspects of Commonwealth–State Relations, 1901–1910*, ANU Press, Canberra.

CONCLUSION

12

AN OVERVIEW AND COMMENTARY

Joan Rydon

I have been given a dangerous freedom in that I have been told I may say what I like. As I cannot adequately summarise the discussions or gather up all the viewpoints which have been expressed, I shall make some comments on the changed attitudes since the conferences and publications of 1949–51 and then indulge in my own reflections on the current state of Australian federalism in the light of both developments in the intervening years and the discussions of the last two days.

Professor Sawer has suggested that the social scientists participating in the earlier conferences had few problems in discussions across their disciplines. Perhaps in 1987 our disciplines are more developed and distinct; perhaps it is merely that the jargon has increased. I have felt the conference valuable for its interdisciplinary exchanges, not so much because such exchanges are difficult, but because they are not frequent enough. Yet we would be mistaken to believe that the development of the social sciences since the Jubilee publications (or, indeed, the founding of the Australian National University) has enabled us to say much that is new; most of the issues we have argued about were considered by our predecessors. The change has been in the context rather than in the questions. In 1950 speakers already deplored the difficulties of amending the Constitution and endeavoured to explain them; we have taken them for granted. Some, like Colin Clark, wanted more genuine decentralisation which might be through new states (a possibility we have ignored—perhaps ruled out) or, as H.P. Brown hoped, through Commonwealth encouragement of local government—a development which was to wait for Whitlam. Lawyers and economists agreed that the states must regain some taxing powers if they were to survive and they talked of improvements in what we now call 'intergovernmental relations'.

They conferred in the post-war atmosphere of optimism and a widespread belief in planning and central financial power. Few would have doubted Colin Clark's assertion that the appreciation of Keynesian principles meant that the USA could be relied upon to prevent another major depression. A number of the participants had worked for the Commonwealth during the war; they generally regarded central influence as benign and progressive. Gordon Greenwood was impatient with the shackles of federalism. He saw greater Commonwealth powers as essential for Australian development in both national and international terms. A politician, Thomas Playford, spoke most strongly for the states–he wished to restore the 'federal balance'. Our forerunners spoke in more absolute terms than we have done. It was indicative that P.H. Partridge could discuss the views of those who saw federalism as a success or failure (though he stressed the Constitution had proved adaptable to changing circumstances). Others saw a millennium—a desirable static condition to be reached. For Playford it was a return to the original compact, for L.F. Giblin and H.P. Burton who hoped federalism was a stage in the development of a unitary state, it was effective national government. These would be tidy solutions, but the idea of progress to some fixed form—usually the states as administrative agencies of the Commonwealth—has often bedevilled the study of federalism, even in Sawer's discussion of the stages towards the development of 'organic federalism'.

Perhaps in 1987 we are more sophisticated, or more cynical. Our discussions have recognised federalism as a complex of rather untidy relationships constantly adjusting to new pressures. Most of us do not see solutions though some of the economists may still hanker after them They have advocated, as did the economists of the fifties, that the states should have greater taxing powers, but they are well aware that uniform taxation has not destroyed the states. Despite the great increase in the powers of the Commonwealth—actual and potential, legislative, financial and coercive—in the intervening years, it is in the appreciation of the strength and resilience of the states that we appear to differ most from our predecessors. Like them, we can probably be divided into 'centralisers' and 'decentralisers', those who put greater emphasis on the national or subnational levels of government, but even the centralisers recognise that independent states are here to stay and that some functions may be best performed at state or local level. Moreover economists and lawyers seem to agree that, while they may delineate principles, rules or plans, the extent to which these are followed or circumvented will be decided by pragmatic politicians pursuing short-term objectives.

What then has changed attitudes since the 1950s? The experience of the Whitlam years is possibly most important. Gough's 'brave new world' in which the Commonwealth would improve the quality of Australian life by coercive use of section 96 grants did not materialise. Many were disillusioned as the Commonwealth demonstrated an incapacity to cope with national questions such as Aboriginal rights, as it indulged in controls through the Assistance Plan, and as the commissions which it established presided over public extravagance. Promised economies due to size were not achieved by Commonwealth planning; both state and federal bureaucracies increased. The Whitlam government showed that the states could be neither side-stepped nor coerced. Through the specific grants and their participation in joint programmes the states have been strengthened in their finances, in their bureaucracies and in their bargaining powers. Measures meant to destroy or, at least, control have brought new life. Modern, innovative state governments have reformed both their constitutions and structures of government and in their reorganisation of public services displayed a new emphasis on efficient management. New Labor governments in the states are long past considering the Whitlam dictum that they should preside over their own abolition. Attitudes may also have been influenced by the Coombs report on the Commonwealth public service which suggested that administration closer to the people might be more efficient and economical. There seems to be an increased belief in democratic participation, probably linked with the large number of organisations and local action groups formed since the Vietnam war, to take up issues previously ignored by parties and parliaments. Then there is what may be called the end of Keynes—the recognition that central governments have no clear solutions to economic problems.

So the pendulum has swung towards greater emphasis on the states; the extent of Commonwealth activity is no longer seen as the sole determinant of the condition of the federation. Yet our discussions have still treated federalism rather narrowly. I see Australia as a federal state, not because of diverse cultural, ethnic or religious traditions, but because it is federally structured and the federal structure extends far beyond government into practically all social and political activities. I realise that some of you would claim that our 'federal culture' embodies social diversity and particular democratic values. Yet the making of the Commonwealth had little to do with the principles of limited government or decentralisation. The existing colonies wished to join together for specified purposes, but to retain their separate identities in all else. Because they found a constitutional model for doing so in the USA, we may have incidentally gained some of the values which Madison and others attributed to the division of powers between two levels of government. But, as one of the contributors to the Jubilee seminar put it, 'forms of government are almost invariably the product of the history and geography of a particular area'. The particular nature of Australian federalism has been determined by local conditions, among the most important being:

1 the pre-existing constitutions of the states, including responsible government and established bureaucracies;
2 the small and fixed number of the states;
3 the pattern of development whereby state communities have remained concentrated and distinct because most have been dominated by one capital city and there has been relatively little settlement near the borders;

4 the centralised nature of government services.

These factors are interrelated and they are basic not only to government, but to practically all activities in Australia. Most organisations are state-based with their headquarters in the respective capital city. Federal administration is organised on the basis of the states in a similar fashion. The small number of states makes such arrangements feasible. His Excellency, the Governor-General, has stressed that most Australians are little concerned with federalism. Yet a minority of them will at some time have been concerned with constitutional questions in federal organisations—of trade unions, or sporting, religious or professional associations. The division of power between central and state authorities, and the basis of representation upon each are perennial questions. There are centralisers and state-righters everywhere. The period from 1901 can be seen as one of nation-building. The aim of the federation movement of 'one nation for a continent' has been fulfilled, but it is essentially a nation of states. More and more of the activities and interests which commenced within states have been gradually linked across the nation. The governmental pattern of citizens being subject to two levels of government and able to participate in the formation of each is usually too complex to be duplicated in other spheres. Most Australian organisations commenced as confederations with weak central bodies composed of delegates from state authorities. With the decline of distance, the increased importance of central government and the growth of national identity, there has often been a shift in the division of powers towards the centre. State organisations have found it necessary to form or strengthen central machinery to deal with central government; there has been a rapid growth of national organisations since the Whitlam government. General meetings on an Australia-wide basis were once impractical; they are becoming increasingly feasible. The Australian Medical Association and the Law Council of Australia are presently both involved in proposals to change their constitutions to shift more power to the centre in line with national developments. But the independent centres of power at state level are resisting. There will be compromises; the results, like many of the organisations now developing, are likely to be neither clearly federal nor confederal. There is now a variety of organisations with different mixes of (in Madison's terms) national and federal elements. The political parties furnish good examples. They commenced as weak confederations in which state parties often asserted their independence (as the Queensland branch of the National Party is now doing). In the two major parties there have been changes involving greater central power and moves to broader participation in the national machinery.

While the Constitution divided powers between the Commonwealth and states it established a central government which guaranteed equal state representation in the Senate. A common theme in our discussions has been a shift from earlier emphasis on the division of powers to the structure of government. Such a shift has been identified in the subject matter of referendums, High Court cases and the proceedings of the Constitutional Convention. This is not to suggest that the balance of power and of activities between Commonwealth and states has remained unchanged. The constitutional division has been changed only by the transfer of the power to legislate for Aborigines from the states to the Commonwealth. Yet the Commonwealth has expanded its activities into many new areas. Some of this expansion has been sanctioned by High Court decisions. Its interpretation of 'postal, telegraphic, telephonic, and other like services' has enabled the Commonwealth to regulate the development of television and assume considerable control of the media generally. Its interpretation of 'excise' has strengthened Commonwealth financial supremacy. We have yet to see the effects of its move to broader interpretations of power over arbitration, corporations and external affairs.

Some participants are worried that the Court is ceasing to defend the states; they hope it may yet find some 'federal principle' by which it limits Commonwealth encroachment. The same worries were expressed in 1951. Then there were frequent references to the *Uniform Tax* case; now they are to the *Dams* case. There is the fear that few, if any, limits on Commonwealth legislative power will remain. Yet whether, and to what extent, the Commonwealth uses its powers is likely to be in the future, as it has been in the past, determined by political circumstances. The Commonwealth did not for many years use its powers to legislate on marriage and divorce. From 1910 on it could have legislated for uniform tax (though the Court might have thrown it out before the *Engineers'* case), but it was only wartime conditions which created the political situation for its introduction. Section 96 was always available, and its use, perhaps more than that of any other power, has been dictated by political considerations. The uneven resources of the two levels of government do not create the need for specific grants; it is political factors that do so. Successive governments have demonstrated how grants can be political favours for regions, states or pressure groups. The entry of the Commonwealth into education (other than at university level) was due to Menzies' effort to secure the Catholic vote. The establishment of the Schools Commission was Whitlam's attempt to defuse the resultant problem of state aid. Future Commonwealth moves to use the external affairs power can be expected to depend on similar vote-winning factors.

The emphasis on the clear division of powers has been fading in another sense. K.C. Wheare read a paper to the Jubilee conference and he has been quoted in 1987. Yet his definition of federalism requiring separate and independent powers for each level of government is barely applicable to Australia. We have been told it is now difficult to find an area of state policy-making in which the Commonwealth is not involved. Many of us would see dual or co-ordinate federalism as a model which never existed in practice. In the Commonwealth Constitution its concepts never applied to the provisions governing finance and the courts. It is in these areas that the greatest intermeshing and confusion of state and federal powers and activities have occurred, but they are apparent in many others. The main emphasis of this conference has been not on the independence but the interdependence of our two levels of government. We have heard of this interdependence in economic policy, resource development, defence activity, trading arrangements, external affairs, treaty-making, etc. We have been told of the intergovernmental machinery, the necessary bureaucratic arrangements which either have been, or should be, established to undertake the necessary negotiations. We have heard, too, of how the operations of the older federal–state bodies, the Premiers' Conference, the Loan Council, the Grants Commission, have changed or should be changed. We know that the coercive commissions of the Whitlam years have largely given way to more traditional intergovernmental bodies. Several speakers have stressed the bargaining strength of the states in such bodies and that their procedures are not zero-sum games. The small number of states makes consultation on specific policies at bureaucratic or ministerial level reasonably easy. Such gatherings are federal in that the Senate principle invariably applies and Tasmania has a voice equal to that of New South Wales. But few of our speakers, in their enthusiasm for intergovernmental policy-making, seem concerned to relate this to parliamentary government or even to ministerial control and responsibility. We have been told that executive federalism is alive and well, but is it imagined that the Premiers' Conference can control or co-ordinate the other mechanisms for intergovernment bargaining?

Copland might well be horrified by the proliferation of such mechanisms. In 1951 he saw the federal structure as promoting bureaucracy and having, as its chief features, administrative irresponsibility and the old game of passing the buck. Have these characteristics lessened or has there been a failure to appreciate the problems of multiplying bureaucratic structures or relating them to party government and electoral federalism? Perhaps these questions can be linked with the shift in interest to the structure of government and the question about how far the interests of states are reflected in the political processes. There have in recent years been referendum proposals relating to concurrent elections and casual vacancies in the Senate. There have been High Court cases dealing with the conditions for double dissolutions and joint sittings of the two Houses of Parliament. In actual politics, double dissolutions may be developing as the electoral norm. Sawer's 'government by double dissolution' is now being practised by Hawke. All these developments involve the Senate. Our predecessors in 1951 believed the Senate had already failed as a states' house, but wondered whether the move to proportional representation (PR) would change much. We can now see that PR plus the more recent enlargement of the Senate—both of which required no constitutional amendment, only legislation—have changed the whole nature of federal politics.

No one would suggest the Senate now represents the states. 1975 saw its power to block supply exercised as part of the struggle for office between the major parties. Yet state-wide constituencies have ensured that the Senate is primarily the House of state parties. PR has allowed state parties (first the Country Party of Western Australia and then the Country (now National) Party of Queensland) to gain representation in their own right rather than in joint party teams. It has meant that splits and divisions in state parties have been reflected in the Senate by the election of Democratic Labor Party (DLP) senators from Victoria and Queensland and a Liberal Movement senator from South Australia. PR has changed the state balance within each party room and ensured that all states will now be represented in the caucuses of the major parties. This assists in giving each state traditional representation in the cabinet and now the shadow cabinet.

More important is the fact that no government can now hope to control a majority in the Senate. Deadlocks between the Houses are unlikely to be resolved by double dissolutions though these may enable contentious legislation to be passed at joint sittings. The power of the executive to control the legislative programme has been seriously weakened. The greater independence of the Senate has seen the development of committees whose workings have occasionally mitigated party divisions. Yet such committees have not been involved in intergovernmental relations or in state affairs. Transfer of funds remains the preserve of executive federalism. Senator Harradine's suggestion for a Senate committee to look at state involvement in international treaties has received no support.

The need for governments to consult and compromise with minority groups in the Senate can be viewed in conjunction with their need to consult and bargain with the states on a host of intermeshing activities. It is not only that intergovernment planning and agreements may destroy accountability and responsibility to ministers and parliaments but they may also seriously weaken responsibility to the electorate. That electorate is dominated by parties which reflect Australian federalism not only in their internal structures, but also in their similarity from state to state. Electoral competition differs from that in most federations in that it is broadly parallel across Australia at state and federal level. David Butler has noted the lack of great variation in party support. It is another expression of the 'never-ending sameness' of the country. Frequent elections at state and Commonwealth level in which the same parties compete and politicians from both levels participate means that electoral politics predominates over interest in government and policy-making. Sawer compared the proceedings of the Commonwealth parliament to one continuous election campaign.

It has always been difficult to separate state and federal issues; a state party has often suffered electorally from the unpopularity of its federal counterpart and vice versa. As the intermeshing of state and federal functions has increased and the organisation of pressure groups at both levels has multiplied it has become difficult for governments to shape policies without taking account of forthcoming elections. Each state election increasingly involves federal policies and is seen as a contest between the federal as well as the state party leaders. The Hawke government modified its policy on Aboriginal land rights to save the Labor government in Western Australia. It modified its uranium policy to save the Labor government in South Australia. Whitlam saw the abolition or weakening of the states as necessary for the implementation of Labor policies at federal level. The present leaders of the federal ALP may well see Labor control of state governments as more essential. In a time of economic depression it has become difficult for the Commonwealth to withdraw from any joint activities—the pressure groups which benefit (including state and federal bureaucratic sections) are joined by the state governments which may be held responsible or may be able to pass the buck according to their political colour. Reactions to moves by both Fraser and Hawke governments to end free tertiary education are examples of these developments. The room in which governments can manoeuvre in policy-making has decreased with the increased interdependence of state and federal functions. The extent to which they can honour promises or fulfil electoral mandates has been decreased by the need for agreement with both state authorities and those who hold the balance of power in the Senate. This makes it difficult to fight elections on issues—personalities, claims to be trustworthy and to be reliable economic managers have become more important. Yet much of the bargaining strength of the states (and the state parties) stems from their separate and regular elections established in their original constitutions.

In 1949 Senator McCallum suggested that it was more necessary to reform the parties than to reform the Constitution. Since then there have been changes but the party discipline which he deplored has not weakened and parties still dominate the political system. As Partridge expected there has been a shift in division of powers within the parties to parallel the shift to the centre in government. This has been most pronounced in the ALP where federal intervention or threats thereof demonstrate the ultimate authority of the national over the state authorities. But, as with government, the result is not simply domination by the centre, but more complex structures allowing for consultation (and therefore more bargaining) at every level of activity. Both major parties have reflected the increased interdependence of the two levels of government by including state parliamentary leaders (together with representatives of women, youth and the territories) in their central authorities. In the ALP the greatest changes are the prohibition on state bodies binding their delegates to the national bodies and the increasing use of PR in internal party elections. These have been accompanied by the emergence and recognition of divergent factions. The previously monolithic structure—the simple tyranny of the majority—has gone and there is a new tolerance of limited disagreements. Whether the factions will each prove as authoritarian as the old structure has yet to be seen. There seems little possibility that they will replace the states as the basis of organisation, but they provide new connections across states. Their recognition has made for more open bargaining within the party, in pre-selection, formation of executives, cabinets and shadow cabinets and even in policy formulation. The growth of more professional party organisations has been accompanied by increased consultation and co-operation between state and federal officials. Labor Party secretaries have regular conferences. Executive federalism is thriving within the parties. Meetings of the leaders of a party have become as necessary as those of heads of government. Meetings of non-Labor premiers to combine in opposition to the Commonwealth became common in the Whitlam years. Meetings of the four current Labor premiers with Hawke appear to be regular events. They are an expression of what may be the most significant change in the parties—the ALP acceptance of federalism and the end of the unreal platform for the abolition of the states. The party has come down to earth. It no longer aims (or can be accused of aiming) to establish a unitary, socialist state. It is now, like its opponents, a pragmatic organisation seeking to control government.

In the 1950s we taught that there were settled policies in Australian government. Most of these have now disappeared or are being questioned. White Australia has been abolished without obvious federal complications. But the acceptance of state aid to denominational schools strained the federal structures of the major parties. The moves away from tariff protection and possibly industrial arbitration will involve even clearer state interests and the conflicts between them may be reflected within the parties. At present Labor controls five of the seven governments. Changes in that combination may have significant effects on intergovernmental relations and the general working of federalism.

Since the Jubilee seminar there has been tremendous growth in the status, power and activities of the Commonwealth. The development of air transport, the establishment of nation-wide newspapers and television networks, the increased involvement with the outside world are only a few of the changes which have cut across state borders and stimulated the nationalisation of attitudes, activities and organisations. The Commonwealth government has become involved in many areas previously seen as outside its constitutional competence. Yet there has been an increased recognition of the interdependence of state and federal units in administration, in policy-making and within political and other organisations. There would seem to be a greater acceptance of pluralism, of bargaining and of compromising as the bases for political and economic decisions. While the courts must still resolve some contentious issues there is probably less emphasis on legal and constitutional questions—certainly less on amending the Constitution—than on working within existing structures and adapting them where possible. These changes are linked with the recognition of the continuing importance of the states and with the new role of the Senate—even with factions in parties.

Such developments underline the basic difficulties in the combination of federalism and responsible government. The new zeal for intergovernmental relations takes little account of duplicating or overlapping bureaucratic structures. It ignores most problems of responsibility and accountability. It is unlikely to disprove the statement of Wilfred Prest in 1951 that federalism is an expensive form of government. We have found no method of reconciling federal–state bargaining and joint decision-making with our version of the Westminster system. Building suitable procedures for consultation and planning does not ensure that recommendations will be implemented. Rational outcomes may often be sacrificed for short-term electoral gains, particularly when distinctions between state and federal issues have blurred and some elections are always imminent.

Parties which compete for control of government know that many of their policies will be subject to negotiation with the states and with minority groups in the Senate. Yet they must fight elections as if control of the House of Representatives still gave the executive control of the legislative programme. They must campaign in terms of promises, mandates and adversary politics which are the trimmings of responsible government. There is the danger that the arguments of electoral campaigns become unreal and that sections of the electorate become cynical or even hostile to the democratic processes. In any case there are likely to be tremendous gaps between the arguments on the hustings and those within the cabinet rooms. Yet the gaps may be just as large between the cabinet room debates and the discussions within intergovernmental bodies.

Eighty-seven years after the inauguration of the Commonwealth Australia remains a federally structured society. It is not a static society for national interests are constantly increasing, but the states remain the basic elements for most activities and organisations. The formative influences: the pattern of settlement, the huge distances, the dominance of the cities and the lack of contact across state borders are being modified only slowly. The pre-existing constitutions of the states still ensure that they retain some bargaining strength through their electoral processes and administrative structures. National and state activities and interests become increasingly interconnected. The result is neither the domination of national bodies nor the destruction of the states. Instead there is an increasing variety of organisations combining state and national interests. Within each there may be conflict, competition and co-operation, shifts in the balance of power or of bargaining strengths. The participants in the discussions in 1949–51 could foresee the growth of national interests. They could not foresee the resilience of the states, the changed role of the Senate, or the endless variety of machinery for bargaining over federal and state interests. Change may be accelerating—if so, many of our conclusions may be even less lasting than those of 1951.

INDEX